DETERMINANTS OF INFANT AND CHILD MORTALITY IN RURAL INDIA

DETERMINANTS OF INFANT AND CHILD MORTALITY IN RURAL INDIA

DR. S. GUNASEKARAN

PUBLICATIONS
KALPAZ PUBLICATIONS
DELHI-110052

Determinants of Infant and Child Mortality in Rural India

Rs. 765

ISBN: 81-7835-709-7

Published in 2008 in India by
Kalpaz Publications
C-30, Satyawati Nagar,
Delhi-110052
E-mail: kalpaz@hotmail.com
Phone : 9212729499

Lasser Type Setting by: Rudra Computer Graphics, Delhi
Printed at : G. Print Process, Delhi

Dedicated
to
My Beloved Parents

Contents

List of Tables

List of Figures

Abbreviations

ANC	Antenatal Care
ANM	Auxilary Nurse and Midwife
ASFR	Age Specific Fertility Rate
CBR	Crude Birth Rate
CEB	Children Ever Born
CMR	Child Mortality Rate
DHS	Demographic and Health Survey
GFR	General Fertility Rate
High	High (under-five) Mortality Group
ICDS	Integrated Child Development Service
IMR	Infant Mortality Rate
Low	Low (under-five) Mortality Group
Medium	Medium (under-five) Mortality Group
NFHS	National Family Health Survey
NNM	Neo-natal Mortality
PNM	Post-Neonatal Mortality
SC	Scheduled Caste
SLI	Standard of Living Index
ST	Scheduled Tribe
TBA	Traditional Birth Attendant
TT	Tetanus Toxoid
TV	Television
WFS	World Fertility Survey

Preface

This book, which emerged from the National Family Health Survey (NFHS) data (1992-93), is intended to assess the determinants of infant and child mortality in Rural India. After the completion of the basic survey reports of all the 25 surveyed states of India, the NFHS data were released in December 1995 for the use of the scientific community to carry out further research. As I was doing my Ph.D. by that time on the topic of 'Infant and Child Mortality' in the Department of Population Studies at Sri Venkateswara University, Tirupati, I found it suitable to use the NFHS data for my Ph.D. as it represented the whole nation with sample selected from almost all states of India, As the infant and child mortality rates were much higher in rural than in urban areas, I chose the rural data related to all the 25 states for further analysis. After the award of my Ph.D. degree, I have revised my thesis, including additional data on various factors influencing infant and child mortality.

In this study, all the states covered under the NFHS-I were classified into three groups of states as High, Medium and Low mortality groups based on their under-5 mortality rates as per the NFHS-I report. The data were analyzed separately for each group of states and the results are presented, comparing the three groups of states. Both univariate and multivariate analysis have been carried out and the salient findings are highlighted in each chapter. Based on the findings, suggestions have been made for devising suitable strategies to reduce infant and child mortality rates in rural India in order to achieve the target of the millennium development goal on child mortality by the year 2015. This book will be very useful to researchers, students, teachers, programme planners and policy makers as a valuable guide for the analysis of data on infant and child mortality as well as to plan programmes and devise strategies to reduce infant and child mortality rates in rural India.

At this juncture, I acknowledge with deep gratitude the valuable support and encouragement given by my parents for my studies since my childhood. I take this opportunity to acknowledge my debt to my research supervisor Prof. P. Ramachandran (Retd.), Department of Population Studies of the Sri Venkateswara University, Tirupati, for all his kind research advice, without which this work would not have been successful. I also thank him for his continued help and encouragement in my professional career. I thank Dr.Damodar Sahu for his kind help to complete the computer analysis of data. I am also thankful to Dr.S.Muthukrishnaveni, Ms.P.Devi, and Ms. T. Latha, research scholars in the Department of Applied Research, Gandhigram Rural University for their valuable help at various stages of the preparation of this book.

I take this opportunity to also acknowledge the computer assistance rendered by Shri. S. Arul Gnanaprakasam, working in the ICMR Project in the Department of Applied Research.

Finally I thank Mr.Amit Garg and Kalpaz Publications, New Delhi, for their professional help and support in publishing this book.

Dr. S. Gunasekaran
Reader
Department of Applied Research
Gandhigram Rural University
Gandhigram-624 302

1

Introduction

Infant and child mortality rates are considered as sensitive indicators of living and socio-economic conditions of a country. This recognition has made the international organisations as well as National Governments to intensify their efforts to reduce infant mortality and improve child survival. As a result, there have been considerable improvements in the infant mortality and Under-five mortality rates for the world as a whole in recent years. The infant mortality rate which was 127 in 1960 has declined to the level of 54 in 2003. Similar1y, the Under-five mortality rate which was 198 in 1960 has declined to the level of 80 in 2003. In spite of the achievements made in the reduction of infant mortality and under-five mortality rates, there appears to be wide disparities among regions, countries and provinces (UNICEF, 2005).

The infant mortality rate during 2003 was just 5 per 1000 live births in more developed countries (Industrialised countries) whereas it was twenty times as great, at 98 in the least developed countries. Within the less developed regions, vast variations were observed in the infant mortality rates ranging from 104 for Africa to 27 for Latin America. The child mortality among the least developed countries was much higher than that for the more developed countries. There was 155 deaths among children under-five years of age in the least developed countries compared with only 6 in the more developed countries in 2003 (UNICEF, 2005).

In 2005, one child in eighteen across the world died during their first year of life. This represents a total of 7.6 million infant deaths in one year.

Most infant deaths occur in developing countries. Africa accounts for 40 per cent of the total, though it comprises only 14 per cent of the world population. There are two reasons for this: many children are born there (24 per cent of the world total) and with 89 deaths per 1,000 live births, Africa has the highest infant mortality rate of all the world's continents.

Table 1.1 Infant mortality in the main regions of the world in 2005

Region	*Deaths of Children under age 1*		*Proportion of newborns dying before age 1 (per 1,000)*
	Number (millions)	*Distribution (%)*	
Asia	4,08	54	52
Africa	3,06	40	89
Europe	0,05	1	7
Latin America	0,05	4	25
North America	0,02	0	7
Oceania	0,02	0	29
World	7,57	100	55

Source : United Nations, World Population Prospects, the 2004 revision.

More than 10 million children die each year in the developing world, the vast majority from causes preventable through a combination of good care, nutrition, and medical treatment. Mortality rates for children under five dropped by 15 percent since 1990, but the rates remain high in developing countries. Child deaths have dropped rapidly in the past 25 years, but progress everywhere slowed in the 1990s, and a few countries have experienced increases in the same period. At current rates of progress, only a few countries are

Figure 1.1

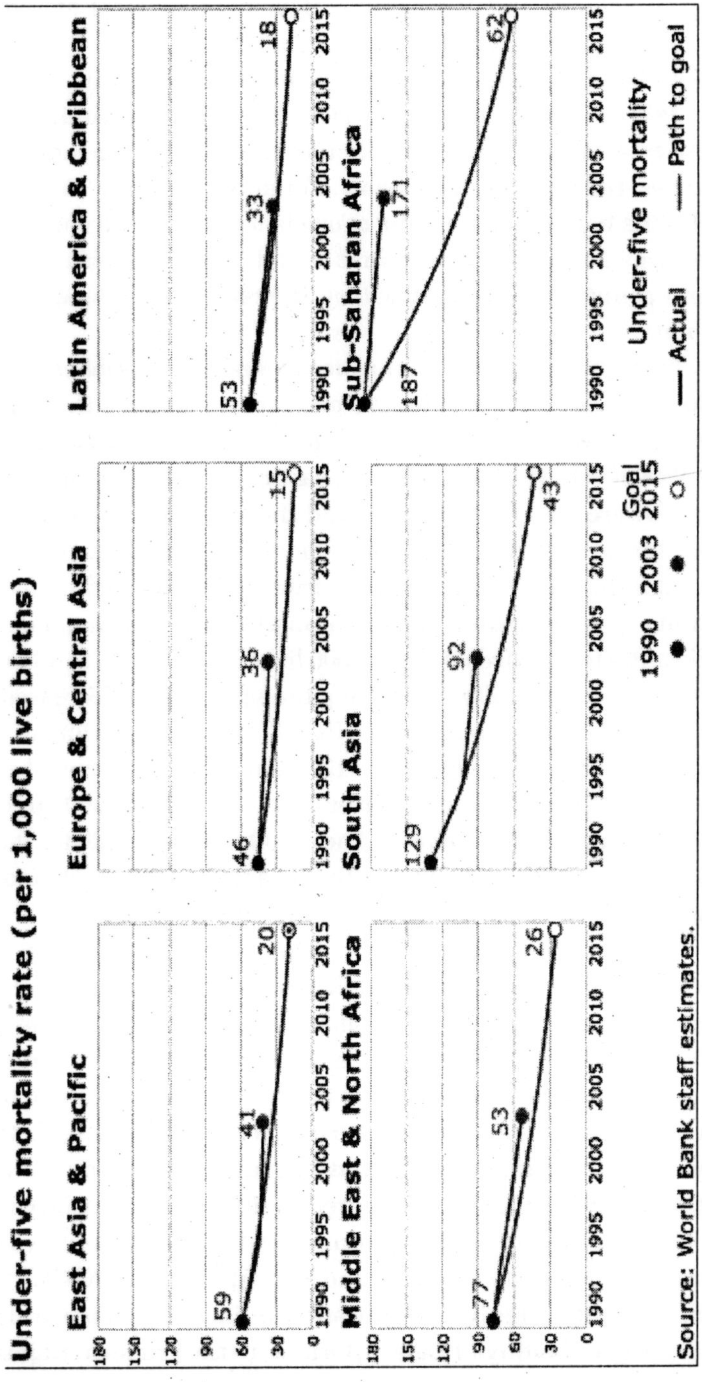

Source : World Bank Staff estimates (2004) Millennium Development Goals. Reduce Child Mortality.

likely to achieve the Millennium Development Goal of reducing child mortality to one-third of their 1990 levels.

In 2003, the average under-five mortality rate was 123 deaths per 1,000 in low-income countries, 39 in lower-middle-income countries, and 22 in upper-middle-income countries. In high-income countries, the rate was less than 7. For approximately 70 percent of the deaths before age five, the cause is a disease or a combination of diseases and malnutrition that would be preventable in a high-income country: acute respiratory infections, diarrhea, measles, and malaria.

No region, except Latin America and the Caribbean as well as Europe and Central Asia are on track to achieve the target of reducing, by 2015, the under-five mortality rates by two thirds of their 1990 levels. Progress has been particularly slow in Sub-Saharan Africa, where civil disturbances and the HIV/AIDS epidemic have driven up rates of infant and child mortality in several countries.

In India, there have been appreciable decline in infant and child mortality in recent years. The infant mortality rate in India declined significantly from 146 deaths per 1000 live births in 1960 to 63 in 2003. The under five mortality rate during the same period decreased from 242 to 87 per 1000 lives births (UNICEF, 2005) The decline of infant mortality was 14.7 percent between 1971 and 1981, 27.3 percent between 1981 and 1991 and by about 15 percent between 1991 to 2000. According to the Registrar General of India, the infant mortality rate for the year 2003 was 60 per thousand live births. The figures for rural areas was 66 and urban areas was 38 (Table 1.2).

With in India, large variations have been observed in infant and child mortality rates across the states as well as between rural and urban areas within states (Table 1.1 and Figure 1.2). The rural-urban differences in the infant mortality rate indicates that the infant mortality rate of 66 in 2003 for Rural India was much higher than the rate of 38 for urban India. Though there has been substantial reduction in the infant and child mortality rates, India's infant mortality rate is still high compared to the infant mortality rate of 7 for U.S. Even china and Mexico-comparable countries – have much lower infant mortality rate of 30 and 23 respectively (UNICEF 2005). Infant mortality rates in India are substantially higher in rural areas particularly in Madhya Pradesh, Orissa, Uttar Pradesh, Rajasthan,

Assam and Andhra Pradesh. The under 5 mortality rate during 1995-99 ranged from 18 in Kerala to 137 in Madhya Pradesh. During the same period the under 5 mortality rate in rural India was 111, which was nearly twice as high as in urban areas, 65 per 1000 live births. (NFHS II, 1998-99).

Table 1.2 : Estimated Infant Mortality rate, 2003

Sl. No	*India / States / Union territories*	*Infant mortality rate*			
		Total	*Rural*	*Urban*	*Difference*
	India*	**60**	**66**	**38**	**28**
	Bigger States				
1.	Andhra Pradesh	59	67	33	34
2.	Assam	67	70	35	35
3.	Bihar	60	62	49	13
4.	Gujarat	57	65	36	29
5.	Haryana	59	61	49	12
6.	Karnataka	52	61	24	37
7.	Kerala	11	12	10	2
8.	Madhya Pradesh	82	86	55	31
9.	Maharashtra	42	48	32	16
10.	Orissa	83	86	55	31
11.	Punjab	49	53	34	19
12.	Rajasthan	75	78	53	25
13.	Tamil Nadu	43	48	31	17
14.	Uttar Pradesh	76	79	55	24
15.	West Bengal	46	48	34	14
	Smaller States				
1.	Arunachal Pradesh	34	35	11	24
2.	Chhatisgarh	70	77	55	22
3.	Goa	16	18	14	4
4.	Jharkhand	51	54	34	20
5.	Himachal Pradesh	49	51	26	25
6.	Jammu & Kashmir	44	46	32	14
7.	Manipur	16	15	19	4
8.	Meghalaya	57	59	44	15
9.	Mizoram	16	18	14	4
10.	Nagaland	N.A	N.A	16	-
11.	Sikkim	33	33	23	10
12.	Tripura	32	32	31	1
13.	Uttaranchal	41	62	21	41

(Contd.)

(Contd. Table 1.2)

Sl. No	India / States / Union territories	Infant mortality rate			
		Total	Rural	Urban	Difference
	Union territories				
1.	Andaman & Nicobar Islands	18	20	11	9
2.	Chandigarh	19	25	18	7
3.	Dadra & Nagar Haveli	54	57	19	38
4.	Daman & Diu	39	41	38	3
5.	Delhi	28	32	28	4
6.	Lakshadweep	26	31	21	10
7.	Pondicherry	24	33	17	16

* : Excludes Nagaland (Rural) due to part-receipt of returns. N. A : Not available due to part-receipt of returns.

Note : Infant mortality rates for smaller States and Union territories are based on three-years period 2001-03.

Source : Registrar General of India, SRS Bulletin 2003.

Reducing child mortality is universally given high priority in the developing world as an important social objective. The United Nations millennium development goal on child mortality has set the target of reducing 1990 child mortality levels by two thirds in 2015. Hence it is essential to focus our attention on child mortality and identify high risk groups which are in need of better health care services.

Though infant and child mortality declined appreciably in both urban and rural areas, the persistence of the high incidence of infant and child mortality in rural areas, the vast gap between the rural and urban areas and the variations among various states within India, have drawn the attention of Governments, to intensify their efforts to improve child health and survival with special emphasis for rural areas.

Considering the present level and trend of infant and child mortality in Rural India, it is imperative to determine the factors influencing infant and child mortality in rural India to achieve the millennium development goal by 2015.

The present study on the level, trends, differentials and determinants of infant and child mortality in Rural India, examines the influence of various socio-economic, demographic and health care factors on infant and child mortality. The uniqueness of the study is that it includes data from the rural areas of 25 states which have participated in the National Family Health Survey of India in 1992-93.

In order to study the variations in infant and child mortality rates among various States of India, all the 25 States were grouped in to three categories as high, medium and low mortality group of states according to their level of under-five mortality rates as per the NFHS, 1992-93. The variations in the infant and child mortality rates among these three groups of States according to various socio-economic, demographic and maternal health care variables are examined in this study to determine the determinants of infant and child mortality in rural India.

2

Review of Literature

2.1 Overview

Infant and child mortality rates are considered to be sensitive indicators of the socio-economic and health conditions prevailing in a community. For infants and young children, the risk of dying is closely related to the environment in which they live, because they are ill-equipped to deal with infection, inadequate food and lack of elementary hygiene. While the baby is in her mother's womb, the health and the nutrition of the mother, her age, the number of children she has had, the interval between them and the care during pregnancy, all have profound influence on its survival. Inadequate care during delivery, incomplete or no immunization, inadequate or no breast feeding and improper supplement feeding practices further enhances the hazards to the child. Thus, the determinants of infant and child survival vary according to various socio-economic, cultural, demographic and health care factors. Hence, a review of literature on the socio-economic, demographic and health care determinants of infant and child mortality is made to get an overview of the existing knowledge on infant and child survival.

2.2 Socio-Economic Variables

The extensive analysis of World Fertility Survey data indicated that the survival chances of children vary widely between socio-economic strata, with the educational attainment of the mother being a particularly strong predictor (Cleland J., 1991). Mother's education might affect child health through five distinct ways. They are : 1. Education may affect the productivity of effectiveness of the health inputs used in the production of child health. 2. Education may affect perceptions about the best allocation of the health inputs. 3. Education may increase total family resources. 4. More educated women may assign a higher value to their own time, particularly, but not only, if they work in the market and receive a higher wage rate; and 5. Education may residually affect preference for child health and family size given total resources, prices and technology (Schultz T., 1984). An examination of the intervention mechanisms through which parental education influences health and survival of children in developing countries found a remarkable sensitivity of childhood survival to the length of formal schooling of the mother. Even after adjustment for economic factors, 1 - 3 years of schooling was associated with a fall of 20 per cent in childhood risk of death and further large decreases were recorded with successive increments in educational attainment. This strong relationship was found in all major regions of the developing world and persists both in countries with accessible and effective health services and in those with weak primary health care system (Cleland J., and Van Ginneken J., 1989).

The demographic and family health survey of Ecuador (1987) indicated a strong correlation between female education and infant and child mortality. Children born to mothers without any schooling have a higher probability of dying before the age of 1 and five times greater before reaching the age of 1-4 in comparison to those women with high school education. Literacy especially maternal education is observed to have consistent and significant relationship with infant and child mortality which are independent of culture or level of economic development (Grosse R., and Auffrey C., 1989).

The joint analysis of WFS and DHS Survey Data for 15 developing countries that have participated in both survey programmes showed that there was little evidence of convergence in relative mortality levels although absolute differences diminished during the period between mid 1970's and mid 1980's. The urban-rural disparity showed a slight tendency to increase rather than decrease. The relative advantage enjoyed by the children of primary school mothers over those of uneducated mothers had remained stable, while the advantage associated with secondary over primary schooling might have widened. In terms of paternal socio-economic status, there is a suggestion of narrowing of the blue collar-white collar divide, but no such tendency was observed for the agrarian - white collar differential. It was concluded that the huge socio-economic inequalities recorded in the 1970's have persisted into the 1980's despite the overall decline in mortality in this decade (Cleland J., 1991). Many studies had indicated a strong inverse relationship between mother's education and child mortality (Behm and Hugo, 1979; Caldwell J.C., 1979; Caldwell J.C. and Mc Donald, 1981; Kathrynkost and Sajeda Amin, 1992 and Pandey A., et al., 1998).

The logistic regression analysis of Egyptian Fertility Survey showed that household income had no effect on survival of infants, but pronounced effects of survival in childhood. The impact of income on childhood mortality persisted even when other variables (sanitation, water sources and maternal demographic factors) were controlled. The impact was somewhat greater for educated mothers, for fathers of higher socio-economic status and for homes with pipe water (Casterline J.B., et al., 1989).

A generalized linear models used to associate five socio-economic variables (mothers education, work status, husband's occupation, husband's education and residence) with the neonatal, post-neonatal and child (1-4 years) mortality rates found that the mother's education and place of residence were highly associated with the three mortality rates. The father's occupation and education were associated with both neonatal and post-neonatal mortality (Hobcraft J.N., et al., 1984).

Using data collected through follow-up home visits to a sample of mothers, whose singleton babies were born at the Dufferin Hospital, Lucknow, during September 1976-August 1977, estimates are made of infant mortality in Lucknow city, and its differentials by socioeconomic, demographic and health care characteristics of the infants and their families. Among socioeconomic factors considered, infant mortality is found to be inversely related with caste status among Hindus, education of mother, father's monthly income, and father's occupation (Srivastava J.N. and Saksena D.N, 1981).

A study conducted on a sample of 2178 children from 2 villages in Kheda District in rural Gujarat state, India revealed that increased maternal education among landless and low status persons was not associated with more equal child survival by gender. Excess female child mortality (EFCM) was higher among those with land ownership and high status, but higher educational level among the upper classes was associated with more gender-equal life chances. Prior research had demonstrated north/south Indian differences and variations in EFCM across various educational levels. The assumption was that education increased parental awareness of health and use of health services and imparted greater concern for a child's quality of life. This research is unique in considering socioeconomic factors in conjunction with the status of membership in social groups (caste and social class). It is assumed in this study that child values vary with social class and status groups (economic class and caste): the Kanbi Patidars (landholders) and the Kolis (peasants). The overall sex ratio of all children born among the sample population was 1.08. The sex ratio of survivorship to 5 years of age had a stronger male bias. Survivorship increased with a higher level of maternal education. Landholding women had sex ratios of 1.10, and landless women had sex ratios of 1.04. When education level was considered, high sex ratios of children ever born were reflected in the landholders with low educational levels and the landless with low educational levels. Sex ratios of survivorship to age 5 years were only improved by maternal educational level among the landholders and not among highly educated landless women. Younger women had more egalitarian sex ratios than older women for children ever born and survivorship, regardless of educational level (Clark A.W. and Shreeniwas S,1994).

An examination of how child mortality changes with different levels of maternal education revealed that child mortality gradients, according to years of education, are rather steep at the primary education level for both male and female children. In post-primary stages of education, incremental gains in mortality reduction are almost nonexistent. Child mortality is inversely related to non maternal education and female labor force participation but disaggregated analysis showed that female labor force participation has no impact on child mortality among females with fewer than 7 years of education. The relative impact of maternal education on child mortality is 3 times stronger than that of female labor force participation. Excess female child mortality prevailing in certain parts of India also has an inverse relationship with the length of mothers' education, and female labor force participation. Female labor force participation has a stronger influence on excess female child mortality than on absolute child mortality (Tulasidhar V.B., 1993).

An impact evaluation study conducted in Panchmahals district of Gujarat State, western India, revealed that the association between age/sex and child deaths that occurred over the 5-year period demonstrated that the number of deaths were highest (70/1000 children) among children who were in the age category of 0-6 months at the baseline evaluation and lowest (8/1000 children) among those in the age category of over 37 months. More male than female children had died in the 7-12 months age group and more females than males had died in the 13-24 months age group. Deaths were 4-fold among the children under 3 as compared to those over 3 years of age. The number of deaths were higher among children of illiterate mothers. Male deaths were higher than female deaths when the birth order was over 4. Among children over 3 years of age birth order seemed to be positively related to male as well as female deaths. More children died when their birth interval was less than 24 months, particularly those under 3 years old. Deaths were higher among children with poor nutritional status especially among females. A significantly higher number of deaths occurred in females over 36 months of age who had poor nutritional status (Gujral S. et al., 1992).

The influence of maternal education, sex and birth order interacted in a complex manner. 2nd and higher order daughters were found to have a higher mortality rate relative to 1st daughters and sons. Children of educated mothers had a lower risk of dying even though the population's education level was very low. Even among educated mothers, daughters of 2nd or higher birth order had abnormally high mortality in the 1st month of life. This is theorized to reflect the fact that resource allocation is devoted to 1st order sons and daughters. Four factors determined the health of the children: 1) the resources like money, time and skills available to the family. 2) the disease environment in which the child lives. 3) the child's genetic endowment. 4) the allocation decisions made by the family regarding distribution of available resources (Amin S, 1990).

A study carried out in Punjab, Ludhiana district showed that the factors significantly associated with child survival were women's autonomy, social class and mother's education (Dasgupta M., 1990). Another study showed that the percapita income did not have a consistent correlation with infant mortality rate in Indonesia. But mother's educational status emerged as one of the strongest determinants of infant and child mortality. Mother's standard of living did not make much influence on infant and child mortality (Utomo B. and Iskandar M.B., 1989). The level of education of mothers plays a more dominant role in influencing the infant and child mortality than their standard of living. The infant mortality for rural India declined by about 50 per cent among women with education atleast up to high school in comparison to the illiterates and this happened irrespective of the standard of living. The infant mortality also declined with an increase in living standard, but the quantum of the decline was relatively less than that in case of the education. The comparison of child loss experiences by rural women in four States (Kerala, Punjab, Maharastra and Orissa) of India showed that per cent of women experiencing child loss declined consistently with the increase in the level of education of women in all the four States. Standard of living also made a difference, but the decline in the per cent of women experiencing child loss according to standard of living was less apparent (Roy T.K and Jayachandran, V. 1996).

Child mortality rates in Madya Pradesh were higher for children of manually employed mothers when compared with children of non-manually employed mothers (Registrar General of India, 1987b). It is also observed that mothers engaged in traditional sector jobs had a lower infant and child mortality rates than those engaged in farming or modern sector jobs (Bailey M., 1989). The infant mortality rate was also observed to be higher among working women in rural Punjab than non working women (Singh K.P., 1989). In another study, it has been demonstrated that greater female autonomy had lowered child mortality in South India than in the North (Dyson T. and Moore M., 1983).

The analysis of census data (1981) related to Tamil Nadu, Madya Pradesh, Uttar Pradesh, Karnataka and Hariyana states of India revealed that child mortality rate was higher among Hindu than others (Registrar General of India 1987 a,b,c,d & e). In both rural and urban areas of Punjab State, infant mortality rate was higher among lower castes which form a fairly high proportion of the total population (Singh K. P., 1989). A prospective study carried out in 14 villages of a rural ICDS block in Rajasthan also showed that the infant mortality rate was higher among the families of Scheduled Caste, Scheduled Tribe and other Backward Castes (Bhandari B. et al., 1988).

A study on the influence of mother's employment on child survival in India indicates that infant mortality did not vary by mother's employment status. Mother's employment had a negative impact on infant survival, especially male infants, if the mother worked away from home for cash, lived in an urban area, or lived in the south of India. Infant girls' survival chances were better in rural areas and worse in urban areas. Maternal employment negatively affected child survival. Male child mortality was greater among mothers working away from home. Female child mortality was greater among mothers working at home. Lower total infant and child mortality in the south and east regions was due to lower female mortality. In the north, mothers' employment was not significantly associated with increased risks of infant and child mortality, except among infant boys. In the south, mothers' employment was associated with increased risks of mortality among boys aged 12-47 months. In the east, it was associated with increased risks for girls. The interaction between birth order and same sex siblings at birth and mothers' employment was unable to be determined (Kishor S. and Parasuraman S., 1998).

Based on the Indian National Family Health Survey data, an analysis was carried-out to examine the relevance of socio-cultural and environmental factors in explaining child mortality in Northeast India, considered to be the most inaccessible region in the country. The results indicate that lack of hygiene in the household and poor women's engagement in physically demanding agriculture based work contributes to higher risk of child mortality. Unlike in other parts of India, female children have an edge over boys in childhood survival and living with paternal grandmother tends to lower the risk of child death in the first five years of life. Community education is found as the dominant factor outside the household to have a significant effect on child mortality (Ladusingh L and Singh C.H., 2006).

An analysis of the National Family Health Survey-2 data on women's empowerment and its relevance to fertility and child mortality in Gujarat state revealed that older women with long marital duration, those residing in urban areas, belonging to high living standard groups, socially better off castes, engaged in higher non-farm type occupations, and Christians are found to have high index value on all indices. The study also found that autonomy indices revealed weak influences on child survival and contraceptive use. However, it is important to note that education of women, a variable highly correlated with female autonomy, has emerged more powerful in the analyses. It is noted that educated women are more likely to have decision making power, freedom of mobility, and access to resources in order, thus enabling them to act upon the aspects that may affect their own health as well as of their children, thereby leading to increased contraceptive use and reduced child mortality (Dey D. and Bhavsar S., 2002).

Using cross-sectional individual-level survey data collected from Maharashtra, Tamil Nadu and Uttar Pradesh under the Indian National Family Health Survey program of 1992-93, statistical modeling was used to analyze the impact of a range of variables on the survival status of children during their first 2 years of life. Attention was focused on the potential impact of the mother's autonomy. The strongest predictors of mortality were demographic and biological factors, breast-feeding behavior, and use and knowledge of health services. Variables that can be interpreted as being related to maternal autonomy, such as the presence of a mother-in-law in the household, did not have a significant direct effect on child survival at the individual level, and their indirect effects were very limited (Griffiths P., et al., 2001).

The comparison of the determinants of infant and child mortality in TamilNadu and Uttar Pradesh, revealed that young-age deaths are influenced by the background characteristics of socioeconomic and demographic variables. In comparing both states, results show that mother's education is an independent determinant in influencing child survival status, more so in Uttar Pradesh than in Tamil Nadu (Srinivasan S, 2000).

An examination of the effect of maternal education on child mortality [in India], shows that education has direct as well as indirect effects through antenatal care and family formation patterns on neonatal mortality. Maternal education also has a substantial effect on later childhood mortality. While improving maternal education is a means of reducing childhood mortality, an immediate reduction in childhood mortality is feasible even under existing social conditions by enhancing accessibility to maternal and child health services and safe drinking water" (Rajna P.N., et al., 1998).

The levels of child mortality in Goa state, India, estimated based on the National Family Health Survey, (1992-93), revealed that about 8 per cent of women had experienced a child death. Mortality was three times higher among children from households without toilets compared to children with toilets. The probability of dying was 6 times higher among children living in households with a low Standard of Living Index (SLI) than in households with a high SLI. Children from middle SLI households had a 3.5 times higher risk than the highest SLI children. The probability of child mortality was very high among children with mothers with just primary education or mothers with no education. Children of working mothers had slightly lower mortality. Child mortality was higher in urban areas. Multivariate models show that children from better socioeconomic backgrounds had significantly lower risks of mortality. Children with a medium SLI had about 40 per cent lower risk of dying than children from low SLI households. The risk of dying was significantly related to presence of a toilet. Religious affiliation did not affect survival chances. Higher maternal education was related to improved child survival. Risk of dying among children of illiterate women was reduced by 65 per cent by increases in maternal education to the primary level (Rao S.R., et al., 1997).

The analysis of Gujarat NFHS (1992-93) data demonstrated the pronounced effect of demographic, economic and social factors on neonatal and post-neonatal deaths. A multivariate hazard analysis is attempted to estimate the relative risk of different factors. Among the socio-economic variables, standard of living index came out as an important factor (statistically significant) in influencing both neonates and post-neonates. The role of education in influencing infant deaths is found to be limited to post-neonates (statistically significant) and insignificant in the case of neonates. The study does not show significant sex differential, urban-rural differential and religious differential in the risk of neonatal and post-neonatal deaths. It is seen that children born to medium and high SLI group mothers faced 47-61 percent less risk of infant deaths as compared to that of low SLI group mothers (> 18 months). (Patel R.M., 2000).

A study on the relative role of public health program and socioeconomic factors in influencing infant mortality in India, traced the pathways between the program, socioeconomic, and infant mortality through selected proximate variables. The study has used data mainly from the 1992-93 National Family Health Survey and Health Statistics published by the Ministry of Health and Family Welfare of the Government of India. Overall, univariate analysis has revealed that survival through infancy is dependent on the socioeconomic level of the household, as well as on the availability of health facility and certain proximate variables like maternal condition, antenatal and natal care, infant feeding practices, malnutrition and environmental sanitation. Multivariate analysis has revealed the equally important role of development and program factors in the reduction of infant mortality. Finally, the direct, indirect and the total effect of various independent variables on the dependent variable through path analysis were identified. These findings suggest that on the one hand it is social change, while on the other it is the effective utilization of the available public health services that has resulted in reducing infant mortality in the country (Das N.P., 1996).

A study on the correlation between infant mortality in India and socioeconomic, demographic, cultural, and community factors conducted in 11 villages in East Godavari (developed) and 21 villages in Medak (underdeveloped) districts of Andhra showed that infant mortality did not differ by caste, family type (nuclear or nonnuclear), or maternal educational level. Infant mortality declined with an increase in socioeconomic status (SES) of nuclear and nonnuclear families. Infant mortality was higher among lower status nonnuclear families compared to higher status nonnuclear families. 21 per cent of the variation in East Godavari was explained by proportion of literates, laborers, and scheduled castes. Infant mortality was higher among those who lived in huts than who lived in "kutcha and pucca" housing (Sandhya S, 1991).

A comparative study of education-specific infant mortality rates (IMR) among women in rural areas of two states in India, Kerala and Uttar Pradesh (UP), showed that female education is complementary to medical services. Kerala has the lowest IMR (42 deaths/1000 births in 1978) and UP has the highest IMR (172 deaths/1000 births in 1978) among the Indian states. The two states differ on a number of characteristics including the degree of political commitment to equitable distribution of food, health and educational services, actual availability of health services and the poverty level of households, with Kerala generally being much better off. In Kerala, the IMR decreases from 55/1000 births among women with no education to 29 among women with at least primary school education. The ratio between these two rates is 0.53 as compared to a ratio of 0.61 in UP. Thus, the effect of female education on infant mortality in both states is in the same order of magnitude (Jain A.K., 1985).

A study on the demographic, socioeconomic, and health and nutritional correlates of infant mortality in Gujarat, India found that the mother's education affects infant mortality more than any other socioeconomic variable. Illiterate mothers experience an infant mortality rate 3 or 4 times greater than more educated mothers and also have a larger infant death concentration during the post-neonatal period. Other socioeconomic factors such as household income and householder occupation influence infant deaths. This study shows a 0.25 per child infant death rate difference between upper and lower socioeconomic classes (Population Research Centre, Baroda, 1983).

An examination of the relevance of socio-cultural and environmental factors in explaining child mortality in Northeast India, considered to be the most inaccessible region in the country using data from the Indian National Family Health Survey, provide evidence that lack of hygiene in the household and poor women's engagement in physically demanding agriculture based work contributes to higher risk of child mortality. Unlike in other parts of India, female children have an edge over boys in childhood survival and living with paternal grandmother tends to lower the risk of child death in the first five years of life. Community education is found as the dominant factor outside the household to have a significant effect on child mortality (Ladusingh L. and Singh C.H., 2006).

Women's empowerment and its relevance to fertility and child mortality was assessed by using data from the National Family Health Survey-II of Gujarat state. It is observed that older women with long marital duration, those residing in urban areas, belonging to high living standard groups, socially better off castes, engaged in higher non-farm type occupations, and Christians are found to have high index value on all indices. The study also found that autonomy indices revealed weak influences on child survival and contraceptive use. However, it is important to note that education of women, a variable highly correlated with female autonomy, has emerged more powerful in the analyses. It is noted that educated women are more likely to have decision making power, freedom of mobility, and access to resources in order, thus enabling them to act upon the aspects that may affect their own health as well as of their children, thereby leading to increased contraceptive use and reduced child mortality (Dey D. and Bhavsar S., 2002).

Using cross-sectional, individual-level survey data from Maharashtra, Tamil Nadu and Uttar Pradesh collected under the Indian National Family Health Survey program of 1992-93, statistical modeling was used to analyze the impact of a range of variables on the survival status of children during their first two years of life. Attention was focused on the potential impact of the mother's autonomy. The strongest predictors of mortality were demographic and biological factors, breast-feeding behavior, and use and knowledge of health services. Variables that can be interpreted as being related to maternal autonomy, such as the presence of a mother-in-law in the household, did not have a significant direct effect on child survival at the individual level, and their indirect effects were very limited (Griffiths P. et al., 2001).

The comparison of the determinants of infant and child mortality in TamilNadu and Uttar Pradesh, revealed young-age deaths are influenced by the background characteristics of socioeconomic and demographic variables. In comparing both states, results show that mother's education is an independent determinant in influencing child survival status, more so in Uttar Pradesh than in Tamil Nadu.

A study on the determinants of child mortality in the major states of India and variations by district revealed that child mortality varied widely from 49/1000 live births in Kottayam district, Kerala state, to 216 in Tikamgarh district, Madhya Pradesh. Districts were grouped as low, moderate, and high child mortality. 83 per cent of the districts in Kerala had low mortality, compared to only 7 per cent and 10 per cent of districts in Tamil Nadu and Karnataka, respectively. Low mortality was not prevalent in northern states, except in Gujarat and West Bengal. 47per cent of all districts had higher female mortality (FM). Female child survival risk was lower in Uttar Pradesh, Bihar, Haryana, and Madhya Pradesh. Excess FM states were mostly in the north. Female literacy, marriage age, percentage of electrified households, and health personnel were highly, negatively correlated with child mortality. Access to safe drinking water, normal rainfall, proportion urban, and sex ratio were negatively, weakly correlated. Child mortality was negatively associated with population density and positively associated with the proportion of scheduled tribes/castes. Over 73per cent of variation in child mortality was explained by socioeconomic, regional dummies, and interaction effects. Female education had the strongest impact on declines in child mortality. An increase to 100per cent female literacy would halve child mortality (Deshpande R.V., 1998).

An examination of the effect of maternal education on child mortality [in India], shows that education has direct as well as indirect effects through antenatal care and family formation patterns on neonatal mortality. Maternal education also has a substantial effect on later childhood mortality. While improving maternal education is a means of reducing childhood mortality, an immediate reduction in childhood mortality is feasible even under existing social conditions by enhancing accessibility to maternal and child health services and safe drinking water" (Rajna P.N., et al., 1998).

An assessment of the levels of child mortality in Goa state, India, based on the National Family Health Survey, (1992-93), revealed that about 8per cent of women had experienced a child death. Mortality was three times higher among children from households without toilets compared to children with toilets. The probability of dying was 6 times higher among children living in households with a low Standard of Living Index (SLI) than in households with a high SLI. Children from middle SLI households had a 3.5 times higher risk than the highest SLI children. The probability of child mortality was very high among children with mothers with just a primary education or mothers with no education. Children of working mothers had slightly lower mortality. Child mortality was higher in urban areas. Multivariate models show that children from better socioeconomic backgrounds had significantly lower risks of mortality. Children with a medium SLI had about a 40per cent lower risk of dying than children from low SLI households. The risk of dying was significantly related to presence of a toilet. Religious affiliation did not affect survival chances. Higher maternal education was related to improved child survival. Risk of dying among children of illiterate women was reduced by 65per cent by increases in maternal education to the primary level. A long birth interval was significantly associated with reduced mortality risk (Rao S.R. et al., 1997).

An examination of the relationship between the socioeconomic factors and child mortality among the four south Indian states—Andhra Pradesh, Karnataka, Maharashtra, and Tamil Nadu, revealed that the factors affecting child mortality differ among the selected states. The developmental variables such as electricity, availability of drinking water and female literacy influence a proportion of married females and thereby affect child mortality in Andhra Pradesh. In Karnataka, female literacy level was observed to be the major determinant, accounting for about 50per cent of variations in child mortality. Moreover, in Tamil Nadu and Maharashtra, household level of literacy and female literacy level were the major determinants of child mortality. The analysis clearly demonstrates that child mortality is highly influenced by community development, female literacy, household literacy, and fertility variables. It is therefore suggested that efforts be made to concentrate on community development programs, adult female education programs, and provision of formal health education to the mothers irrespective of age, thereby enhancing child survival (Prakasam C.P. et al., 1991).

India's 1981 Census data on child mortality differentials revealed that India's child mortality rate was 115/1000 live births. This rate was 123/1000 in rural areas and 67/1000 in urban areas. A closer analysis revealed substantial variation by state in under one year mortality (ranged from 33/1000 in the Hyderabad district of Andhra Pradesh to 280/1000 in the East Kaweng district of Arunachal Pradesh). In terms of under-2 mortality, the states of Orissa, Madhya Pradesh, Rajasthan, Uttar Pradesh, Arunachal Pradesh, and Lakshadweep had districts with rates in the 146-180/1000 range. The census data further indicated an inverse relationship between child mortality and maternal educational level. By 5 years of age, child mortality was 170/1000 among offspring of illiterate women, 107/1000 in cases where the mother was literate but has not gone beyond primary school, 71/1000 when the mother has completed middle school only, 48/1000 for the offspring of matrics, and 32/1000 for the children of women who completed school or pursued graduate studies. In general, these data confirm a strong association between both sociocultural factors and the devaluation of female children and child mortality in India (Ghosh S, 1989).

The analysis demonstrated the pronounced effect of demographic, economic and social factors on neonatal and post-neonatal deaths. A multivariate hazard analysis is attempted to estimate the relative risk of different factors. The influencing of standard of living index in affecting the infant mortality stands common to both neonatal and postneonatal deaths. The analysis shows that the demographic factors like mother's age at birth, experience of earlier child deaths and previous birth interval are directly associated (statistically significant) with neonatal death, but the latter two has insignificant relationship with post-neonatal deaths. Among the socio-economic variables, standard of living index came out as an important factor (statistically significant) in influencing both neonates and post-neonates. The role of education in influencing infant deaths is found to be limited to post-neonates (statistically significant) and insignificant in the case of neonates. The study does not show significant sex differential, urban-rural differential and religious differential in the risk of neonatal and post-neonatal deaths. It is seen that children born to medium and high SLI group mothers faced 47-61 percent less risk of infant deaths as compared to that of low SLI group mothers (Patel R.M., 2000).

Socio-cultural factors related to the persistent high infant mortality are identified as widespread poverty and its consequences, severe malnutrition, and early age at marriage. Mortality is high despite major medical interventions in rural and urban areas. Women are valued less, cared for less, and protected less. A single model is not appropriate for implementing reductions in infant and child mortality. Improvements in diet and an increase in women's status will impact favorably on reductions in infant and child mortality. These and other nonmedical interventions are relatively new concepts for addressing mortality decline. A number of conceptual frameworks for explaining intermediate or proximate determinants of fertility or mortality have been developed. For instance, Jain identified six proximate determinants: prenatal medical care, postnatal preventive nonmedical care, medical care at birth, postnatal nonmedical care, postnatal preventive medical care, and postnatal curative child care. Other key factors identified by Jain and Talwar are conception variables, prenatal variables, delivery variables, and postnatal variables. The interaction and impact of these factors is best analyzed in a micro context. Low age at marriage is a cultural factor which places the infant at greater risk. Marriage age is low due to conformity with tradition, to the need to assure the chastity of daughters, and to reduce financial liabilities. Other factors influencing infant mortality are the subordinate status of women, childbearing practices, and breast feeding and weaning practices (Khan M.E., 1993).

The findings of the review indicated that the socio-economic factors, particularly education of mother is significantly influencing infant and child mortality.

2.3 Demographic Variables

Demographic factors such as maternal age at the time of child birth, birth order, the occurrence of multiple births and the duration of previous birth intervals are the important predictors of child survival. Especially significant is the birth interval where infant is born within two years of another child, both children are at greater risk of dying (Chidambaram V.C. et al., 1985). Evidence from around the world showed that illness and death in both the industrialized and developing countries are highest in four specific type of pregnancy. 1. Before 18 years of age; 2. After 35 years of age; 3. After four deliveries; and 4. Less than two years apart (Idayatullah, 1986 and Singh K. et al., 1987).

The health of the infant is affected by the mother's age at the time of birth. The very high rate of infant death among women below 20 years of age is due to biological immaturity as well as their inability to care for their children due to economic instability or lack of experience of motherhood. Infant mortality is also high among children born to women aged 35 or more resulting from biological complications that may occur during their older ages. These women are usually high parity and repeated births have weakened them and made them anaemic. Consequently their babies have lower birth weight and are more likely to succumb to infections and illness. If child bearing is confined to the optimal ages of 20 to 34, then not only maternal mortality but infant mortality as well can be reduced to the minimum possible levels (Hemant Tiwari, 1989).

The net effect of maternal age on neonatal and post neonatal mortality examined in a study conducted in Gujarat State of India showed that only the offspring of the youngest mothers (less than 20 years old) were exposed to high risk of death during neonatal period, while the babies born to older mothers (30 years and older) were exposed to a much higher risk of death during the post neonatal period (Gandotra M.M. 1988). Many studies in India showed extremes of maternal age (< 20 and > 30 years) and multi parity as risk factors associated with infant mortality (Choudhery S.R. and Jayaswal, O.N., 1989; Bhandari B. et al., 1988 and Roy T.K., 1996). The examination of the determinants of infant and child mortality variations in Jordan, Yemen, Egypt and Tunisia using data from WFS Surveys indicated that mortality risk was higher for infants born to very young and very old mothers with short previous birth interval of higher birth orders and where previous infants had died (Adlakha A.L., and Suchindra C.M., 1985).

The analysis of Gujarat NFHS (1992-93) data demonstrated the pronounced effect of demographic, economic and social factors on neonatal and post-neonatal deaths. A multivariate hazard analysis is attempted to estimate the relative risk of different factors. The analysis shows that the demographic factors like mother's age at birth, experience of earlier child deaths and previous birth interval are directly associated (statistically significant) with neonatal death, but the latter two has insignificant relationship with post-neonatal deaths. Children born to mothers' have experience of earlier child deaths faced 41 percent more risk than that of mothers' who did not have such experience. Similarly, the births with a short preceding birth interval (</= 18 months) faced more than twice the risk of neonatal deaths than that of births with longer duration (> 18 months) (Patel R.M., 2000).

A study on the correlation between infant mortality and socioeconomic, demographic, cultural, and community factors conducted in 11 villages in East Godavari (developed) and 21 villages in Medak (underdeveloped) districts of Andhra showed that first conception, maternal age, birth order, birth interval, age, and sex of the child were important demographic determinants of infant mortality. Poor survival chances were given to births among young mothers with a first birth. Increased birth interval only in Medak contributed to lower infant mortality. A male infant death led to a shorter birth interval than a female death (Sandhya S, 1991).

A study on the demographic, socioeconomic, health and nutritional correlates of infant mortality in Gujarat, India found that lowest neonatal mortality rates occur for women aged 20-34, and the highest for women under age 20 or over age 35. The 2nd birth has the lowest mortality, unless it happens to a mother under age 20. 1st births have the highest mortality risk since these births often occur before the mother's 20th birthday. Higher order births also have increased mortality rates, even when the mother's increasing age is controlled. 25 per cent of rural births and 23 per cent of urban births in India are order 5 or above. Shifting the high proportion of lower order births into the low mortality risk group and ending the high proportion of higher order births in advanced age would reduce the infant mortality rate considerably. Birth spacing of less than 18 months results in an infant mortality rate greater than 200 per 1000 live births; 36 month intervals reduce infant mortality to 1/3 this level. Even for higher order births, greater spacing lowers mortality, unless the mother's advancing age also exerts an influence. Children spaced 30 months or more, and born to women aged 20-29, have the greatest chances for survival (Population Research Centre, Baroda, 1983).

A study conducted in rural Chithoor district of Andra Pradesh found a high correlation of birth order to both infant and child mortality and number of living children to childhood mortality (Mahadevan K. et al., 1985). A classic 'U' shaped relationship of age of mother at birth and mortality during the first year of life is evident from many studies (Ahmed Alkabir, 1984; Hement Tiwari, 1989 and Gunasekaran, S, 1988). The multivariate analysis of WFS data from rural Bangaladesh showed that the strongest determinants of infant and child mortality in rural Bangaladesh were the length of the previous birth interval and the birth order (Ahmed Alkabir, 1984). The results of another study showed that the infant mortality rate was high for first and second birth, then decreased from the third to eighth birth and increased again for births of order 9 or higher. This study showed a different pattern of child mortality, the birth order first rising and then falling (Chen C. et al, 1981).

Short birth intervals affect child survival through three mechanisms first, short birth intervals can retard fetal growth resulting in low birth weight and increased death risks due to endogenous causes. Second, they may impair the potential milk production for the child whose birth closes the interval. A third effect results from restrictions imposed by too closely spaced births on the distribution of resources including maternal care among children in the household (Palloni A. and Tienda M. 1986).

The analysis of WFS data established a strong relationship of birth spacing to infant and child survival in developing countries. The WFS data showed that the short birth interval (less than 2 years) endanger the births of both the child born at the start of the interval and the child born at the end of the interval. The effect of short interval is greater in infancy. The effect of birth spacing lasts at least 5 years. Children born either at the start or at the end of a short interval are about 50 per cent more likely than other children to die at ages 1-4 (Maine D. and Mc Namara R., 1985). It is also found that very short intervals have an adverse effect on child survival and the birth interval effects were strongest in situations where infant and child mortality were already high (Winikoff, B., 1987).

A study carried out in rural Uttar Pradesh of India found high mortality to be casually related to short birth spacing. Where mothers in spacing categories under 3 years to increase to intervals of 3 or more years, a 51 per cent reduction in infant mortality and a 42 per cent reduction of total mortality in early childhood would be realised (Srivastava J.N., 1990).

Children throughout the developing world are much more likely to die if they are born less than 2 years after the mothers previous birth than they are, if the birth interval is longer (Koenig et al., 1988; Pebley A.R. and Millman. S, 1986 and Gubhaju B.B., 1986). Both preceding birth interval and following birth interval had substantial effect on infant mortality, but the birth interval effects are smaller in the case of child mortality (Rutherford R.D. et al., 1989).

The detrimental impact of short preceding birth intervals on infant and early childhood mortality is well documented in demographic literature, although the pathways of influence within the relationship remain an area of debate. An examination of the impact of the length of the preceding birth interval on under-two mortality in India, and the pathways through which short preceding birth intervals may lead to an increased risk of mortality. Short preceding birth intervals (<18 months) are associated with an increased risk of child mortality and the effect is particularly marked in the early post-neonatal period. Significant interactions were found between the length of the preceding birth interval and maternal education, gender and the survival status of the previous child. The significance of these interactions varied with the age of the child. The results highlight the diluting effect that a higher level of maternal education has on the relationship between short preceding birth intervals and mortality risk. There is evidence to suggest that sibling rivalry is a pathway through which short birth intervals influence mortality, with the death of the previous sibling removing the competition for scarce resources, and resulting in lower risks of mortality than if the previous sibling was still alive. The greatest risks of an infant following a short birth interval are among those whose previous sibling died, high parities, those with young mothers, and those whose previous sibling was breastfed for a short duration (Whitworth A. and Stephenson R, 2002).

The comparison of the determinants of infant and child mortality in TamilNadu and Uttar Pradesh, revealed young-age deaths are influenced by the background characteristics of socioeconomic and demographic variables it is also noted that birth intervals and child deaths are negatively related (Srinivasan S, 2000)

The findings of the analysis of NFHS-I (1992-93) data on the patterns and determinants of infant and child mortality (IM/CM) in India indicate that adjusted IM and CM rose with increasing birth order. Third order births had the lowest IM. Higher mortality of first births was related to mother's young age. Maternal age at childbirth at second and higher birth orders was related to mortality in a U-shaped pattern. CM was higher among children born with a short birth interval (SBI), and children with an older sibling who died (Pandey A. et al., 1998).

A multivariate hazard models analysis of 1988-89 retrospective survey from 39 villages selected randomly in the Karimganj district of Southern Assam representing 1805 scheduled caste households revealed that babies born between 15 and 27 months and >or= 27 months from the preceding birth were 25 per cent and 72 per cent, respectively, less likely to die in the first 24 months. Children born to a mother younger than 25 years were more likely to die early compared to mothers 25-35 years or older. The risk of death increased by 1.085 times for every increase in parity of children. The relative risk of death of a male child compared to a female child was 0.4 (Nath D.C. et al., 1994).

The risk of infant death fell as maternal age at 1st conception increased from 15 to 25 years. First birth order infants were at greater risk of infant mortality than other orders (52.15 per cent vs. 2.45-30.06 per cent), probably due to early age at 1st conception, untrained birth attendants, and improper delivery care. A higher incidence of infant mortality for the index child existed for mothers whose succeeding birth interval or whose preceding birth interval was less than 24 or 12 months, respectively. Infant deaths were rare and almost nonexistent when the succeeding birth interval was 36 and 48 months, respectively (Dhanalakshmi N, 1993).

A study conducted in 5 Primary Health Centers (PHCs) in Bangalore Division of Karnataka State in India between August 1977-November 1977 to determine the infant mortality rate (IMR), its components, and correlates found that male infants were more likely to die than female infants (113 vs. 90; $p<.05$), especially in the neonatal period (76 vs. 48; $p<.01$). Further, IMR was highest among 15-19 year old mothers and 35-44 year old mothers (115 and 128 respectively compared to 87-101 for all other mothers). Infants of birth order 2 had the lowest IMR (85 vs. 102-109 for other orders). Mothers who had experienced a previous stillbirth were more apt to experience infant death than those who had not had a previous stillbirth (150 vs. 90; $p<.05$) (Badari S. et al., 1991).

A study on 'Infant Mortality and Its Causes in Gujarat,' conducted by the Population Research Centre, Baroda found that although the crude effects for most of the variables are similar to the findings reported by other investigators, when the effects of various factors are adjusted by the binary variable regression analysis method, the effect of some of the variables is found to be very different. For example, the net effect of maternal age on neonatal and post-neonatal mortality shows that only the offspring of the youngest mothers (less than 20 years old) are exposed to a high risk of death during the neonatal period, while the babies born to older mothers (30 years and older) are exposed to a much higher risk of death during the post-neonatal period. Male babies are exposed to a higher risk of death in the neonatal period but female babies are exposed to a higher risk of death in the post-neonatal period. 1st order births may not be at as high a risk of death as those which follow quickly after short intervals irrespective of their order (Gandotra M.M. and Das N., 1988).

Although there is lack of consensus, the evidences indicating association between levels of infant and childhood mortality with that of fertility has been well documented in the research carried out in the past in both developed and developing nations. Some researches have shown that the existing levels of high mortality, particularly during the infancy and early childhood along with strong preference for sons, reinforce couples to go for as many children as possible, resulting in higher fertility levels. This happens in order to ensure that few of the children would survive to adulthood and be able to provide their parents with the support in old age. Contrary to this, some others have stated that those women who have children in rather quick succession (with shorter birth intervals) also experience higher infant mortality. Nevertheless, there seem to be short of consensus in taking infant mortality levels as a single most important indicator not only for assessing the quality of public health care but also for assessing the over all development status of the population. In addition to this, a number of studies have also suggested that the environmental factors play crucial role in determining the levels of mortality during early childhood which, beside infant mortality, also reflect on the general health conditions in a population. Incidentally, in comparison to the later ages, the gaps between levels of mortality during infancy and early childhood are widest across developed and developing nations (Lahiri S. and Ram U., 2004).

The results of the review indicated that demographic factors such as age at birth, parity, and birth interval are having significant relationship with infant and child mortality.

2.4 Sex of the child

In most societies where differential treatment has been observed, female children are disadvantaged relative to male children. Discrimination may operate in many different areas, including health care, educational opportunities, feeding practices, household chores and the distribution of family resources (Fred Arnold, 1991). Discriminatory practices against girls have been widely reported in countries where son preference is strong (Ravindran S., 1986). At moderate to low levels of mortality, males typically have higher mortality rates than females at every age (United Nations, 1988 a,b). However, excess female mortality for infants and children has been observed in a few developing countries, primarily in South Asia, the Middle East and Northern Africa (United Nations 1988a; Arriaga et al., 1985 and Rutstein Shea Oscar, 1984). Many studies in India found higher infant and child mortality rates for females than males (Abel Rajaratinam, 1988 and Dasgupta M., 1990). After the first year of life, the risks of mortality for girls are greater than those for boys. Moreover this excess mortality appears as early as the first month of life, while the child is still totally dependent on the mother. From the 1970's to the 1980's excess female child mortality declined only slightly (Dominique Tabutin and Michel Williams, 1995).

An analysis of data from the 1988 two-per-thousand survey of fertility and birth control, in china found that among first born children, the difference between male and female childhood mortality was not statistically significant, but among others, female children between ages 1 and 5 experienced higher mortality than male children. Childhood mortality was slightly higher for children who have older brothers only than who have older sisters only and it is highest for those who have both older brothers and sisters (Minja Kim Choe, et al., 1995).

The analysis of longitudinal data from rural Bangladesh found an acute disadvantage of female with respect to mortality during early childhood. Analysis of data from several groups of Bangladesh children showed that female mortality began to systematically exceed male mortality during the second half of the first year of life and that there after the differential became increasingly more pronounced (Koeing M.A. and Stan D'Souza, S., 1986). The analysis of 1981 Indian census data for Karnataka State showed that infant mortality rate was higher for males than females irrespective of area and the mortality differentials beyond infancy were not very clear (Ram F. et al., 1985).

The comparison of age specific probabilities of dying at ages 0-5 in the republic of Korea showed a relatively high female mortality. The higher female mortality was more pronounced during childhood than during infancy. The multivariate analysis of life tables using hazard models showed that co-variates influencing the mortality at young ages differ for male and female children and suggested that male and female children received unequal care by the parents (Choe M.M., 1987). The assessment of the WFS data showed that death rates during the first year of life seemed to be higher for males than for females (Chidambaram V.C. et al., 1987). The results of an another study based on WFS data showed that neonatal, post neonatal and infant mortality rates were higher for boys than for girls, but child mortality was lower for boys (Ahmed Alkabir, 1984). The same pattern was also observed in other WFS surveys (Rutstein Shea and Oscar, 1984). A study of change in mortality differentials between boys and girls over time by examining the changing regional patterns in the Juvenile sex ratio in rural India using district level data from the census of 1961 and 1971 indicated that sex differentials in childhood mortality were increasing overtime in favour of boys and to the detriment of girls (Miller B.D., 1989).

The analysis of data from census reports, sample registration schemes, statistical abstracts and other published research studies showed that female mortality in Punjab State was higher than male mortality at every age. Various studies seemed to suggest that there was a tendency in Punjab to give preferential treatment to boys over girls (Singh K.P., 1989). Though infant mortality rate for boys was higher, boys received better care and this is expressed in the child mortality differential (Chen C. et al, 1981).

Cultural pattern in India discriminate against female children and this has translated into poorer health for this group. Indian culture confers greater value on male infants seeing them as both producers and heirs. Traditionally, the male infant death rate was always greater than that of female infants. But in India, the female infant death rate was only lower during the first week of month of life, after which it surpasses male infant death (Ghosh, S. 1991).

India's 1981 Census data on child mortality differentials revealed that the sex differential in child mortality showed a pattern of reversal with increasing age. At 2 years of age, female child mortality exceeded that among males in only 142 (35 per cent) of

India's 401 districts. However, this statistic increased to 172 districts (42 per cent) by age 3 years and to 224 districts (55 per cent) by age 5 years. In terms of region, there was an overall pattern of an excess of female child mortality in the northern districts and an excess of male child mortality in southern India (Ghosh, S. 1989).

Comparison of the incidence of infant and child mortality and sex preference in India and some selected Indian states, such as West Bengal, Punjab, Gujarat, Karnataka, and Andhra Pradesh over the periods 1992-93 and 1998-99 revealed that variation in the intensity of son preference over the states seems consistent to a large extent with the changes in sex differentials in the mortality under age-5 over the two NFHS surveys. The extent of decline in the under-5 mortality among female children compared to their male counterpart is much faster in Karnataka followed by West Bengal and Gujarat, which, in turn, become more favorable among females compared to Punjab and Andhra Pradesh (Lahiri S. and Dutta P., 2002).

The National Family Health Survey (NFHS) conducted in 1992 revealed lower levels of infant and child mortality among females than among males in Andhra Pradesh. However, this advantage for females was mainly because of the high neonatal mortality rate among males than that among females. The postnatal mortality and child mortality between 1-4 years of age were unfavorable to females. The results from the survey showed that the female mortality rate during both the post neonatal and childhood periods was higher than the male rates (about 21 per cent in both). However, neonatal mortality which accounts for 64 per cent of the total infant deaths was much lower among females and as a result the infant mortality rate was lower for girls (James K.S., 2001).

The analysis of data derived from different sources including NFHS and SRS revealed that the decline in infant and child mortality would be favorable only to boys and not to girls. The analysis determined that there is no significant difference between rural and urban residence. However, maternal educational level was found to affect the sex disparity in infant and child mortality in a different manner in different states. States such as Rajasthan, Uttar Pradesh, Haryana, Madhya Pradesh, and Bihar are those where girls are in a disadvantaged position, whereas in states such as Andhra Pradesh,

Tamil Nadu, Karnataka, and Maharashtra girls are in an advantaged position, as expected. In the former group of states more women are illiterate, which leads to sex disparity in the nutritional, preventive, and curative aspects and to son preference. However, the latter group of states, due to maternal educational achievement, shows less sex disparity in the same set of indicators. The correlation results show, as expected, that where son preference is more prevalent disparity in child mortality is greater, though the same result is not seen with regard to the disparity in infant mortality (Banerjee S, 2000).

The reviews of literature on gender differences in child mortality (CM) in India and the analysis of the impact of development on excess female mortality (FM) showed that socioeconomic development may not help reduce excess FM, as suggested by the modernization theories. The review indicates how excess FM is affected by cultural factors as well as by economic factors, and other indicators. Cultural factors appear to have the strongest impact on gender differences in mortality. Development increases sex differences in CM. Gender differences occur regardless of a household's availability of resources. Female survival appears to be greater in rice cropping areas. It appears that the best strategy is to increase the cultural and economic worth of females, where their cultural or economic worth is low. It is widely understood that under-allocation of food and medical services to women leads to excess FM, but little is known about the motivations. Trends indicate that females have a mortality advantage during infancy in some states, which disappears at age 5 in all states, with the exception of Kerala and Andhra Pradesh. Excess FM is greater in the north, where the highest levels of mortality are found (Kishor S, 1998).

The analysis of NFHS (1992-93) data from eight states: Goa, Kerala, Tamil Nadu, Punjab, Orissa, Haryana, Rajasthan, and Uttar Pradesh, Haryana, Rajasthan, and Punjab showed the strongest son preference. Son preference was weak in Kerala, Goa, and Tamil Nadu. Hazard models are constructed for each family size group. The effects of family composition on parity progression were strongest in Punjab and Haryana. The effects were least strong in Kerala, Tamil Nadu, and Uttar Pradesh. Women were less likely to continue childbearing if they were literate, older, living in urban areas, and had a recent birth. Women were more likely to continue childbearing if they experienced a child death. There were no significant effects of sex composition on child mortality in Goa, Kerala, and Tamil Nadu. Sex composition affected excess female mortality in Punjab, Rajasthan, Uttar Pradesh, and Haryana in families with an increased number of girls. In Uttar Pradesh, however, girls with a number of older brothers had higher child mortality. Orissa showed unusual patterns. Higher levels of fertility and mortality were associated with higher excess female child mortality. Parity progression was higher after a female child in states where excess female mortality was observed (Arnold F. et al., 1996).

It is expected that maternal education would diminish the social effects on son preference in some castes and social classes. It was found that increased maternal education among landless and low status persons was not associated with more equal child survival by gender. Excess female child mortality (EFCM) was higher among those with land ownership and high status, but higher educational level among the upper classes was associated with more gender-equal life chances. Prior research had demonstrated north/south Indian differences and variations in EFCM across various educational levels. The assumption was that education increased parental awareness of health and use of health services and imparted greater concern for a child's quality of life. This research is unique in considering socioeconomic factors in conjunction with the status of membership in social groups (caste and social class). It is assumed in this study that child values vary with social class and status groups (economic class and caste): the Kanbi Patidars (landholders) and the Kolis (peasants). The overall sex ratio of all children born among the sample population was 1.08. The sex ratio of survivorship to 5 years of age had a stronger male bias. Survivorship increased with a higher level of maternal education. Landholding women had sex ratios of 1.10, and landless women had sex ratios of 1.04. When education level was considered, high sex ratios of children ever born were reflected in the landholders with low educational levels and the landless with low educational levels. Sex ratios of survivorship to age 5 years were only improved by maternal educational level among the landholders and not among highly educated landless women. Younger women had more egalitarian sex ratios than older women for children ever born and survivorship, regardless of educational level (Clark A.W. and Shreeniwas S., 1994).

An analysis of the 1970-73 data on 4943 rural and 2947 urban infants from North Arcot District in Vellore, southern India, revealed that there were essentially no differences between male and female infant mortality when analyzed by community type, educational status, type of housing, family size, and occupation of mother and father. On the other hand, female mortality was higher among Muslims than women of other religions in both rural and urban areas. For example, 17.9 per cent of 0-12 months old females infants died compared with 8.2 per cent of male infants in rural areas. These corresponding numbers were 16.3 per cent and 14.9 per cent in urban areas. Female mortality was also more prevalent among literate parents who had not attended formal schooling in both rural and urban areas (for 0-12 month old infants, 12.5 per cent vs. 4.8 per cent and 15.2 per cent and 11.3 per cent, respectively). Yet none of the aforementioned differences were statistically significant. These patterns were also similar for postneonatal mortality. The differences between male and female postneonatal mortality were statistically significant (Rao P.S., 1991).

The positive effect of son preferences on IMRs was especially apparent in Rajasthan, Gujarat, Maharashtra, Haryana, and Punjab. For example, in Punjab, which had both a high IMR and a high domestic product, there was a marked son preference, and in 1968-71, Punjab's IMR for males was 97 compared to 111 for females. The impact of son preference on Punjab's IMR is further confirmed by a recent study which was conducted in Punjab's Ludhiana district. The district is highly developed and has a good health care program. An analysis of health program records revealed that in 1983, female deaths accounted for 85 per cent of all the deaths recorded for children aged 7 months to 36 months (Miller B, 1985).

An examination of the some of the socioeconomic and demographic differentials of male and female infant mortality in a rural area in Uttar Pradesh showed that Muslims experienced a higher infant mortality rate among both males and females as compared with the Hindus, but these differences were statistically insignificant. Among the Hindus, the highest infant mortality was observed in the lower socioeconomic group. Their living conditions, particularly their environment and sanitary conditions, food habits, and child care were responsible for the high level of infant mortality.

In joint families, a female birth is generally unwelcome due to the existing norms of society. This is probably the reason for the infant mortality rates being relatively higher in the case of females, but no statistical significance was found in infant mortality rates in either joint or in nuclear families. The highest infant mortality was observed among the agricultural laborers; the lowest was found among the cultivators. A similar pattern was seen when male and female infant mortality rates were considered separately. A declining trend was observed in infant mortality by level of education with a similar pattern emerging for male and female infant mortality rates. The differences between male and female infant mortality rates were not statistically significant in any educational category. Statistical testing revealed no significant differences between male and female infant mortality rates for any of the age groups of mothers (Bhattacharya B.N. et al., 1980).

The results strongly suggest that discrimination against female children is more prevalent in most of the developing countries including India.

2.5 Maternal Health Care Variables

Maternal care services, such as Tetanus Toxoid immunisation, iron and folic acid tablets, attendance for a check up during pregnancy, delivery assistance by trained health personnel during pregnancy and institutional deliveries play a vital role in improving the survival status of children. In developing countries, child survival is affected by prenatal care, prenatal management, maternal age, maternal nutrition, the process of child birth, treatment of obstetric emergencies and treatment of birth injuries (Rajaram P., 1990). The importance of maternal health services in reducing infant morbidity and mortality has received significant recognition in the past decade (Ebrahim G., 1982). Under utilisation of maternal health services has been identified in a number of studies as an important factor in maternal and infant mortality (Bhandari B. et al., 1989 and Paul B., 1991).

A Study in Sri Lanka found that the decline in the neonatal mortality rate in the non-estate sector of Sri Lanka was due to the factors such as proportion of mothers receiving antenatal care and the proportion having institutionalised births (Meegama S.A., 1980). A comparative study of infant mortality between two development blocks in Tamil Nadu, found that the infant mortality rate was lower in both the blocks among the children of mothers who have received antenatal checkups (from any agency), TT immunisation, children born in institutions and children whose birth were attended by ANMs (Rajaratinam T., 1989). Another study carried out in Madurai district of Tamil Nadu revealed that immunisation (TT) during pregnancy significantly affect neo-natal mortality (Gunasekaran S., 1988). The comparison of the determinants of infant and child mortality in TamilNadu and Uttar Pradesh, revealed that, antenatal care and immunization is highly significant among the two states (Srinivasan S, 2000)

Percentage of births attended by trained medical personnel and poverty were the two important determinants of neo-natal mortality. Availability of medical facilities and the extent of vaccination coverage were the two important determinants of post-neonatal mortality. The influence of adult women's literacy on infant mortality is explained by better medical care at birth and preventive and curative medical care during the post-neonatal period. Medical factors have been shown to be slightly more important than non-medical, suggesting possible reduction of high level of infant mortality prevalent in many states in India by simple preventive medical intervention. An examination of the difference between the death rates among infants whose birth were attended to by trained personnel (including Doctors, LHVs, ANMs and Trained Dais) and untrained personnel revealed that mortality rate were comparatively higher among infants whose birth were attended by untrained personnel (Jain A.K., 1985). The use of maternal care (modern pre-natal and birth delivery) were the important determinants of infant mortality (Luis Tam, 1991). Similar findings were observed in a number of other studies carried out in India (Khan M.E. 1988 and Badari S. et al., 1991).

A comparative analysis of child loss experiences of women from four States of India (Kerala, Punjab, Maharastra and Orissa) according to their level of utilisation of maternal care services found that the survival chances of births which were delivered with the assistance of relatives or friends were significantly less than those which were delivered with the assistance of health professional. Similarly, births to mother who took antenatal care during pregnancy had a significantly higher chance of survival compared to those where the mother did not receive the antenatal care. In Punjab, none of the maternal care factors seemed to have any influence on the survival chance of infants. In Maharastra, the survival chances of infants were lower among births attended by trained health personnel. In the case of place of delivery, births which occurred in institutions had higher chance of dying during infancy. The deliveries conducted with the assistance of relatives and friends and the practice of not taking antenatal care during pregnancy significantly decreased the chances of survival of infants in Orissa. It was also observed that births, where the mothers did not receive any antenatal care during pregnancy, but the delivery took place in an institution, had higher chance of dying during infancy (Roy T.K. and Jeyachandran V., 1996).

In 49 randomly selected villages from two adjoining blocks of rural Varanasi, all pregnant women and live births were followed for perinatal and infant mortality, during the years 1988-92. Both PMR and IMR were significantly higher if weight gain during pregnancy was <7.0 kg. Low weight gain during pregnancy was also associated with significantly higher low birth weight deliveries and to some extent increased still birth rate. PMR and IMR decreased with higher levels of hemoglobin in third trimester and socioeconomic index. However, the calculated relative risks were not significant. Low weight gain during pregnancy is an important risk factor for PMR and IMR (Agarwal D.K. et al., 1998).

A study conducted in five primary health centers (PHCs) in Bangalore Division of Karnataka State in India between August 1977-November 1977 to determine the infant mortality rate (IMR), its components and correlates found that untrained traditional birth attendants delivered 69 per cent of all live births. IMR for these infants was considerably higher than that for trained attendants (108 vs. 87; p<.1). Most women delivered at home and IMR was much higher for home births than institution births (103 vs. 89), especially after the first 28 days (43 vs. 11; p<.1) (Badari S. et al., 1991).

A study on the correlates of infant mortality in Tamil Nadu, conducted in two rural areas of Madurai district found that antenatal care of the mother affected the level of neonatal mortality though not the post-neonatal risk of death. Likewise, the availability of health personnel within the village was associated with a lower neonatal mortality; but it did not have a similar effect on post-neonatal mortality. The length of the gestation period affected both the neonatal and the post-neonatal risks of death. Contrary to received wisdom, parity did not show a significant relationship with neonatal mortality rates but showed a J-shaped relationship with post-neonatal death. The quarter of birth showed a surprising association with neonatal mortality. Both neonatal and post-neonatal mortality rates showed a surprising relationship with the average monthly expenditure on food (Gunasekaran S., 1988).

An examination of the development of the health care system in Kerala and its impact on infant mortality reveal that neonatal mortality in the rural areas is 1.8 times that in the urban, and 1.4 times greater than the postnatal mortality rate. In contrast, the infant mortality rate in Kerala is lower for rural areas than for urban. Medical expenditures, the number of institutions and health care personnel per capita have increased dramatically in Kerala since the 1950s. The government expenditure on medicine and public health shows a 13.04 per cent growth rate from 1957-81, while the total state government expenditure had a growth rate of 12.45 per cent for the same period. There has also been a spread of maternity and child welfare centers and health education campaigns. The health care system in Kerala is characterized by a more even spatial distribution of medical care institutions. However, intra-regional differences exist in the availability and accessibility of these facilities. Data are presented for the distribution of medical institutions and beds for each district, as well as for the distribution of medical care facilities among the natural divisions (lowland, midland, highland). Infant mortality rates in Kerala are presented for each natural division and are divided into the different periods within which the infant death occurred. There has been a steady rise in medical attendance at birth in rural areas, which corresponds to an over all increase in the percent of live births in lowland, midland and highland areas. Overall, the evidence suggests that the infant mortality rate has responded favorably to the expansion of health and medical facilities. The high level of education and health consciousness of the parents are also identified as primary factors in the declining infant mortality rate in Kerala (Panikar P.G., 1985).

A comparative study of education-specific infant mortality rates (IMR) among women in rural areas of two states in India, Kerala and Uttar Pradesh (UP), showed that female education is complementary to medical services. Kerala has the lowest IMR (42 deaths/1000 births in 1978) and UP has the highest IMR (172 deaths/1000 births in 1978) among the Indian states. The two states differ on a number of characteristics including the degree of political commitment to equitable distribution of food, health and educational services, actual availability of health services and the poverty level of households, with Kerala generally being much better off. In Kerala, the IMR decreases from 55/1000 births among women with no education to 29 among women with at least primary school education. The ratio between these two rates is 0.53 as compared to a ratio of 0.61 in UP. Thus, the effect of female education on infant mortality in both states is in the same order of magnitude. The correlation between these ratios and the percentage of villages within 2 kilometers of a medical facility for 15 major states in India is -.27. These results indicate that higher female education and better availability and utilization of medical services are the two factors responsible for lower IMR in Kerala. The IMR of 188 among illiterate women in UP provides an estimate of infant mortality that can be expected in the absence of both education and medical services. (Conversely, the IMR of 29 among women with at least primary school education in Kerala provides an estimate of infant mortality that can be expected in the presence of both education and medical services.) The improvement of education and availability of medical services, especially for primary medical care, is therefore advised. Vaccinations for mothers and infants and utilization of safe delivery kits are suggested (Jain A.K., 1985).

A 1981 survey revealed 1) a low IMR for the state of Kerala, one which was comparable with Western nations, despite the fact that nearly half of the population in Kerala lived below the poverty line; 2) a very high IMR for the state of Uttar Pradesh, even though the number of people living below the poverty line was not significantly different from the state of Kerala; and a moderate IMR reduction in the state of Punjab, even though only 15 per cent of the population was below the poverty line. Favorable factors for low IMR appear to be a high female literacy rate, good medical and educational facilities close to the place of residence, and an excellent transportation and communication system. To significantly reduce IMR in a short period of time, it is necessary to adopt certain immediate measures. Nearly 55 per cent of infant deaths occur in the 1st month of life and these generally are not amenable to general measures and technological interventions. The problem is difficult, but a solution can be found by reaching a broad consensus among professionals and administrators. The major recommendations of a seminar on the Strategies for Reducing infant Mortality in India, held during January 1984, were: provide antenatal care to 100 per cent of pregnant women; work for early registration of pregnancy and identification of high risk pregnancies; immunize 100 per cent of pregnant women with tetanus toxoid; make available intrapartum care for all pregnant women; delineate anticipated job requirements, duties, and functions of village level health workers; make presterilized packaged delivery kits available to all female health workers; and implement secondary level perinatal care (Ghai O.P., 1985).

An examination of the differences between death rates among infants whose births were attended by trained personnel e.g. doctors, lady health visitors (LHVs), auxiliary nurse-midwives (ANMs), trained dais or traditional birth attendants and untrained personnel showed that mortality rates are somewhat higher among infants whose births were attended by untrained personnel; but the differences are not statistically significant. The two exceptions to the general trend relate to Muslims among the religious groups and to the 30-34 age span among mothers' age groups; the rates of these two groups were higher for births attended by trained personnel, but again the differences are not statistically significant (Reddy P.H. and Sholapurkar M.V., 1983)

The results of the review clearly indicate the influence of maternal care such as antenatal checkup, T.T immunization and place of delivery on infant and child mortality.

2.6 Immunization

Immunisation of children against six vaccine preventable diseases (tuberculosis, diphtheria, pertussis, tetanus, poliomyelitis, and measles) in the first year of life is observed to have significant effect in reducing infant mortality. A population-based, case-control study conducted at Ballabgarh (an area in rural northern India) showed that children from lower caste households who were not vaccinated in infancy had the highest risk of mortality (odds ratio, 8.9). A 27 per cent increase in child mortality was attributable to failure to vaccinate against measles in the study population. Measles vaccine seems to have a non-specific reducing effect on overall child mortality in this population. If true, children in lower castes may reap the greatest gains in survival (Zubair Kabir. et al, 2003).

In a special project area of rural India, the age-specific mortality rates of a birth cohort of 0-59 months old were calculated from 1991 to 1999. The mortality rates were lower than the national average, but the common causes of child deaths were similar. Since 1985, when the Universal Immunization Programme of India introduced routine measles vaccination, there has been a proportionate decline in child deaths unlike other parts of India. The absolute numbers of child deaths from 'all' causes have also declined significantly over the same period of time. The vaccination coverage in the project area is higher than the national average. This suggests a possible 'beneficial' non-specific effect of measles vaccination on child survival over this time period (Kabir Z. and Long J., 2002).

A double blind study conducted during January 90-March 91 in a rural part of Varanasi district in Uttar Pradesh state of India on 9987 and 5260 children under six years of age demonstrated that administration of vitamin A reduced overall mortality by 14.0 per cent. The additional data collected from January 1991 to February 92 under similar settings on 1314 and 1200 children of same age in the experimental and control groups respectively and from all children suffering from xerophthalmia who received mega dose of vitamin A (200,000 I.U.), taken together, show that vitamin A supplementation results in 16.9 per cent reduction in mortality. Mortality was reduced in unimmunized children by 22.0 per cent, diarrhea by 18.8 per cent and measles by 9.0 per cent. However, significant reduction in mortality in vitamin A supplemented group was observed only for deaths due to severe malnutrition. No death was recorded in xerophthalmia children who received mega dose of vitamin A (200,000 I.U.). The child survival pattern remained unaltered and mortality pattern remained unchanged significantly even after one year of withdrawal, thus denying the possibility of any substantial change in the study area for births and deaths. Thus the finding that vitamin A supplementation protects against overall mortality and in particular deaths due to gastroenteritis, severe malnutrition and in unimmunized children is of significance (Agarwal D.K. et al., 1995).

The comparison of the determinants of infant and child mortality in TamilNadu and Uttar Pradesh, revealed antenatal care and immunization is highly significant among the two states (Srinivasan S, 2000).

2.7 Breast feeding

The development potential of the society depends upon the level of physical and mental state of its children, for which early child hood lays the foundation. The infant mortality rate in India is very high and deaths during the period of weaning are 10 to 15 times higher than industrialized countries. Better infant feeding practice can make an important contribution to the reduction of mortality rates and in protection against the infantile malnutrition during the formative years of human life. Breast feeding practices vary according to various socio-economic, demographic, maternal care, mass media and family factors.

A study on the association between use and knowledge of colostrum on neonatal and post-neonatal deaths conducted in Varanasi found that the neonatal and post-neonatal deaths were very low for females familiar with the importance of colostrum and feeding it. Findings also revealed that there was no effect of social status on the use and knowledge of colostrum but at the same time a highly significant effect of residence was found on the use and knowledge of colostrums (Singh K. and Srivastava P, 1992).

Delays in initial breast feeding deprive the infant of colostrum. Pre-lactation beverages may be administered without hygienic practices. Supplementary food may be introduced too late and in too small a quantity. Milk is sometimes diluted because of poverty or the misguided belief that digestion is improved with dilution (Khan M.E, 1993).

A study conducted on a sample of 912 children born during 1990-1994 in Tamilnadu revealed that only 28 per cent of mothers had practiced ideal infant feeding practice. It was more among urban women (32 per cent) as compared to their rural counterparts (26 per cent). Place of residence, age at marriage, sex of the child, number of antenatal visits during pregnancy and place of delivery had played significant role on infant feeding practices (Gunasekaran S. et al, 1995).

Another study on infant feeding practices of working and non-working urban mothers found that a majority (80 per cent) of the working mothers fed colostrums due to its beneficial and immunity to fight against infections where as 24 per cent of the non-working mothers did so on doctors advices. Ninety per cent of the infants of non-working mothers were fed with breast milk alone upto 3 months where as 70 per cent children of the working mothers were getting supplementary milk feed with or without breast milk. However, 22 and 18 per cent of the non-working mothers had started giving supplementary milk feed only between the age of 6-9 and 9-12 months, respectively. Semi-solid and solid supplementary foods were started before 6 months by a majority of the working mothers where as the non-working mothers started giving these foods only between 6-9 months of age (Sarojadahiya and Sehgal, 2001).

A study on weaning in the perspective of breast-feeding in a rural area revealed that 93 per cent of mothers initiated breast-feeding within three days of birth, while only 50 per cent started on the first day. Only 8 per cent of the mother's were aware of colostrum, 75 per cent of mothers stated that breast milk had substance to protect against diseases; 20 per cent of mothers did not know about colostrum. The study also revealed that most of the (95 per cent) babies had been deprived from the colostrum feeding. It is also observed that 88 per cent of mothers breast-fed their children up to two years. 70 per cent fed up to 3 years and 12 per cent up to 4 years (Sangeethapanday, et al. 2001).

Another study on some aspects of feeding and weaning practices in an urban slum community found that breast-feeding was started by 85 per cent on the third day, 10 per cent on the second day and by 1.7 per cent on the fourth day. The commonest reason offered for delayed initiation of breast-feeding was lack of milk formation during the first few days. Specific enquiry revealed that 'fenush' (local term for colostrums) was secreted in the first few days. But it was not fed because it was not considered as milk and that it was harmful to babies (Gayatri ray and Reddy, D.C.C., 1988).

A study on maternal nutrition, breast feeding and growth of young children among urban population revealed that among the 43 women who were studied, only one women did breast fed as she was medically advised not to do. Another woman stopped breast-feeding even during the first month of breast-feeding because she did not want to feed the infant and her family instructed her to follow certain dietary restrictions during the period of nursing the child for which she was unwilling. Out of 31 women who breast-fed beyond the first few weeks, some had started supplementing before one month; earliest was 0.2 months. Four mothers introduced supplements after 4 months (Neena Joshi, et al., 1999).

A study among 400 nursing women found 9 per cent of them breast-feed their infants for 6 months. About a half of the infants were at breast fed till one year. This prolonged period of lactation may be due to the beliefs that the breast-feeding prolongs the poor mothers to continue lactation even till the onset of next pregnancy (Das, et al., 1992).

A study conducted in Patna found that 98.2 per cent mothers were breast-feeding their children and only 17 per cent mothers fed their babies with colostrums and even they were ignorant of its advantages. The age of weaning preferred was after one year by 91 per cent (Sharma R. and Kumar, 1991).

Another study conducted in Mumbai slum found that 19 out of 26 children received breast milk for 12 to 15 months and 22 out of 36 infants continued breast-feeding (Bavedkar S.B., et al., 1994).

The data on breast-feeding and complementary feeding obtained from a series of questions in the woman's questionnaire of NFHS-2 (1998-99) revealed that the proportion of children who begin breast feeding within an hour of birth ranges from 25 per cent in Nagaland to 54 per cent in Mizoram. A substantial proportion of woman who gave birth to children during the three years preceding the survey squeezed the first milk from the breast before they began breast-feeding contrary to recommendations regarding infant feeding (NFHS, 1998-99).

A study on feeding pattern practiced by the mothers attending an under five clinic revealed that by third month 36 per cent babies were on breast fed, 19 per cent were on artificial and 45 per cent were on mixed feeding. In the study, lactation failure (5 per cent) may be one of the important causes for such a low level of acceptance of breast-feeding (Mrinal Kanti Chatterjee, 1990).

The results of a study conducted in Srinagar revealed that 96 per cent of the infants were breast fed and the important reasons responsible for adopting breast feeding were, nutritional quality, free of cost, satisfaction to the mother, safe and protected feeding to the infant, eliminates preparation of milk, is available at proper temperature and child does not take artificial feed. Breast feeding was stopped by 65.7 per cent of the mothers at the age of 7 to 9 months while 52 per cent of the mothers felt that breast feedings should be terminated at 18 months of age. Fifty seven per cent of the mothers did not feed their infants with colostrums as they felt that colostrums is an unhygienic product. Forty four per cent of the mothers who fed colostrums stated that it was given to their infants on doctor's advice. Decisions regarding breast-feeding and bottle feeding prior to pregnancy were made by 72 per cent and 36 per cent of mothers respectively. Semi-solid foods were introduced to 71.2 per cent of the infants and the different semi-solids introduced were farex, cerelac, spinach soup, suji kheer, tea, roti, suji, halwa and meant soup. Seventy per cent of illiterate and 69 per cent of literate mothers introduced semi-solids at the age of 7 to 9 months (Ganjoo C. and Rowlands, R., 1988).

A study on the effect of the socio-economic level on the infant weaning practices in maharastrians revealed that by 4-6 months of age, weaning was started for 60 per cent of the infants from high income group (HIG) as compared to 7.5 per cent in middle income group (MIG) and 22.5 per cent in low income group (LIG). For most of the infants from MIG (65 per cent) weaning was started at 6 – 9 months whereas in LIG, even by 15 months of age, the mothers have not weaned their infants (Nina S.Dodd and Sunanda Datta, 1993).

A study on breast-feeding and weaning practices in Uttar Pradesh revealed that as many as 91.5 per cent of the women breast-fed their infants. Breast-feeding on the second day was observed in 44.3 per cent of the women, 35.5 per cent of new born infants got breast milk after a lapse of three days, 17.5 per cent on the fourth day of birth and only 2.6 per cent got it a day after birth. None of the infants received breast milk on the day of birth. Though colostrums is regarded as an ideal food for the newborn, only 25 (11.8 per cent) of the women gave colostrums to their infants following counseling (Bhardwaj N. et al., 1991).

Another study on knowledge, attitude and practices of breast-feeding in a rural area of East Delhi revealed that majority of the respondents had good knowledge and a positive attitude towards breast-feeding. Colostrum was thought to be harmful for the baby. According to 52 per cent of the mothers all of them had breast fed their children but the breast feed was given within one hour by only 9.1 per cent of the mothers. Pre-lacteal foods were given by 82 per cent of mothers. Majority (83.5 per cent) of the children were breast fed till one year of age. Literate mothers were more likely to initiate breast feeding early and gave pre-lacteal feeds less often. Illiterate mothers breast fed for long duration and on demand. Thus, early feeding and colostrum feeding have to be promoted among the mothers (Vijay L. Grover, et al., 1997).

A study on the impact of action programme on health, hygiene and feeding practices of mothers in slum areas revealed that all the mothers preferred breast-feeding to bottle-feeding except three per cent who had no breast milk. The infants were at breast normally for one and a half years, and for most of these mothers breast-feeding duration were longer because of economic problems. Fifty per cent of the infants were weaned at 9 to 10 months of age and very few before 7 months, and thirty per cent of the infants were weaned at one year of age (Suhasini Ramisetty, 1988).

Another study on weaning and feeding practices of urban, rural and tribal children revealed that all the tribal and rural mothers were discarding the colostrum while 48 per cent of urban mothers were given colostrum to their children; the majority of rural (94 per cent) and tribal (75 per cent) children were breast fed for one year or more as compared to 60 per cent of urban children. Thirty eight per cent of urban mothers stopped breast-feeding before one year of age while only 6 to 25 per cent of rural and tribal mothers stopped at this age. The liquid supplementary/ weaning food were given by 60 per cent of urban mothers between the age3-6 months while 80 per cent of rural and 50 per cent of tribal mothers were not giving any liquid foods, but semi-solid food known as 'Rab' was commonly used by these mothers. Urban mothers also introduced solid foods at an early age 3-9 months, while rural and tribal mothers introduced after one year of age (Muktaparashar and Mayachoudhary, 1986).

A study on food, dietary intake and feeding practices in urban slum of Visakhapatnam revealed that all children were breast-fed till the end of first year. A gradual decrease has been noted from then onwards, with 25 per cent of females being breast fed till 4th year and 11 per cent of males till 5th year. Such prolonged breast-feeding was not reported in other studies (Muktaparashar and Mayachoudhary, 1986).

The above reviews of literature on infant feeding practices in various parts of India revealed that a high percentage of mothers did not feed colostrums because they did not know its importance and majority of the mothers exclusively breast-fed the child upto 6 months and beyond. A significant proportion of mothers breast-fed beyond one year. Introduction of timely supplement feeding was observed to be very poor in many studies. Very small percentage of mothers stopped breast-feeding before 6 months, as they were not aware of the importance of breast milk. The above review of literature indicated the prevalence of poor infant feeding practices in different parts of India.

3

Methodology

The aim of the present study is to examine the socio-economic, demographic and health care determinants of infant and child mortality in Rural India. In order to have a better understanding of the variations in infant and child mortality among various states of India, all the 25 states for which data are available for the present study are grouped into three categories as high, medium and low mortality groups according to their level of under five mortality rates as per the NFHS 1992-93. This design has the advantage of knowing intragroup and intergroup variations in infant and child mortality among the three mortality group of states. The objectives and methodology of the study are presented in detail in the following sections.

3.1 OBJECTIVES

General Objective

The general objective of the study is to identify the socio-economic, demographic, maternal health and child care determinants of infant and child mortality in Rural India.

Specific objectives

1. To study the variations in the fertility behaviour and the utilisation of maternal health care services by mothers in the three mortality group of states.

2. To study the levels, trends and differentials in infant and child mortality rates among the three mortality group of states;
3. To study the influence of socio-economic, demographic, maternal health, child care and mass media variables on infant and child mortality;
4. To study the effect of selected socio-economic, demographic and maternal health care variables on infant and child mortality; and
5. To suggest viable strategies to reduce infant and child mortality in Rural India.

3.2 Hypotheses

1. Increase in mother's education decrease infant and child mortality.
2. Higher the standard of living, lower will be the infant and child mortality.
3. Infant and child mortality are higher among children of mothers from lower caste groups (SC/ST) than others.
4. Infant and child mortality are lower among children of mothers age 20-29 years than those born to very young (<20 years) and very old (>30 years) mothers.
5. Infant and child mortality are higher among children born with short birth interval (<24 months) than those born with longer birth interval (>24 months).
6. Infant and child mortality are higher among children of higher order births than others.
7. Infant mortality is lower among children of mothers who have availed antenatal care than those who have not.
8. Infant mortality is lower among children of mothers who have received tetanus toxoid vaccine during pregnancy than those who have not.
9. Infant mortality is lower among children whose births were attended by trained health personnel than those attended by untrained personnel.
10. Infant mortality is lower among children born in institutions than those born at homes.

A few more hypotheses, based on the available data, have been considered and tested in different chapters.

3.3 Theoretical Frame Work

The mechanism through which various factors operate to influence infant and child mortality are complex because of the synergism of social, economic and biological process. A variety of conceptual models/theoretical frameworks have been developed by different authors for the study of child survival (Mosely and Chen, 1984; Schultz, 1985; Jain, 1985; Mahadevan, 1986). Among the various theoretical frame works, the proximate determinant frame work developed by Mosley and Chen is the most widely adopted model.

Mosley and Chen identified a set of 14 intermediate or proximate determinants that directly influence the risk of morbidity and mortality among infant and children. All social and economic determinants must operate through these variables to affect child survival. Mosley and Chen grouped these proximate determinants into five categories, viz. 1. Maternal factors; 2. Environmental contamination; 3. Nutrient deficiency; 4. Injury; and 5. Personal illness control.

Mosley and Chen's proximate determinants framework is the tool for the development of theoretical framework for the present

Figure 3.1

A theoretical framework for child survival analysis

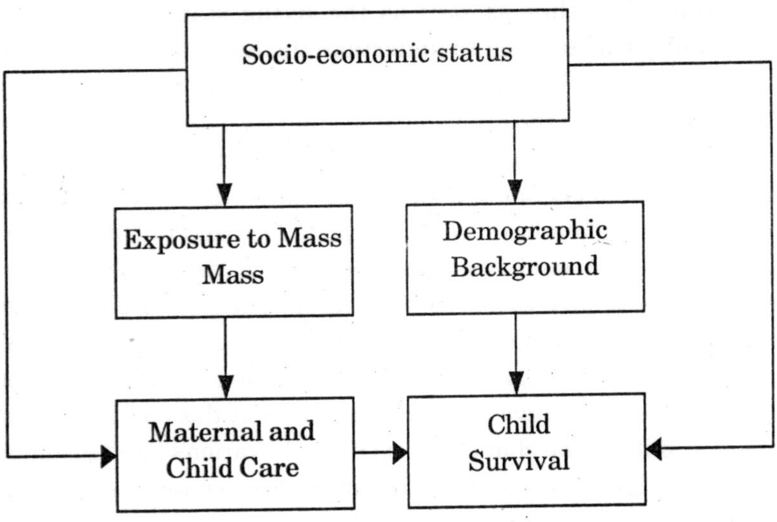

study. Based on the limited range of variables, for which data are available, a simplified theoretical framework is developed for the study and is shown in figure 3.1.

Mother's exposure to mass media which depend on the socio-economic status of the mother, influences the practice of maternal and child care, which inturn affect child survival. Demographic background of mother such as age at marriage and parity are influenced by their socio-economic status are expected to influence the maternal and child care practices, which in turn affect the child survival. Demographic background of mother is also expected to affect child survival directly.

The relationship between the socio-economic status of the mother and the maternal and child care practices is evidenced from many studies. Several studies have shown that women in higher socio-economic groups tend to exhibit more frequent use of maternity care services than women in the lower socio-economic groups. The socio-cultural background of women also plays an important role in the utilisation of maternity care services (Leslie and Gupta, 1989; Petto, 1987; Roy 1996). The factors that deny women, the right to reproductive choices and dignity (Germain, 1987) inhibit their utilisation of maternal health care services. In both high and low access setting, more educated women will use health care services to a much greater extent than the uneducated (George, 1991). Education of mother as well as the living standard, influence significantly the decision to undertake the antenatal care services (Roy, 1996). Thus the socio-economic variables affect survival status of children through the maternal and child care practices of mother.

The direct relationship of socio-economic variables with survival status of children is evident from the fact that children of higher socio-economic status families receive adequate food and nutrition, timely medical attention and hygienic and preventive care which will result in the improved survival status of children. The relationship of socio-economic variables with the demographic characteristics of mother is evident from the fact that women of higher socio-economic status tend to marry later and have smaller families than those of lower socio-economic status. The chances of exposure to various mass media are also much higher for mothers of higher socio-economic status than those of lower socio-economic status.

The relationship between age-parity and utilisation of maternal health care is not only negative but also linear (Lesile and Gupta, 1989). The greater confidence and experience of the older women and high parity women together with greater responsibilities within the household and for child care, have been suggested as explanatory factors for their tendency to use maternal health care services less frequently (Kswast, 1988). Mass media such as radio, television and cinema play a vital role in disseminating information on nutrition, health, family welfare and other health care practices. Thus, mass media act together with socio-economic characteristics, to determine the extent of the use of maternal health care services which in turn affect child survival. Thus the present model is conceptualised based on the existing literature on the determinants of child survival.

3.4 Data Source

The data for the present study were taken from the National Family Health Survey (NFHS) conducted during 1992-93 in 25 states of India. The National Family Health Survey was sponsored by the Government of India and funded by United States Agency for International Development (USAID). A total of 62,243 ever married women in the age group 13-49 years in rural and 27,534 ever married women in the age group of 13-49 years in urban areas were interviewed for the NFHS. As the study related to Rural India, the data related to rural areas of the 25 states of India were taken for the analysis of the present study.

The National Family Health Survey provides vital information on fertility, nuptiality, family planning, utilisation of maternal and child care services, breast feeding, supplementation and immunisation practices, child health and nutrition, infant and child mortality. The information on infant and child mortality were taken from the birth history data which include information on the dead children, their sex, date of birth and date of death.

3.5 Grouping of States

According to the findings of the NFHS, 1992-93, the variation in under-five mortality rates in India is great, ranging from 142 per 1000 live births for Assam to 21 per 1000 live births for Nagaland. In order to have a better understanding of the reasons for the variations and to identify the specific factors operating on infant and child mortality, all the 25 states were grouped into three categories as Low, Medium and High mortality groups according to their level of under-five mortality rates as per the NFHS, 1992-93 (Table 3.1).

The groupings of states were made based on the following procedure.

All the 25 states were arranged in descending order according to their level of under-five mortality rates. The cumulative total of under-five mortality rates of all the 25 states was divided into three equal intervals viz. 33.3 percentile, 33.4 to 66.6 percentile, 66.7 percentile and above. Those states which fall in the first 33.3 percentile are considered as HIGH mortality group. States which fall between 33.4 to 66.6 percentile are considered as MEDIUM mortality group and states which fall above 66.6 percentile are considered as LOW mortality group. The details of under-five mortality rate for each state and the cumulative total rates are given in Table 3.2.

Table 3.1 Distribution (Grouping) of States according to their level of under - five mortality rates (1992-93)

High Mortality Group (105-142)	*Medium Mortality Group (87-104)*	*Low Mortality Group (86 or less)*
Assam	Gujarat	TamilNadu
Utter Pradesh	Rajasthan	Delhi
Orissa	West Bengal	Arunachal Pradesh
Madhya Pradesh	Haryana	Maharastra
Bihar	Andhra Pradesh	Himachal Pradesh
Tripura	Karnataka	Punjab
	Mehalaya	Manipur
		Jammu
		Goa
		Kerala
		Mizoram
		Nagaland

Note : Figures in parentheses are the range of under 5 mortality rates of the states included in the group.

3.6 Analysis of Data

After having grouped the states into three categories as Low, Medium and High mortality groups, the data related to the rural areas of the three groups of states were analysed separately and compared.

First a tabular analysis (percentage distribution) was made on the background characteristics of the study area, fertility behavior and utilisation of maternal health care services,

Table 3.2 States grouped according to their level of under - five mortality rates, NFHS, India, 1992 - 93.

S.No	*Name of the State*	*Under – 5 Mortality Rate*	*Rank*	*Cumulative Total*	*Mortality Group*
1	Assam	142.2	1		High
2	Uttar Pradesh	141.3	2	283.5	
3	Orissa	131.0	3	414.5	
4	Madhya Pradesh	130.3	4	544.8	
5	Bihar	127.5	5	672.3	
6	Tripura	104.6	6	776.9	
7	Gujarat	104.0	7	880.9	Medium
8	Rajasthan	102.6	8	983.5	
9	West Bengal	99.3	9	1082.8	
10	Haryana	98.7	10	1181.5	
11	Andhra Pradesh	91.2	11	1272.7	
12	Karnataka	87.3	12	1360.0	
13	Meghalaya	86.9	13	1446.9	
14	Tamil Nadu	86.5	14	1553.4	Low
15	Delhi	83.1	15	1616.5	
16	Arunachal Pradesh	72.0	16	1688.5	
17	Maharashtra	70.3	17	1758.8	
18	Himachal Pradesh	69.1	18	1827.9	
19	Punjab	68.0	19	1895.9	
20	Manipur	61.7	20	1957.6	
21	Jammu	59.1	21	2016.7	
22	Goa	38.9	22	2055.6	
23	Kerala	32.0	23	2087.6	
24	Mizoram	29.3	24	2116.9	
25	Nagaland	20.7	25	2137.6	

immunization and breast feeding practices and child nutrition for the three mortality groups and compared to see the differences if any, which might have resulted in the variations in infant and child mortality rates among the three mortality groups.

Secondly, an univariate analysis of infant and child mortality rates by different background characteristics of mother and child was made.

The mortality measures used in this study are:

1. Neonatal mortality : the probability of dying during the first month of life.
2. Post neonatal mortality : the difference between infant mortality and neonatal mortality.
3. Infant mortality (1q0) : the probability of dying before 12 months of age.
4. Child mortality (4q1) : the probability of dying between exact ages 1 and 5 years.
5. Under-five mortality (5q0) : the probability of dying before five years of age.

The mortality estimates are not rates, but are true probabilities, calculated according to the conventional life table approach. For any calendar period, deaths and exposure in that period are first tabulated for the age intervals 0, 1-2, 3-5, 6-11, 12-23, 24-35, 36-47 and 48-59 months. Then age-interval-specific probabilities of survival are calculated, denoted as qi. Finally, probabilities of death over larger age intervals are calculated by multiplying the relevant age-interval survival probabilities together and subtracting the product from one.

The trends in infant and child mortality rates were derived directly from the maternity history data for three quinquennial period preceding the survey for the three mortality groups. The mortality estimates by demographic and socio-economic characteristics were made for 10 years period preceding the survey. However, the mortality estimates by maternal care variables were made for the four years period preceding the survey as these information were collected only for four years preceding the survey.

The univariate analysis of mortality estimates was made to see the intragroup and inter-group variations according to selected background characteristics of the parents and child.

Some of the variables used in the univariate analysis are associated with each other and hence it is difficult to interpret the mortality differentials observed in the univariate analysis. Hence, multivariate approach is also adopted in order to estimate independent effects of each variable when other variables are controlled. The method adopted for the multivariate analysis is the proportional hazard models.

3.7 Variables

A. Dependent Variables

1. Infant mortality and its components (Neonatal and Post-neonatal mortality).
2. Child mortality.

B. Independent Variables

1. Demographic Variables

i. Age of mother
ii. Birth order
iii. Previous birth interval
iv. Sex of child
v. Birth weight

2. Socio-economic Variables

i. Religion
ii. Caste
iii. Education of mother
iv. Education of father
v. Working status of mother
vi. Standard of Living Index (SLI)

3. Maternal Care Variables

i. Antenatal visits
ii. Medical maternity care
iii. Tetanus Toxoid (TT)

iv. Place of birth
v. Birth attendant
vi. Complications at delivery

4. Child care variables

i. Breast feeding
ii. Immunisation
iii. Nutritional status of children

5. Mass Media Variables

i. Exposure to mass media
ii. Watch T.V. once a week
iii. Listen to Radio once a week
iv. Visit Cinema once a month

4

Housing Characteristics

Illness and death among young children is mainly caused by germs which get into the child's mouth via food and water. In communities without latrines, without safe drinking water and without safe refuse disposal, it is very difficult for families to prevent the spread of germs. Housing conditions such as type of materials used for roofing and flooring, number of rooms (number of person per sleeping room) and electrification are also play an important role in the child survival.

Considering the influence of housing condition on child survival, the variation in the housing characteristics among the three mortality group of states are examined and presented in the following sections.

4.1 Type of House

The materials used in the roof and floor of the house play an important role in infant and child survival because of the underlying fact that the children of mothers living in thatched roof and mud flooring houses are more exposed to the risk of respiratory and other infection.

Based on the materials used for the construction of walls, roof and floor, a house in the NFHS is classified as either kachcha, pucca or semi-pucca. Kachcha houses are made from mud, thatches or other low quality materials. Pucca houses are made from high quality materials throughout, including roof, walls and floor. Semi-Pucca houses are made partly with low quality and partly with high quality materials.

The distribution of households by type of house is presented in table 4.1. A substantially higher proportion of kachcha houses (made from mud, thatch or other low quality materials) were observed in the high mortality group, followed by medium and low mortality groups. It is found that nearly three fourth of households (74 per cent) in high mortality group, a little over half of the households (52 per cent) in medium mortality group and a little over two-fifth of households (42 per cent) in low mortality group were kachcha houses.

4.2 Electrification

It is generally believed that children of mothers living in households with electrification facilities are having higher chances of survival than the children of mothers living in households without electrification. The results presented in table 4.1. supports the above notion. It is observed that a substantially higher proportion of households (64 per cent) in low mortality group were using electricity for lighting which was followed by medium (46 per cent) and high (22 per cent) mortality groups.

4.3 Sources of Drinking Water

The importance of safe drinking water in reducing infant and child mortality has been well established in many studies. Among the various causes for infant and child death, water-borne diseases play a significant role. Hence, provision of potable water is expected to bring down infant and child mortality to a considerable extent.

The distribution of households by sources of drinking water among the three mortality groups presented in table 4.1 revealed that the main source of drinking water was hand pump in the high and medium mortality groups (53 per cent and 38 per cent respectively) where as it was pipe water in the low mortality group (40 per cent). The results indicate that infant and child mortality are low among communities where the use of pipe water for drinking is high.

4.4 Persons per Sleeping Room

Acute lower respiratory tract infections, primarily, pneumonia and bronchia ties are the major type of Acute Respiratory Infection responsible for childhood mortality. Many socio-economic status studies indicate a clear relationship between socio-economic status as measured by household size, number of rooms and persons per room and the incidence of respiratory infection.

The per cent distribution of households by number of persons per sleeping room is presented in table 4.1. The proportion of households having one or two persons per sleeping room was 64 per cent in low mortality group where as it was 55 per cent in medium and 59 per cent in high mortality groups. The mean number of persons per sleeping room was observed to be low (2.6) in the low mortality group as compared to medium (3.0) and high (2.8) mortality groups. The results indicate the significance of less crowding in reducing childhood mortality.

4.5 Toilet Facility

Many studies have proved the relationship of toilet facilities at home with infant and child mortality. The distribution of households according to toilet facilities presented in Table 4.1 revealed that about 78 per cent of households in low mortality group, 88 per cent in medium mortality group and 91 per cent in high mortality group were not having toilet facility at home. Though a majority of households in all mortality groups were not having toilet facility at home, a higher proportion of households (about 22 per cent) in low mortality group were having toilet facility as compared to only 12 per cent in medium and just 10 per cent in high mortality group.

4.6 Place of keeping Animals at Night

It is common practice in most of the households in rural areas to keep animals inside the house at night. Such practices increase the risk of morbidity and mortality among young children. The distribution of households according to the place of keeping animals at night presented table 4.1 showed that comparatively higher proportion of households (25 per cent) in the high mortality group were having the practice of keeping animals inside the house during night hours where as it was only 19 per cent in medium and just 9 per cent in low mortality groups.

4.7 Summary

The comparative analysis of the housing characteristics of the three mortality groups showed that a substantially higher proportion of households (74 per cent) in high mortality group were having kachcha houses, followed by medium (52 per cent) and low (42 per cent) mortality groups. Only 22 percent of households in high mortality group were having electrification facility where as it

Table 4.1 Percent distribution of households by selected housing characteristics, Rural India, 1992 – 93.

Housing Characteristics	*Mortality group*		
	High N = 29517*	*Medium* N = 21042*	*Low* N = 13579*
Type of House			
Kachcha	74.4	52.4	42.3
Semi Pucca	19.8	31.4	42.5
Pucca	5.8	16.2	15.2
Electricity			
Yes	21.7	46.2	64.1
No	78.3	53.8	35.9
Source of Water for Drinking			
Piped	5.5	25.5	39.6
Hand pump	53.0	37.9	22.3
Well Water	35.4	29.3	29.1
Surface Water	5.0	5.1	5.3
Others	1.1	2.2	3.5
Persons Per sleeping Room			
< 2	58.7	54.8	64.1
3 – 4	25.8	26.8	22.3
5 – 6	10.3	12.5	9.6
7 +	5.1	5.8	3.9
Dk/missing	0.1	0.1	0.0
Mean	2.8	3.0	2.6

(Contd)

(Contd. Table 4.1)

Housing Characteristics	*Mortality group*		
	*High N = 29517**	*Medium N = 21042**	*Low N = 13579**
Sanitation Facility			
Flush	3.3	6.6	15.3
Pit Toilet/Latrine	6.1	5.6	6.2
Others	0.1	0.1	0.1
No facility	90.6	87.7	78.4
Where Animals kept at Night			
Inside the House	24.5	19.0	9.2
Outside the House	48.4	48.3	44.3
No Livestock	27.1	32.7	46.4

* Weighted Numbers

was more than two fifth (46 per cent) and nearly two third (64 per cent) in the medium and low mortality groups respectively. Hand pump was the major source of drinking water in the high and medium mortality groups where as it was pipe water in the low mortality group. The mean number of persons per sleeping room was low at 2.6 persons per room in the low mortality group as compared to 3.0 persons in medium and 2.8 persons in high mortality groups. With regard to the place of keeping animals at night, it is found that one fourth of households (25 per cent) in the high mortality group, nearly one fifth of households (19 per cent) in the medium and nearly one tenth of households (9 per cent) in low mortality groups had the practice of keeping animals at home. The results indicate that housing conditions are better in the low mortality group, comparatively poor in the high mortality group and moderate in medium mortality group.

5

Fertility Behaviour of Women

It is generally believed that reduction in fertility improves the survival status of infant and children by decreasing the high risk pregnancies such as closely spaced births, those from very young and very old women and those of higher order births. This chapter compares the fertility behaviour of women among the three mortality groups in order to have an understanding of the relationship of fertility with infant and child mortality.

5.1 Current Fertility

The general fertility rate, total fertility rate and the age specific fertility rates derived for the three years preceding the survey (1990-92) are presented in Table 5.1. The crude birth rate derived from the household data for the period 1-24 months before the survey indicate that the estimated crude birth rate for the high mortality group was much higher (33 births per 1000 population) than the crude birth rate estimated for medium (27) and low (23) mortality groups. The general fertility rate was 150 births per thousand women in the reproductive age of 13-49 in the high mortality group where as it was 121 for medium and 113 for low mortality groups. The total fertility rate (TFR) which is the sum of the age specific fertility rates was also observed to be very high (4.3 births per women) for high mortality group compared to 3.2 for the medium and 3.1 for the low mortality groups. The total fertility rate was nearly same for both medium and low mortality groups.

The age specific fertility rates indicate that the fertility was peak at 20-24 age group in all mortality groups. While the fertility decline was greatest among women age 30-34 in the medium and low mortality groups it was greatest among women age 35-39 in the high mortality group (see Figure 5.1). The results indicate that the fertility continues to be high and the decline is very slow in the high mortality group as compared to the medium and low mortality groups. There is not much difference in the fertility rates between the medium and low mortality groups.

Table 5.1 Age specific and cumulative fertility rates and crude birth rates by mortality groups, Rural India, (1990 - 92)

Age	*High*	*Medium*	*Low*
15 – 19	122	133	152
20 – 24	252	231	243
25 – 29	215	147	140
30 – 34	152	78	60
35 – 39	80	36	19
40 – 44	31	10	7
45 – 49	9	4	2
TFR (15 - 49)	4.3	3.2	3.1
GFR	150.0	121.0	113.0
CBR (Based on household birth record)	32.9	26.8	23.4

Note : Rates are for the period 1- 36 months before the interview except for the CBR which is based on the period 1-24 months before the interview.

TFR : Total Fertility Rate, expressed per woman

GFR : General Fertility Rate (births to women age 13 - 49 divided by women-years lived between age 15 and 49 expressed per 1000 women)

CBR : Crude Birth Rate, expressed per 1000 population

5.2 Total Fertility Rates and Mean Number of Children Ever Born

The total fertility rates for three years preceding the survey (1990-92) and the mean number of children ever born to women age 40-49 by selected background characteristics are presented in Table 5.2. Both the total fertility rate and the mean number of children

Figure 5.1
Age Specifi Fertility Rates by Mortality Groups

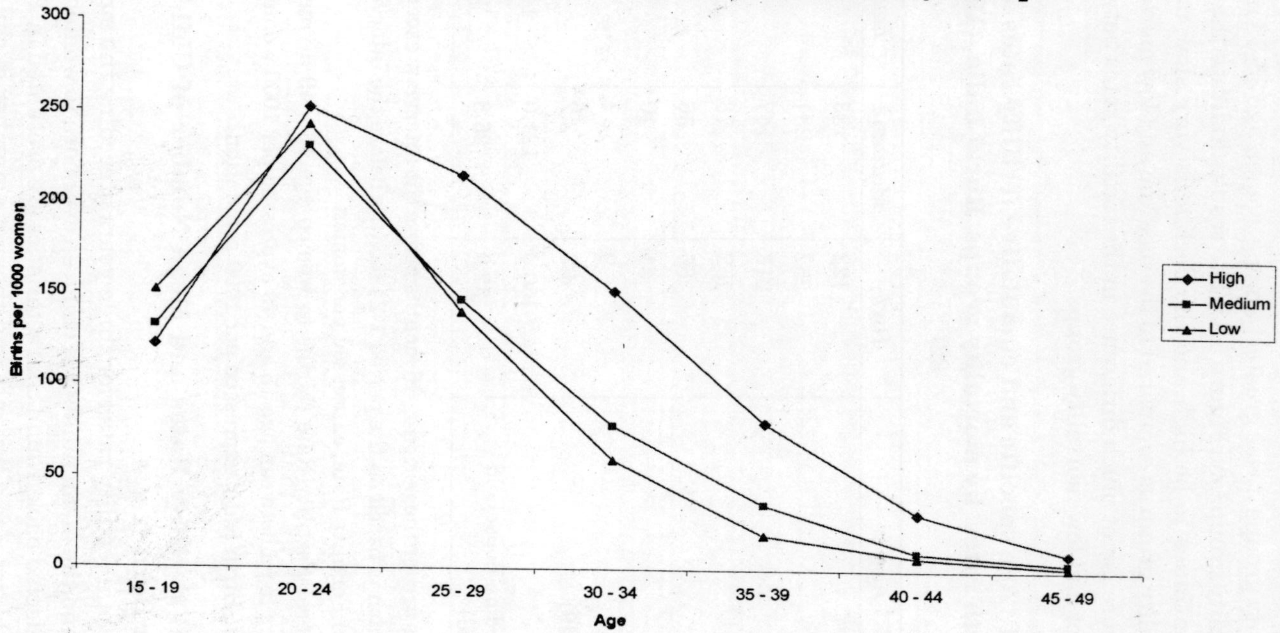

Note : Rates are for the three years period before the survey (1990-92)

NFHS, Rural India, 1992–93.

ever born were substantially high in the high mortality group as compared to medium and low mortality groups (See Figure 5.2). It is observed that the total fertility rate declined with increase in education in all mortality groups. In the high mortality group, it has decreased from 4.6 for illiterates to 2.4 for high school and above level of education. In the medium mortality group, it has decreased from 3.5 to 1.9 and in the low mortality group, it has decreased from 3.4 to 2.4. The differences observed between the high and low mortality groups narrowed down with the increase in

Table 5.2 Total fertility rate for the three years period preceding the survey (1990 – 92) and mean number of children ever born to women age 40-49 years by selected background characteristics, Rural India, 1992 - 93.

	Total Fertility Rate			*Mean number of children ever born*		
	High	*Medium*	*Low*	*High*	*Medium*	*Low*
Education						
Illiterate	4.6	3.5	3.4	5.8	5.0	4.6
Literate < Middle Complete	3.7	2.8	2.9	5.5	4.6	4.0
Middle Complete	3.2	2.2	2.2	4.8	3.6	3.5
High School & Above	2.4	1.9	2.4	4.3	3.1	2.7
Religion						
Hindu	4.1	3.0	2.9	5.6	4.8	4.2
Muslim	5.2	4.3	3.6	6.4	6.0	5.5
Christian	4.1	2.6	2.8	5.1	4.6	3.9
Sikh	2.5	2.9	2.4	6.0	4.4	4.1
Others	3.7	2.4	2.8	4.9	4.4	4.6
Caste						
Scheduled Caste	4.8	3.5	3.4	6.2	5.3	4.8
Scheduled Tribe	3.7	3.5	3.5	5.1	4.7	4.9
Others	4.1	2.9	2.9	5.7	4.8	4.2
Total	**4.2**	**3.1**	**3.0**	**5.7**	**4.9**	**4.3**

Figure 5.2
Total Fertility Rate and Mean Number of Children Ever Born by Mortality Groups

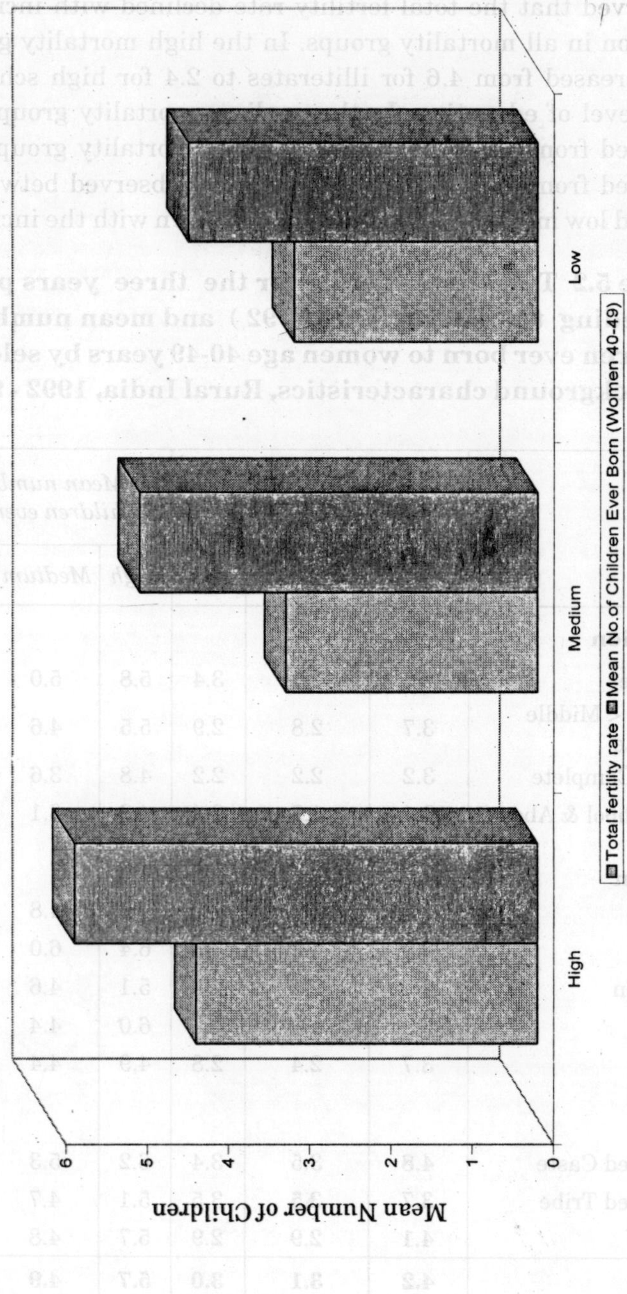

NFHS, Rural India, 1992-93

education of women. Muslim women tend to have high fertility than others in all mortality groups. Scheduled Caste women tend to have high fertility in high mortality group where as in medium and low mortality groups, both Scheduled Caste and Scheduled Tribe women tend to have high fertility than other caste groups.

The mean number of children ever born was 5.7 for women in the high mortality group, where as it was 4.9 and 4.3 for women in the medium and low mortality groups respectively. Number of children ever born declined considerably with increase in education in all mortality groups. The mean number of children ever born was high among Muslim women than others in all mortality groups. Scheduled caste women have more number of children than other caste groups in the high and medium mortality groups, where as in the low mortality group, Scheduled Tribe women have more number of children. Overall, both total fertility rate and mean number of children ever born were high for high mortality group as compared to medium and low mortality groups.

5.3 Children Ever Born and Living

The mean number of children ever born and still living to currently married women in the age 13-49 years are presented in Table 5.3. The results showed that the mean number of children ever born was high (3.4) for high mortality group compared to medium (3.0) and low (2.9) mortality groups. The difference between the mean number of children ever born and living was 0.6 children in the high mortality group, 0.4 in the medium mortality group and 0.3 in the low mortality group. The results confirm the belief that high fertility leads to high child mortality.

The child loss as measured by the difference between the mean number of children ever born and mean number of children living indicate that the child loss was slightly more among male than female children in the high (1.4 vs 1.3) and low (1.2 vs 1.1) mortality groups and there was no sex difference observed in child loss in the medium mortality group (1.2).

In the high mortality group, the mean number of children ever born increased from 0.6 children for women aged 15-19 years to 6.0 children for women aged 45-49 years and the mean number of children living increased from 0.5 for women aged 15-19 years to 4.5 for women aged 45-49 years. The results indicate a consistent increase in child loss at all ages of women in the high mortality group. In the medium mortality group, the mean number of children ever born increased from 0.1 for women aged 13-14 years to 5.3 for women aged 45-49 years and the mean number of children living increased from 0.1 for women aged 13-14 years to 4.3 for women aged 45-49 years. In the low mortality group, the mean number of children ever born increased from 0.1 for women aged 13-14 years to 4.8 for women aged 45-49 years and the mean number of children living has increased from 0.1 for women aged 13-14 years to 3.9 for women aged 45-49 years. The results indicate that the mean number of children ever born was nearly same in all mortality groups up to 20-24 age group and after that the mean number of children ever born in high mortality group was substantially higher than the medium and low mortality groups.

Increase in education has significant effect on the number of children ever born and living in all mortality groups. In the high mortality group, the mean number of children ever born has decreased substantially from 3.6 among illiterates to just 2.0 for women with high school and higher level of education. In the medium mortality group, the mean number of children ever born decreased from 3.3 among illiterates to 1.6 for women with high school and higher level of education. In the low mortality group, it has decreased from 3.4 to 1.8. Even at the higher level of education, the mean number of children ever born was substantially higher among women in high mortality group (2.0) compared to women in medium (1.6) and low (1.8) mortality groups.

Among the three major religious groups, Muslim women seemed to have more number of children ever born than women in Hindu and Christian families in all mortality groups. In the case of caste, scheduled caste women seemed to have more number of children ever born in the high and medium mortality groups where as in low mortality group, both the scheduled caste and scheduled tribe women were having more number of children ever born than women in other caste groups.

The analysis of data on mean number of children ever born and surviving by background characteristics of the women revealed that the mean number of children ever born increased with age of mother in all mortality groups. The difference between the mean

Table 5.3 Mean number of children ever born and living to currently married women by selected background characteristics, Rural India,1992- 93.

Characteristics	*HIGH*						*Medium*					
	Male		*Female*		*All*		*Male*		*Female*		*All*	
	E.B	*L*	*E.B*	*L*	*E.B*	*L*	*E.B*	*L*	*E.B*	*L*	*E.B*	*L*
Age												
13 – 14	0.0	0.0	0.0	0.0	0.0	0.0	0.1	0.0	0.0	0.0	0.1	0.1
15 – 19	0.3	0.3	0.3	0.2	0.6	0.5	0.3	0.3	0.3	0.3	0.7	0.6
20 – 24	0.9	0.7	0.8	0.7	1.7	1.5	0.9	0.8	0.9	0.8	1.8	1.6
25 – 29	1.6	1.4	1.5	1.3	3.2	2.7	1.5	1.4	1.4	1.3	3.0	2.6
30 – 34	2.3	1.9	2.1	1.7	4.5	3.6	1.9	1.7	1.8	1.6	3.8	3.3
35 – 39	2.7	2.2	2.5	1.9	5.2	4.1	2.2	1.9	2.1	1.7	4.3	3.6
40 – 44	3.0	2.4	2.8	2.1	5.8	4.5	2.5	2.1	2.3	1.9	4.9	4.1
45 – 49	3.1	2.4	2.9	2.1	6.0	4.5	2.7	2.2	2.5	2.0	5.3	4.3
Education												
Illiterate	1.9	1.5	1.7	1.4	3.6	2.8	1.7	1.4	1.6	1.3	3.3	2.8
Literate<Middle complete	1.6	1.4	1.5	1.3	3.1	2.7	1.4	1.2	1.3	1.2	2.7	2.1
Middle Complete	1.2	1.1	1.1	1.0	2.3	2.1	1.0	0.9	1.0	0.9	2.0	1.9
High School & Above	1.0	1.0	1.0	0.9	2.0	1.9	0.8	0.8	0.8	0.7	1.6	1.5
Total	**1.8**	**1.4**	**1.6**	**1.3**	**3.4**	**2.8**	**1.6**	**1.4**	**1.5**	**1.3**	**3.0**	**2.6**

E.B - Ever Born L - Living

(Contd.)

(Contd. Table 5.3)

Characteristics		*Low*					
		Male		*Female*		*All*	
		E.B	*L*	*E.B*	*L*	*E.B*	*L*
Age							
13 – 14		0.0	0.0	0.1	0.1	0.1	0.1
15 – 19		0.4	0.3	0.4	0.4	0.7	0.7
20 – 24		0.9	0.8	0.8	0.8	1.7	1.6
25 – 29		1.3	1.2	1.2	1.1	2.6	2.4
30 – 34		1.7	1.5	1.6	1.5	3.3	3.0
35 – 39		2.0	1.7	1.8	1.6	3.8	3.3
40 – 44		2.2	1.9	2.1	1.8	4.3	3.6
45 – 49		2.5	2.0	2.3	1.9	4.8	3.9
Education							
Illiterate		1.8	1.5	1.6	1.4	3.4	2.9
Literate<Middle complete		1.4	1.3	1.3	1.2	2.8	2.5
Middle Complete		1.1	1.0	1.0	0.9	2.0	1.9
High School & Above		0.9	0.8	0.9	0.9	1.8	1.7
Total		**1.5**	**1.3**	**1.4**	**1.3**	**2.9**	**2.6**

(Contd.)

(Contd. Table 5.3)

Characteristics	HIGH						Medium					
	Male		Female		All		Male		Female		All	
	E.B	L	E.B	L	E.B	L	E.B	L	E.B	L	E.B	L
Religion												
Hindu	1.7	1.4	1.6	1.3	3.4	2.7	1.5	1.3	1.4	1.2	3.0	2.6
Muslim	1.9	1.6	1.9	1.6	3.9	3.2	1.8	1.6	1.7	1.5	3.5	3.0
Christian	1.8	1.5	1.8	1.6	3.6	3.1	1.6	1.4	1.5	1.3	3.0	2.7
Sikh	2.0	1.7	1.8	1.6	3.7	3.3	1.3	1.2	1.4	1.3	2.8	2.5
Jain	1.0	1.0	2.0	1.8	3.0	2.8	1.2	1.1	1.3	1.2	2.6	2.4
Buddhist	2.6	2.2	1.8	1.2	4.4	3.4	1.4	1.4	1.1	1.0	2.5	2.3
Others	1.5	1.2	1.1	0.9	2.6	2.2	1.7	1.4	1.7	1.5	3.3	2.9
Caste												
Scheduled Caste	1.8	1.4	1.7	1.2	3.5	2.7	1.7	1.4	1.6	1.3	3.2	2.7
Scheduled Tribe	1.6	1.3	1.5	1.3	3.2	2.6	1.6	1.4	1.5	1.3	3.1	2.7
Others	1.8	1.5	1.7	1.3	3.4	2.8	1.5	1.3	1.5	1.3	3.0	2.6
Total	**1.8**	**1.4**	**1.6**	**1.3**	**3.4**	**2.8**	**1.6**	**1.4**	**1.5**	**1.3**	**3.0**	**2.6**

(Contd.)

(Contd. Table 5.3)

Characteristics	*Low*					
	Male		*Female*		*All*	
	E.B	*L*	*E.B*	*L*	*E.B*	*L*
Religion						
Hindu	1.5	1.3	1.4	1.2	2.9	2.5
Muslim	1.7	1.6	1.6	1.5	3.3	3.0
Christian	1.4	1.2	1.4	1.3	2.7	2.5
Sikh	1.5	1.4	1.4	1.3	2.9	2.7
Jain	1.1	1.1	2.1	2.1	3.2	3.2
Buddhist	1.6	1.3	1.4	1.2	3.1	2.5
Others	1.5	1.3	1.5	1.2	3.0	2.5
Caste						
Scheduled Caste	1.7	1.4	1.5	1.3	3.2	2.7
Scheduled Tribe	1.6	1.5	1.6	1.4	3.2	2.9
Others	1.5	1.3	1.4	1.2	2.8	2.5
Total	**1.5**	**1.3**	**1.4**	**1.3**	**2.9**	**2.6**

Fig. 5.3 Mean Number of Children Ever Born and Living

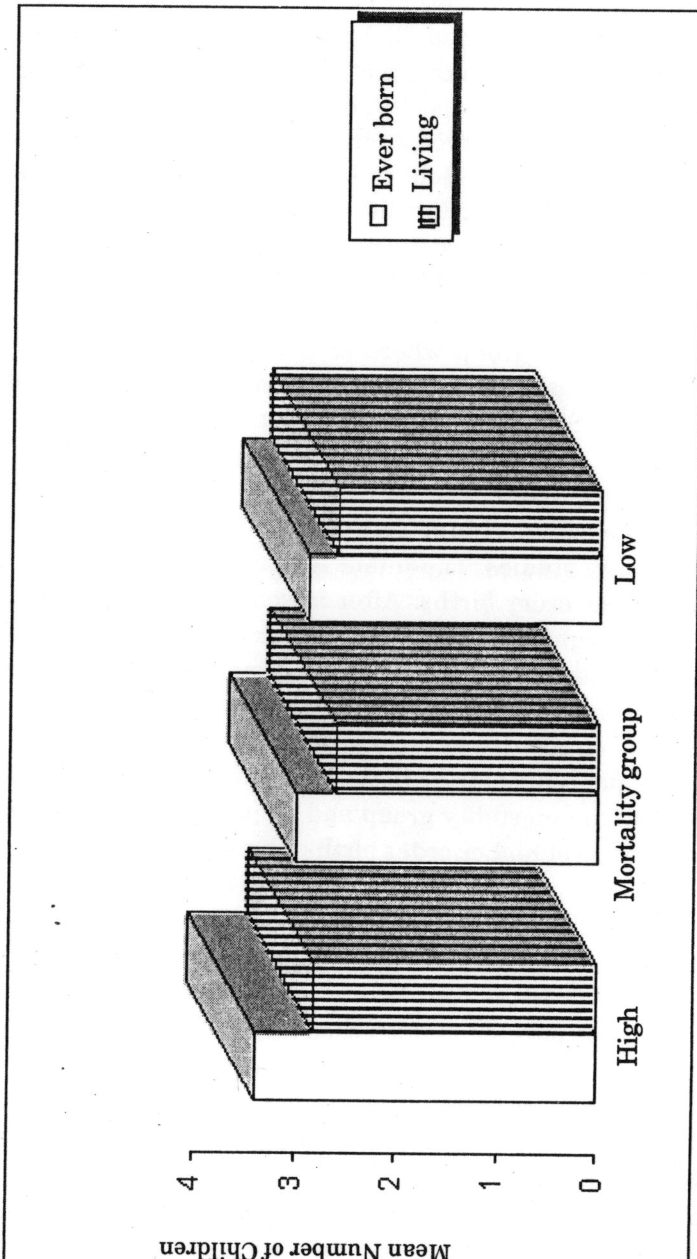

NFHS, Rural India 1992- 93.

number of children ever born and still living is widening with age of mother which indicate that both fertility and child mortality are low among young women. Both fertility and child loss were observed to be high among illiterate mothers in all mortality groups. Among the four major religions (Hindus, Muslims, Christians and Sikh), muslim women observed to have higher fertility in all mortality groups. While the Scheduled Caste women experienced a comparatively higher fertility in the high and medium mortality groups, both Scheduled Caste and Scheduled Tribe women have experienced higher fertility in the low mortality group. The child loss was high among Hindu Muslim and other caste women in the high mortality group where as it was high among Muslim and Scheduled Caste women in the medium mortality group and among Hindu and Scheduled Caste women in the low mortality group.

5.4 Birth order

The relationship of birth order with child survival is evidenced from many studies. The infant mortality risk is high for the first and higher order births. After a women has had three children, further pregnancies bring greater risk to the life and health of both mother and child. Hence it is important to limit child bearing in order to have safe motherhood and child survival. The per cent distribution of births by order of birth presented in Table 5.4 revealed that 57 per cent of births in the high mortality group, 47 per cent in the medium mortality group and 41 per cent in the low mortality group were of higher order births (three and above).

The proportion of higher order births decreased with increase in education in all mortality groups. In the high mortality group, the proportion of higher order births decreased from 60 per cent for illiterates to 30 per cent for high school and above. In the medium mortality group, it has decreased from 53 per cent for illiterates to 15 per cent for high school and above and in the low mortality group, it has decreased from 51 per cent for illiterates to 18 per cent for high school and above level of education. The results indicate that there was not much difference in the level of fertility between the low and medium mortality groups. However, the proportion of higher order births was high among all categories of women in the high morality group as a compared to their counterparts in the medium and low mortality groups. The results indicate that improvement

Table 5.4 Percent distribution of births during the three years period preceding the survey (1990- 92) by order of birth and education of women, Rural India, 1992 - 93.

Education	*Order of Birth*						*Number*
	1	*2*	*3*	*4*	*5*	*6+*	
High							
Illiterate	21.3	18.9	16.7	13.6	10.2	19.4	12365
Literate < Middle Complete	26.1	23.8	19.7	12.6	7.4	10.5	1709
Middle Complete	37.7	30.3	15.6	6.0	5.1	5.3	634
High School & Above	41.1	29.0	15.7	7.6	3.1	3.5	599
Total	**23.3**	**20.3**	**16.9**	**13.0**	**9.4**	**17.2**	**15307**
Medium							
Illiterate	24.2	23.1	19.5	12.7	8.5	12.0	6430
Literate < Middle Complete	36.4	27.3	16.4	8.7	5.3	5.9	1553
Middle Complete	44.3	30.3	15.7	5.5	2.5	1.8	476
High School & Above	54.3	30.6	10.5	3.5	0.7	0.5	433
Total	**28.9**	**24.6**	**18.3**	**11.2**	**7.2**	**9.9**	**8892**

(Contd.)

(Contd. Table 5.4)

Education	Order of Birth						Number
	1	2	3	4	5	6+	
Low							
Illiterate	24.3	25.4	22.0	12.9	6.6	8.8	2642
Literate < Middle Complete	32.1	26.8	20.6	10.9	5.8	3.7	1333
Middle Complete	43.4	33.6	15.1	5.1	2.1	0.7	574
High School & Above	46.6	35.7	12.6	3.4	1.1	0.7	588
Total	**31.0**	**27.8**	**19.8**	**10.4**	**5.3**	**5.7**	**5137**

Fig 5.4 Higher Order Birth (b+) by education of mother

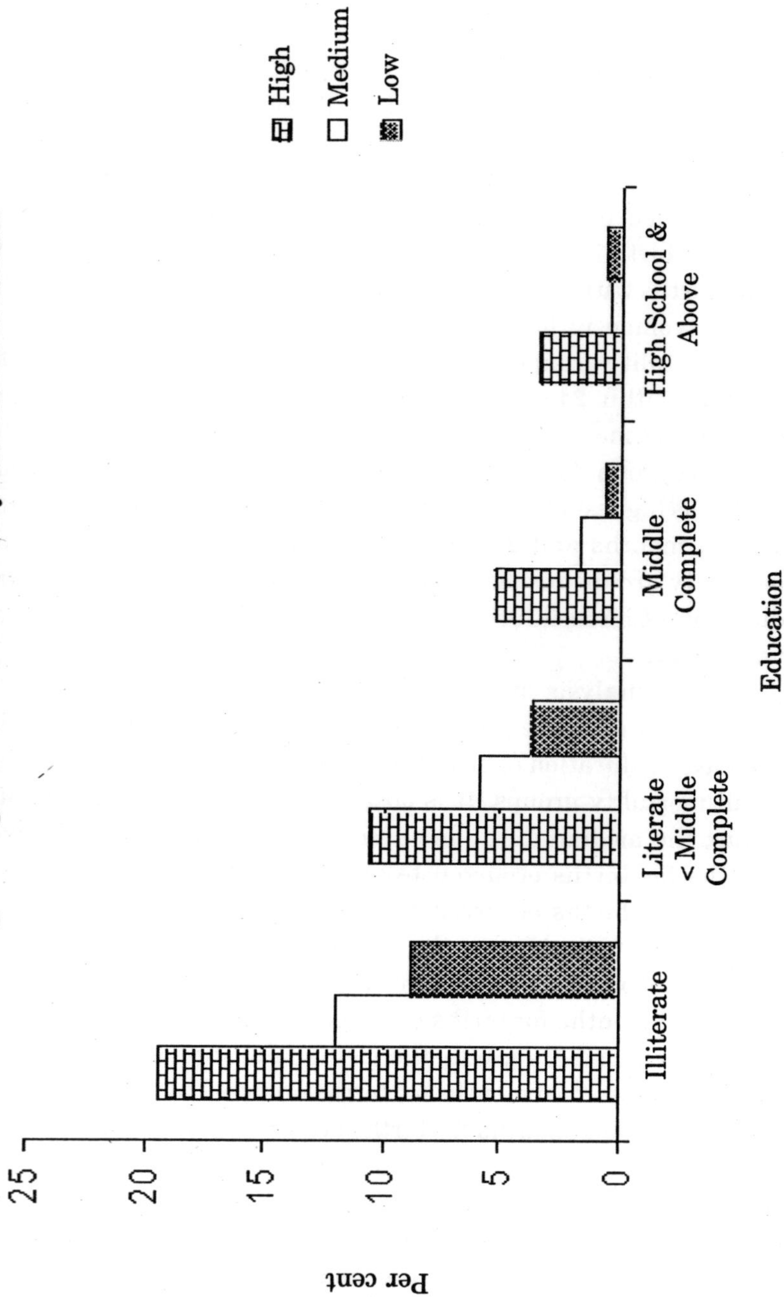

in the education of women will result in the substantial reduction of higher order births in rural India.

5.5 Birth Interval

Children born with short birth interval of less than 24 months are more exposed to the risk of dying than those children born with longer birth interval. The per cent distribution of births in the five years period preceding the survey by number of months since previous birth is presented in Table 5.5. The proportion of higher order births within 24 months of previous birth was slightly higher among women in low mortality group compared to medium and high mortality groups. It is observed that the proportion of births occurred within 24 months of previous birth was 26 per cent in each of high and medium mortality groups and 29 per cent in the low mortality group. The median duration of birth interval since previous birth was highest at 32.6 months for high mortality group compared to 31.4 months and 29.9 months observed for medium and low mortality groups respectively. Variations observed in the median duration of birth interval among the three mortality groups are very small.

The analysis of the median duration of birth interval by background characteristics of women and children revealed that the median duration of birth interval increased with age of mother in all mortality groups. It is observed that in the high mortality group, the median duration of birth interval increased from 24.3 months for births occurred to women aged 15-19 years to 40.1 months for births occurred to women aged 45-49 years. In the medium mortality group, the median duration of birth interval increased from 25.2 months for births occurred to women aged 15-19 to 48.9 months for births occurred to women aged 45-49 years. In the low mortality group, the median duration of birth interval increased from 24.6 months for births occurred to women aged 15-19 years to 50.1 months for births occurred to women aged 45-49 years. In the case of religion, the median duration of birth interval was high among Christians in low and high mortality groups and in the medium mortality group, it was high among the Hindus.

It is also observed that the median duration of birth interval was substantially higher when the previous birth was still living in

Table 5.5 Percent distribution of births during the five years period preceding the survey (1988-92) by interval since previous birth and selected background characteristics, Rural India, 1992 - 93.

Characteristics	*High*					*Medium*				
	Months since previous birth					*Months since previous birth*				
	N	*<12*	*12-23*	*24 +*	*Median*	*N*	*<12*	*12–23*	*24 +*	*Median*
Age										
15 – 19	455	4.0	44.5	51.6	24.3	422	3.8	37.1	59.0	25.2
20 – 24	4733	2.6	29.1	68.3	28.6	3359	2.7	28.6	68.8	28.6
25 – 29	6627	1.8	24.7	73.4	32.4	3637	1.4	23.2	75.4	31.9
30 – 34	4303	1.2	19.5	79.3	34.9	1863	1.0	18.6	80.3	35.6
35 – 39	2146	2.0	19.8	78.3	35.9	752	0.8	16.6	82.8	37.5
40 – 44	758	1.4	11.4	87.1	40.8	250	0.9	12.8	86.4	37.6
45 – 49	244	1.3	7.5	91.3	40.1	60	0.0	8.7	91.2	48.9
Birth Order										
1	5143	1.9	26.1	71.9	31.5	3500	1.9	26.9	71.2	30.6
2	4218	1.9	22.5	75.7	32.7	2645	1.8	21.7	76.6	31.6
3	3214	1.9	22.9	75.2	33.0	1691	1.8	22.1	76.2	31.9
4	2393	1.8	23.3	74.9	33.9	1070	1.8	23.2	75.1	32.6
5	1675	1.4	23.4	75.2	33.3	629	1.4	23.4	75.2	31.9
6+	2623	2.5	23.3	74.2	32.5	808	1.6	23.3	75.2	31.1
Sex										
Male	9712	1.8	23.7	74.6	32.9	5040	1.8	23.4	74.8	31.9
Female	9553	2.1	23.9	74.0	32.2	5304	1.8	24.3	73.9	31.0

(Contd.)

(Contd. Table 5.5)

Characteristics	*Low*				
	Months since previous birth (years)				
	N	*<12*	*12-23*	*24 +*	*Median*
Age					
15 – 19	222	3.3	43.2	53.6	24.6
20 – 24	1880	2.1	33.6	64.3	26.7
25 – 29	2104	1.9	25.9	72.2	31.2
30 – 34	1018	1.7	21.1	77.1	35.4
35 – 39	372	1.6	17.3	81.2	37.8
40 – 44	108	3.7	14.1	82.3	37.9
45 – 49	23	0.0	21.7	78.3	50.1
Birth Order					
1	2327	1.4	30.7	68.0	29.1
2	1617	3.1	24.5	72.5	30.4
3	853	1.0	26.6	72.3	30.5
4	448	1.4	24.0	74.7	30.9
5	218	1.3	27.1	71.6	33.6
6+	265	5.2	25.7	69.1	28.7
Sex					
Male	2870	1.9	27.0	71.1	29.9
Female	2857	2.0	27.9	70.0	29.9

(Contd.)

(Contd. Table 5.5)

Characteristics	*High*					*Medium*				
	Months since previous birth					*Months since previous birth*				
	N	*<12*	*12-23*	*24 +*	*Median*	*N*	*<12*	*12–23*	*24 +*	*Median*
Survival of Prior Birth										
Still living	16095	1.3	21.2	74.4	33.6	9091	1.2	21.9	76.9	32.2
Deceased	3170	5.3	36.7	57.8	26.3	1253	6.1	38.1	55.9	25.2
Education										
Illiterate	16119	2.0	23.1	74.9	32.9	8081	1.8	23.1	75.2	31.7
Literate < Middle complete	2024	1.3	26.3	72.3	31.6	1555	1.8	23.9	74.4	31.4
Middle Complete	582	1.1	28.9	70.0	30.4	405	1.7	30.1	68.2	29.1
High School & Above	540	1.6	32.0	66.3	29.4	303	2.2	36.1	61.6	27.6
Religion										
Hindu	16183	1.9	23.7	74.3	32.6	8539	1.7	23.8	74.6	31.7
Muslim	2849	2.0	24.8	73.2	31.9	1462	2.2	24.3	73.5	30.3
Christian	141	0.6	22.0	77.3	33.9	177	2.9	20.8	76.4	30.2
Sikh	27	0.6	34.7	64.7	26.0	76	3.0	36.9	60.0	27.4
Jain	9	0.0	30.5	69.6	33.6	19	0.0	39.8	60.2	32.8
Buddhist	6	0.0	0.0	100.0	39.1	15	0.0	24.3	75.8	36.1
Others	50	1.8	14.3	83.9	34.7	57	0.0	19.3	80.7	35.1
Caste										
Scheduled Caste	2673	1.7	25.8	72.5	32.2	1692	2.4	23.5	74.1	31.5
Scheduled Tribe	2143	1.9	21.9	76.3	32.2	1265	1.9	25.8	72.4	31.2
Others	14450	2.0	23.8	74.2	32.7	7386	1.6	23.6	74.7	31.4
Total	**19266**	**1.9**	**23.8**	**74.2**	**32.6**	**10344**	**1.8**	**23.9**	**74.3**	**31.4**

(Contd.)

(Contd. Table)

Characteristics	Low				
	Months since previous birth				
	N	*<12*	*12-23*	*24 +*	*Median*
Survival of Prior Birth					
Still living	5224	1.5	26.0	72.4	30.5
Deceased	503	6.7	41.6	51.8	24.4
Education					
Illiterate	3321	2.5	26.0	71.5	30.2
Literate < Middle complete	1429	1.4	28.7	69.8	29.6
Middle Complete	522	1.0	29.1	70.1	27.8
High School & Above	456	1.6	31.6	66.8	32.1
Religion					
Hindu	4110	1.9	26.6	71.5	30.1
Muslim	680	2.1	27.3	70.6	29.9
Christian	293	1.8	27.6	70.6	31.5
Sikh	449	2.1	33.5	64.5	28.3
Jain	5	2.5	0.0	97.5	30.0
Buddhist	132	3.2	29.0	67.8	31.2
Others	58	3.9	37.6	58.6	25.5
Caste					
Scheduled Caste	865	2.0	24.1	73.9	30.4
Scheduled Tribe	599	2.8	31.2	65.9	27.4
Others	4264	1.9	27.6	70.6	30.2
Total	**5727**	**2.0**	**27.4**	**70.6**	**29.9**

(Contd.)

all mortality groups. In the high mortality group, the median duration of birth interval was highest at 33.6 months when the previous birth was still living compared to 26.3 months when the previous birth was deceased. In the medium mortality group, the median duration of birth interval was 32.2 months when the previous birth was still living compared to 25.2 months when the previous birth was deceased. In the case of low mortality group, the median duration of birth interval was 30.5 months when the previous birth was still living compared to 24.4 months when the previous birth was deceased. Thus the results indicate the tendency of women to go for the next birth at a very short interval when the previous child died in order to compensate the child loss. It is very surprising to note that the median duration of birth interval decreased with increase in education in the high and medium mortality groups. This may be due to the fact that the illiterate mothers with low level of education tend to have longer duration of breast feeding than the mothers with high level of education. Thus the longer duration of breast feeding might have resulted in the longer duration of birth interval in the high and medium mortality groups. However, in the low mortality group, births occurred to women with high school or more level of education tended to have longer duration of birth interval than others. There was not much difference in the median duration of birth interval with regard to birth order, sex of child and caste in all mortality groups.

5.6 Age at First Birth

The median age at first birth among women aged 20-49 years is presented in Table 5.6. The results indicate that there was not much variation in the median age at first birth among women in the three mortality groups and it was lingering around 19 years in all mortality groups. The median age at first birth was 19.2 years for high mortality group, 18.9 years for medium mortality group and 19.8 years for low mortality group. The median age at first birth increased with education in all mortality groups. In the high mortality group, the median age at first birth increased from 18.9 years for illiterate women to 23.9 years for women with high school or higher level of education. In the medium mortality group, the median age at first birth increased from 18.3 years for illiterates to 22.6 years for mothers with high school or higher level of education.

Table 5.6 Median age at first birth among women age 20 - 49 years by current age and selected background characteristics, Rural India, 1992 - 93.

Characteristics	*High*						
	Current Age (years)						
	20-24	*25-29*	*30-34*	*35-39*	*40-44*	*45-49*	*20-49*
Education							
Illiterate	19.0	18.8	18.8	18.8	18.9	19.0	**18.9**
Literate < Middle Complete	20.3	19.5	19.1	19.2	18.8	19.1	**19.4**
Middle Complete	21.8	20.0	19.8	19.8	20.4	20.4	**20.6**
High School & Above	*	22.5	21.4	20.8	19.9	19.9	**23.9**
Religion							
Hindu	20.0	19.1	18.9	18.9	19.0	19.0	**19.2**
Muslim	19.4	19.0	18.7	19.0	18.4	18.9	**19.0**
Christian	21.1	20.7	20.6	18.9	21.0	19.7	**20.1**
Sikh	*	24.2	18.5	20.5	18.6	19.4	**20.5**
Others	21.7	19.3	21.4	19.3	18.5	18.3	**19.4**

(Contd.)

(Contd. Table 5.6)

Characteristics	*Medium*						
	Current Age (years)						
	20-24	*25-29*	*30-34*	*35-39*	*40-44*	*45-49*	*20-49*
Education							
Illiterate	18.3	18.0	18.4	18.1	18.7	18.9	**18.3**
Literate < Middle Complete	19.6	19.0	18.6	18.6	18.5	18.6	**18.9**
Middle Complete	21.0	20.0	19.2	19.1	19.9	22.5	**20.2**
High School & Above	*	23.0	22.3	22.8	22.5	21.9	**22.6**
Religion							
Hindu	19.6	18.6	18.7	18.5	18.8	18.9	**18.9**
Muslim	18.4	17.6	18.1	17.7	17.9	18.2	**18.0**
Christian	22.4	19.4	18.2	19.2	18.7	19.3	**19.4**
Sikh	*	21.5	20.7	20.1	21.6	21.1	**20.9**
Others	20.5	20.2	19.8	17.7	19.8	19.6	**19.6**

(Contd.)

(Contd. Table 5.6)

Characteristics	*Low*						
	Current Age (years)						
	20-24	*25-29*	*30-34*	*35-39*	*40-44*	*45-49*	*20-49*
Education							
Illiterate	18.4	18.5	18.6	18.7	18.9	19.1	**18.8**
Literate < Middle Complete	20.1	19.8	19.9	20.1	19.9	20.5	**20.1**
Middle Complete	21.5	21.0	20.9	21.6	20.9	21.0	**21.1**
High School & Above	*	24.0	23.8	23.9	23.7	25.1	**24.2**
Religion							
Hindu	19.9	19.6	19.5	19.5	19.2	19.4	**19.6**
Muslim	19.0	18.8	18.5	17.9	18.3	18.3	**18.4**
Christian	*	22.8	22.6	21.9	22.2	21.3	**22.2**
Sikh	*	22.0	21.6	20.8	21.4	21.6	**21.3**
Others	20.7	18.3	19.1	18.5	20.6	18.8	**19.4**

(Contd.)

(Contd. Table 5.6)

Characteristics	*High*						
	Current Age (years)						
	20-24	*25-29*	*30-34*	*35-39*	*40-44*	*45-49*	*20-49*
Caste							
Scheduled Caste	19.2	18.5	18.8	18.8	19.1	19.3	**18.9**
Scheduled Tribe	19.0	18.9	18.9	18.5	19.0	19.2	**18.9**
Others	20.3	19.3	19.0	19.1	19.0	19.0	**19.4**
Total	**20.0**	**19.2**	**18.9**	**19.0**	**19.0**	**19.0**	**19.2**

(Contd.)

(Contd. Table 5.6)

Characteristics	*Medium*						
	Current Age						
	20-24	*25-29*	*30-34*	*35-39*	*40-44*	*45-49*	*20-49*
Caste							
Scheduled Caste	18.4	18.2	17.9	17.9	18.1	18.4	**18.2**
Scheduled Tribe	19.6	19.0	18.9	18.7	19.0	19.6	**19.1**
Others	19.8	18.6	18.7	18.4	18.9	18.9	**18.9**
Total	**19.6**	**18.6**	**18.6**	**18.4**	**18.8**	**18.9**	**18.9**

(Contd.)

(Contd. Table 5.6)

Characteristics	*Low*						
	Current Age						
	20-24	*25-29*	*30-34*	*35-39*	*40-44*	*45-49*	*20-49*
Caste							
Scheduled Caste	19.4	19.1	19.1	19.1	19.2	19.5	**19.2**
Scheduled Tribe	18.3	19.2	18.8	18.5	19.5	19.1	**18.8**
Others	20.5	20.1	20.0	19.9	19.6	19.7	**19.9**
Total	**20.1**	**19.9**	**19.8**	**19.6**	**19.5**	**19.6**	**19.8**

In the low mortality group, the median age at first birth increased from 18.8 for illiterates to 24.2 years for mothers with high school or higher level of education. The results indicate that education of women up to a minimum of high school level helped to increase the median age at first birth to a minimum 4 years in all mortality groups.

The education effect on age at first birth is substantial only among the younger age group (20-29 years) in the high mortality group. However, in the medium and low mortality groups, the education effect was nearly same among the women of all age groups. This is so because of the early marriage and subsequent childbirth practices followed in the high mortality group of states in the past. Sikh women in the low and medium mortality groups and Christian women in high mortality groups tend to have their first birth at a later age than others. In the case of caste groups, other caste women in the high and low mortality groups and Scheduled Tribe women in the medium mortality group have higher median age at first birth than others. In general, there was not much difference in the age at first birth among women in all mortality groups due to religion or caste.

5.7 Age at Last Birth

The median age at last birth among ever married women age 40-49 years presented in Table 5.7 revealed that the median age at last birth was highest at 33.2 years for women in the high mortality group as compared to 30.2 years and 29.1 years observed for women in the medium and low mortality groups respectively. The median age at last birth was observed to be high among illiterate women, Muslim women and Scheduled Caste women in all mortality groups.

The median duration of child bearing as measured by the difference between the median age at first birth and last birth presented in table 5.8 indicate that the median duration of child bearing was highest at 14.2 years for women in high mortality group compared to 11.4 years and 9.5 years observed for women in medium and low mortality groups. Thus the results indicate that the women in high mortality group stop child bearing at later ages than women in medium and low mortality groups.

Table 5.7 Percent distribution of ever married women age 40 - 49 years by age at last birth and selected background characteristics, Rural India, 1992 – 93.

Characteristics	*High*						
	Age at last birth (years)						
	N	*No Birth*	*< 20*	*20-29*	*30-39*	*40-49*	*M*
Education							
Illiterate	4927	2.4	1.9	26.8	56.3	12.6	**33.4**
Literate < Middle Complete	545	1.1	1.3	35.7	55.8	6.1	**32.1**
Middle Complete	98	1.0	0.8	46.0	51.4	0.9	**30.3**
High School & Above	71	1.5	-	37.3	61.2	..	**32.5**
Religion							
Hindu	4938	2.2	1.9	28.9	55.7	11.4	**33.1**
Muslim	601	3.2	0.8	21.6	59.7	14.8	**34.7**
Christian	52	-	1.1	28.3	62.7	7.8	**32.5**
Sikh	12	-	1.3	12.9	85.8	-	**34.5**
Buddhist	7	6.6	-	40.5	52.8	-	**34.2**
Jain	6	-	-	4.6	81.7	13.7	**32.0**
Others	25	-	3.3	49.1	47.6	-	**29.7**

(Contd.)

(Contd. Table 5.7)

Characteristics	Low				
	Months since previous birth (years)				
	N	*<12*	*12-23*	*24 +*	*Median*
Age					
15 – 19	222	3.3	43.2	53.6	24.6
20 – 24	1880	2.1	33.6	64.3	26.7
25 – 29	2104	1.9	25.9	72.2	31.2
30 – 34	1018	1.7	21.1	77.1	35.4
35 – 39	372	1.6	17.3	81.2	37.8
40 – 44	108	3.7	14.1	82.3	37.9
45 – 49	23	0.0	21.7	78.3	50.1
Birth Order					
1	2327	1.4	30.7	68.0	29.1
2	1617	3.1	24.5	72.5	30.4
3	853	1.0	26.6	72.3	30.5
4	448	1.4	24.0	74.7	30.9
5	218	1.3	27.1	71.6	33.6
6+	265	5.2	25.7	69.1	28.7
Sex					
Male	2870	1.9	27.0	71.1	29.9
Female	2857	2.0	27.9	70.0	29.9

(Contd.)

(Contd. Table 5.7)

Characteristics	Low						
	Age at last birth (years)						
	N	No Birth	< 20	20-29	30-39	40-49	M
Education							
Illiterate	1979	2.8	4.1	48.1	41.4	3.5	**29.4**
Literate < Middle Complete	689	3.6	1.9	53.3	38.5	2.7	**28.6**
Middle Complete	149	3.3	1.1	64.6	29.7	1.3	**28.0**
High School & Above	156	2.9	0.1	54.7	40.6	1.7	**29.0**
Religion							
Hindu	2177	3.4	3.9	53.3	36.6	2.7	**28.6**
Muslim	217	2.3	2.4	33.7	53.6	8.0	**31.3**
Christian	252	1.9	2.0	46.3	45.8	4.1	**30.0**
Sikh	236	1.5	-	48.5	48.7	1.2	**30.0**
Buddhist	6	-	-	67.1	-	32.9	**24.5**
Jain	73	2.8	0.1	35.7	60.8	0.5	**31.2**
Others	12	7.3	1.8	52.4	31.3	7.2	**28.8**

(Contd.)

(Contd. Table 5.7)

Characteristics	*High*						
			Age at last birth (years)				
	N	*No Birth*	< 20	20-29	30-39	40-49	*M*
Caste							
Scheduled Caste	674	1.6	0.2	23.0	59.5	15.8	34.8
Scheduled Tribe	616	3.8	3.5	35.8	48.6	8.3	31.3
Others	4351	2.1	1.8	27.8	56.8	11.4	33.2
Total	**5641**	**2.2**	**1.8**	**28.1**	**56.3**	**11.6**	**33.2**

(Contd.)

(Contd. Table 5.7)

Characteristics	*Medium*						
	Age at last birth (years)						
	N	*No Birth*	*< 20*	*20-29*	*30-39*	*40-49*	*M*
Caste							
Scheduled Caste	515	1.3	5.2	36.3	52.2	5.1	**30.9**
Scheduled Tribe	483	5.3	2.6	43.5	40.0	8.6	**29.8**
Others	3085	3.6	3.6	41.9	46.6	4.2	**30.1**
Total	**4083**	**3.5**	**3.7**	**41.5**	**46.5**	**4.8**	**30.2**

(Contd.)

(Contd. Table 5.7)

Characteristics	Low						
	Age at last birth (years)						
	N	*No Birth*	*< 20*	*20-29*	*30-39*	*40-49*	*M*
Caste							
Scheduled Caste	427	2.7	2.8	43.2	47.2	4.0	**30.2**
Scheduled Tribe	185	0.7	8.2	43.3	41.2	6.7	**29.8**
Others	2361	3.3	2.9	52.4	38.7	2.7	**28.8**
Total	**2973**	**3.0**	**3.2**	**50.5**	**40.1**	**3.1**	**29.1**

M - Median age at last birth

\- Less than 0.05 percent

Table 5.8 Median age at first birth and median age at last birth for women age 40 - 49 years, by mortality groups, Rural India, 1992 - 93.

Category	*Median Age*		
	First Birth	*Last Birth*	*Difference*
High	19.0	33.2	14..2
Medium	18.8	30.2	11.4
Low	19.6	29.1	9.5

5.8 Summary

The comparison of different fertility measures among the three mortality groups revealed that the crude birth rate, total fertility rate and general fertility rate were high for the high mortality group as compared to medium and low mortality groups. However, there was not much difference between the medium and low mortality groups with regard to various fertility measures.

The fertility was peak at 20-24 years in all mortality groups. While the fertility was greatest among women age 30-34 years in the medium and low mortality groups, it was greatest among women age 35-39 years in the high mortality group. The total fertility rate decreased with the increase in education in all mortality groups. The differences observed in the total fertility rate among the three mortality groups, narrowed down significantly with the increase in education. The results indicate that increase in education of women will help to reduce fertility. Muslim women experienced higher fertility than the women of other religions in all mortality groups.

The mean number of children ever born to women age 40-49 years was 5.7 for high mortality group, 4.9 for medium and 4.3 for low mortality groups. The child loss as measured by the differences between the mean number of children ever born and surviving among currently married women age 15-49 years in the three mortality groups revealed that the mean number of child loss was higher (0.6) among children of high mortality group as compared to medium (0.4) and low (0.3) mortality groups. Contrary to expectations, the median duration of birth interval was low (29.9 months) for low mortality group as compared to medium (31.4 months) and high (32.6 months) mortality groups. Nearly two fifth

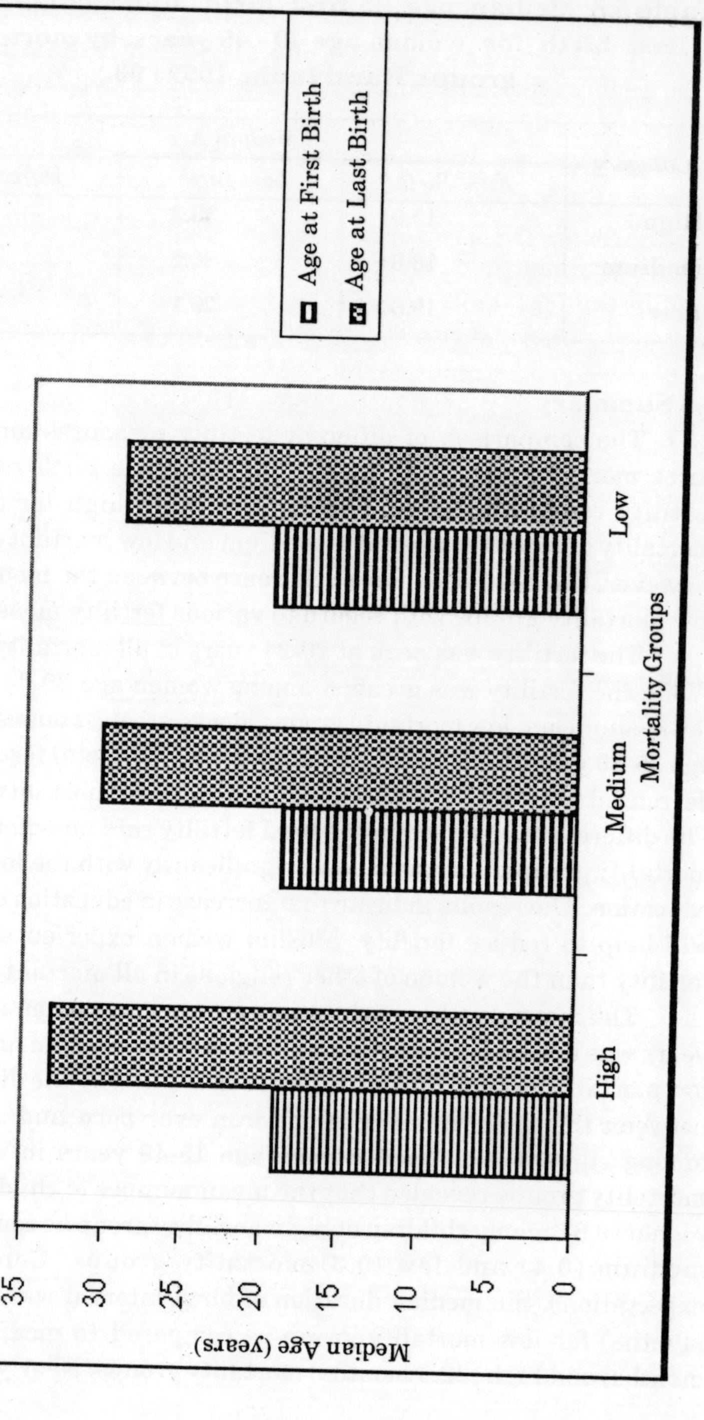

Fig 5.5 Median Age at First Birth and Last Birth by Mortality Groups

of births (40 per cent) in the high mortality group were of higher order (four and above) where as it was only a little over one fourth (28 per cent) in the medium and a little over one fifth (21 per cent) in the low mortality group. Women in the low mortality group start their child bearing a little later and stop earlier than the women in the medium and high mortality groups. The median duration of child bearing was 9.5 years for low, 11.4 years for medium, and 14.2 years for high mortality group.

The findings indicate vast variations in the fertility behaviour of women among the three mortality groups. Though variations are observed among the three mortality groups, there is not much difference between the low and medium mortality groups in terms of various fertility measures. However, women in high mortality group experience high fertility, more child loss and exposed to longer duration of child bearing than women in the medium and low mortality groups.

6

Utilisation of Maternal Health Care Services

Maternal health care services play an important role in reducing maternal and infant morbidity and mortality. Prenatal care, Tetanus Toxoid (TT) immunisation and administering of iron and folic acid tablets during pregnancy, hospital delivery and availability of trained personnel to attend women during labour and delivery are some of the important factors contributing significantly to the maternal, child health and survival. The social status of women and the cultural practices influence the health-care-seeking-behaviour of women during pregnancy and child birth. The details of the health-care-seeking-behaviour of women during pregnancy and child birth among the three mortality groups are presented in the following sections.

6.1 Antenatal Care Visits

Gynecologists, generally recommend that antenatal care be started at 12 weeks of gestation and visits be made on a monthly basis to the 28th week, fortnightly to the 36th week and then weekly until the 40th week or delivery. As per this schedule, a total of 12 visits are required during pregnancy. The National Safe Motherhood and Child Survival Program has suggested at least three antenatal check-ups for all pregnant women. (Ministry of Health and Family Welfare, 1992).

The per cent distribution of live-births in the last four years preceding the survey by number of antenatal care visits and months of pregnancy at first visit are presented in Table 6.1. Among the women who have received antenatal care, the median number of antenatal care visits of any type (either home or outside visits) was 2.9 for high mortality group, 3.8 for medium mortality group and 4.4 for low mortality group. The results indicate that women who have received antenatal care in all mortality groups have met the minimum requirement of three visits as recommended under the National Safe Motherhood and Child Survival Program. However, it is important to note that more than four-fifth (82 per cent) of women in the high mortality group, and a little over two-third (68 per cent) both in the medium and low mortality groups were not visited by the female health workers during pregnancy.

Home visits indicate the extent of antenatal coverage by the female health worker and the outside visit indicate the extent of awareness of women on the importance of antenatal care. Both home visits and outside visits were very low in the high mortality group as compared to medium and low mortality groups.

The median age of gestation at the time of first antenatal care visit of either type (home or outside) was around five months (5.4 for high, 5.1 for medium and 4.9 for low mortality groups) in all mortality groups. There was not much difference between the home visits and outside visits in all mortality groups.

The results indicate that a comparatively high proportion of women both in the medium and low mortality groups have received antenatal care visits at home as compared to high mortality groups. The proportion who have made outside visits for antenatal care was high in the low mortality group as compared to medium and high mortality groups. Among those who have received antenatal care visits, the median number of antenatal care visits was high for the low mortality group followed by medium and high mortality groups. There was not much difference in the median months of gestation at first antenatal care visit among the three mortality groups.

Table 6.1 Percent distribution of live births during the four years period preceding the survey by number of antenatal care (ANC) visits and by the stage of pregnancy at the time of first visit, Rural India, 1992 - 93.

ANC visits/Months pregnant	*High (N = 19862)*			*Medium (N = 11624)*			*Low (N = 6642)*		
	Home Visits	*Outside Visits*	*Any type*	*Home Visits*	*Outside Visits*	*Any type*	*Home Visits*	*Outside Visits*	*Any type*
Antenatal Care Visits									
None	81.9	72.5	57.7	68.2	48.9	31.7	67.6	29.6	15.4
1 visit	4.0	5.3	7.7	4.4	6.2	6.0	4.1	6.0	5.3
2 - 3 visits	11.2	17.2	26.2	15.0	27.8	31.0	16.0	32.0	33.4
4+ visits	1.9	4.4	7.3	11.7	16.8	30.6	11.6	31.8	45.1
Don't know/ missing	1.1	0.6	1.1	0.7	0.4	0.7	0.7	0.6	0.8
Median number of visits (for those with ANC)	**2.8**	**2.9**	**2.9**	**3.5**	**3.4**	**3.8**	**3.6**	**3.8**	**4.4**

(Contd.)

(Contd. Table 6.1)

ANC visits / Months pregnant	*High (N = 19862)*			*Medium (N = 11624)*			*Low (N = 6642)*		
	Home Visits	*Outside Visits*	*Any type*	*Home Visits*	*Outside Visits*	*Any type*	*Home Visits*	*Outside Visits*	*Any type*
Months Pregnant at 1st Visit									
No Antenatal Care	81.9	72.5	57.7	68.2	48.9	31.7	67.6	29.6	15.5
First Trimester	4.1	8.4	12.2	10.3	16.7	24.7	9.8	25.3	32.0
Second Trimester	9.1	12.6	20.5	15.7	23.4	31.9	16.2	29.0	37.1
Third Trimester	4.0	5.9	8.7	5.3	10.7	11.2	5.6	15.5	14.8
Don't Know Missing	0.9	0.6	0.9	0.5	0.4	0.4	0.7	0.6	0.6
Median months pregnant at first visit (for those with ANC)	**5.6**	**5.4**	**5.4**	**5.2**	**5.3**	**5.1**	**5.1**	**5.1**	**4.9**

Fig 6.1 Per cent received two dozes of TT vaccine by education

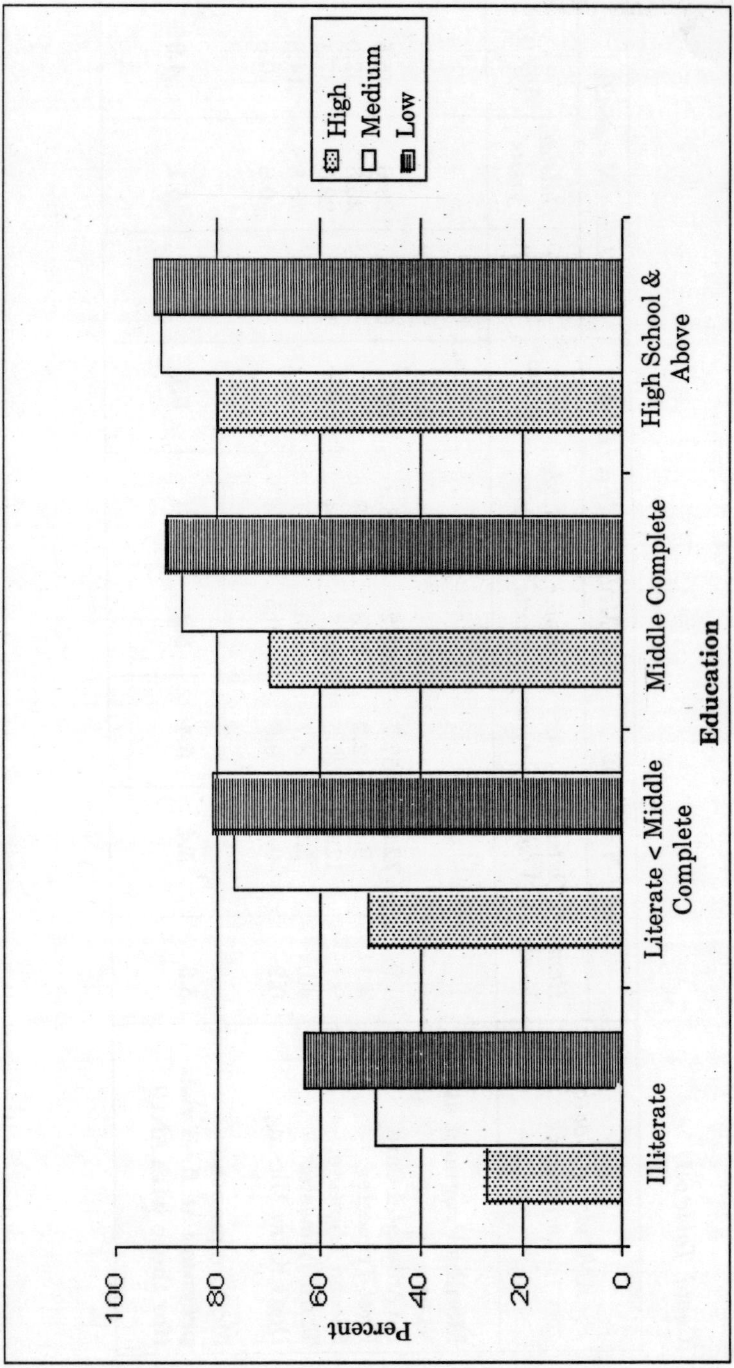

6.2 Tetanus Toxoid (TT)

Percent distribution of women who received tetanus toxoid injection during pregnancy for births in the four years period preceding the survey is presented in Table 6.2.

Substantial variations in the proportion of women who have received tetanus toxoid vaccination during pregnancy was observed among the three mortality groups. Nearly one-third (33 per cent) of women in the high mortality group, nearly three-fifth (58 per cent) of women in the medium mortality group and nearly three-fourth (74 per cent) of women in the low mortality group have received two doses of TT vaccine during pregnancy. It is very surprising to note that about three-fifth (60 per cent) of women in the high mortality group have not availed even a single dose of TT vaccine during pregnancy whereas it was only a little over one-third (35 per cent) in the medium and less than one-fifth (17 per cent) in the low mortality groups.

The tendency to ignore the importance of TT vaccine increased with age of women and birth order in all mortality groups. It is observed that in the high mortality group, the proportion of women who have availed two or more doses of TT vaccination during pregnancy decreased from 35 per cent for women aged less than 20 years to 20 per cent for women aged 35 years or more. In the medium mortality group, it has decreased from 63 per cent for women aged less than 20 years to 32 per cent for women aged 35 years or more and in the low mortality group, it has decreased from 70 per cent for women aged 20 years or less to 56 per cent for women aged 35 years or more.

In the case of birth order, the proportion of women who have availed two or more doses of TT vaccination decreased from 42 per cent for first order births to 20 per cent for birth order of 6 or more in the high mortality group. In the case of medium mortality group it has decreased from 68 per cent for first order births to 36 per cent for birth order of 6 or more and in the case of low mortality group, the decline was from 82 percent for first order births to 55 per cent for birth order of 6 or more. The proportion of women who had availed two doses of TT vaccination was observed to be comparatively low among illiterate women and Scheduled Tribe women in all mortality groups.

Table 6.2 Percent distribution of live births during the four years preceding the survey by number of tetanus toxoid injection availed during pregnancy by selected background characteristics, Rural India, 1992 -93.

Variable & Category	*High*				*Medium*				*Low*			
	N	*Not availed*	*One Dose*	*Two Doses **	*N*	*Not availed*	*One Dose*	*Two Doses **	*N*	*Not availed*	*One Dose*	*Two Doses **
Age (years)												
< 20	4297	57.5	7.4	35.0	3406	29.6	7.6	62.6	1744	19.3	10.4	70.2
20 - 34	14087	58.6	7.2	34.0	7746	35.9	7.1	56.9	4699	15.9	7.9	76.1
35+	1478	74.7	5.4	19.8	473	58.9	8.7	32.3	199	34.0	10.4	55.5
Birth Order												
1	4622	50.3	7.3	42.2	3328	25.1	6.8	67.9	2063	11.6	6.4	81.8
2	4102	55.3	7.5	37.1	2829	29.6	7.8	62.4	1852	14.9	8.7	76.3
3	3315	58.0	7.4	34.4	2105	36.6	6.8	56.3	1296	19.7	10.2	70.0
4	2574	61.6	7.2	31.2	1347	41.9	7.6	50.4	689	24.6	9.3	65.9
5	1865	64.8	7.8	27.4	849	47.1	8.0	44.6	361	21.0	12.2	66.6
6+	3384	74.7	5.7	19.5	1167	56.5	7.4	36.1	380	35.4	9.7	54.9
Education												
Illiterate	16140	65.9	7.1	26.9	8517	42.9	8.1	48.8	3475	26.6	10.1	63.2
Literate < Middle Complete	2199	41.1	8.1	50.5	1983	17.2	5.5	77.1	1710	10.3	8.5	81.0
Middle Complete	773	23.5	6.5	69.8	603	8.4	4.2	87.0	732	3.7	5.7	90.2
High School & Above	749	14.2	6.0	79.8	522	4.2	4.1	91.4	725	2.8	4.7	92.5

(Contd. Table 6.2)

(Contd. Table 6.2)

Variable & Category	*High*				*Medium*				*Low*			
	N	*Not availed*	*One Dose*	*Two Doses **	*N*	*Not availed*	*One Dose*	*Two Doses **	*N*	*Not availed*	*One Dose*	*Two Doses **
Religion												
Hindu	16818	58.6	7.2	34.2	9716	35.4	7.3	57.2	4322	16.6	9.1	74.2
Muslim	2785	66.4	7.0	26.5	1535	32.2	7.0	60.7	708	19.4	9.3	71.1
Christian	142	61.5	5.7	32.8	179	39.2	6.9	52.9	365	25.7	6.0	67.9
Sikh	28	38.3	7.6	54.2	105	34.0	10.7	55.3	518	13.1	4.3	82.5
Buddhist	5	84.6	0.0	15.4	7	44.8	0.0	55.2	161	14.5	10.5	75.0
Jain	15	0.0	0.0	100.0	21	8.8	5.5	80.6	3	17.4	0.0	82.6
Others	69	55.1	8.3	36.7	62	43.1	8.5	47.2	64	42.2	8.0	49.9
Caste												
Scheduled Caste	2716	62.9	7.2	29.7	1764	42.7	5.8	51.2	963	19.3	7.8	72.7
Scheduled Tribe	2301	67.6	7.7	24.4	1390	51.8	9.5	38.4	617	37.6	14.8	47.5
Others	14845	57.7	7.0	35.2	8470	30.6	7.2	62.0	5061	14.5	8.0	77.4
Total	**19862**	**59.6**	**7.1**	**33.2**	**11624**	**35.0**	**7.3**	**57.5**	**6642**	**17.3**	**8.6**	**74.0**

Note : Total percentage not equal to 100 in some categories due to the omissions of don't know/missing values in the table.

* Include women who have received more than two doses.

Variations due to educational background of women was substantial in all mortality groups. Proportion of women who had received two doses of TT vaccination increased from 27 per cent for illiterates to 80 per cent for high school education and above in the high mortality group. In the medium mortality group the proportion of increase was from 49 per cent to 91 per cent and in the low mortality group, the proportion of increase was from 63 per cent to 93 per cent.

In the high mortality group, among the four major religious groups, (Hindu, Muslim, Christian and Sikh) higher proportion of Sikh women observed to have two or more doses of TT vaccination during pregnancy than others. It was highest at 54 per cent among the Sikh followed by Hindu (34 per cent), Christian (33 per cent) and Muslims (27 per cent). In the medium mortality group, higher proportion of Muslim women (61 per cent) seemed to have availed two or more doses of TT vaccine compared to 57 per cent among Hindus 55 per cent among Sikh and 53 per cent among Christians. In the low mortality group, comparatively higher proportion of Sikh women (83 per cent) have availed two or more doses of TT vaccine than Hindu (74 per cent), Muslim (71 per cent) and Christian (68 per cent).

The comparison of the coverage of TT vaccine among different caste groups revealed that in the high mortality group, the proportion of women who had availed two or more doses of TT vaccine was highest at 35 per cent among other caste women compared to 30 per cent among scheduled caste women and 24 per cent among scheduled tribe women. In the medium mortality group, the proportion of women who had availed two or more doses of TT vaccine was observed to be high among other caste women (62 per cent) which was followed by scheduled caste (51 per cent) and scheduled tribe women (38 per cent). In the low mortality group also it was high among other caste women (77 per cent) which was followed by scheduled caste (73 per cent and scheduled tribe women (48 per cent).

6.3 Iron and Folic Acid Tablets

The per cent distribution of women who had availed iron and folic acid tablets during pregnancy for births during the four years preceding the survey is presented in Table 6.3. It is observed that

Table 6.3 Percent distribution of live births during the four years preceding the survey by whether the mother availed Iron / Folic tablets during pregnancy according to selected background characteristics, Rural India, 1992 - 93.

Variable & Category	*High*			*Medium*			*Low*		
	N	*Availed*	*Not Availed*	*N*	*Availed*	*Not Availed*	*N*	*Availed*	*Not Availed*
Age									
< 20	4297	28.2	71.8	3406	61.5	38.5	1744	72.4	27.6
20 – 34	14087	29.3	70.7	7746	56.8	43.2	4699	75.3	24.7
35+	1478	17.4	82.6	473	38.1	61.9	199	61.7	38.3
Birth Order									
1	4622	35.3	64.7	3328	66.2	33.8	2063	78.8	21.2
2	4102	31.4	68.6	2829	61.1	38.9	1852	77.3	22.7
3	3315	28.6	71.4	2105	55.5	44.5	1296	73.4	26.6
4	2574	26.5	73.5	1347	51.4	48.6	689	66.5	33.5
5	1865	23.7	76.3	849	47.1	52.9	361	68.1	31.9
6+	3384	18.0	82.0	1167	41.4	58.6	380	55.7	44.3
Education									
Illiterate	16140	22.6	77.4	8517	50.9	49.1	3475	64.7	35.3
Literate < Middle Complete	2199	44.9	55.1	1983	70.1	29.9	1710	79.5	20.5
Middle Complete	773	59.8	40.2	603	79.1	20.9	732	88.6	11.4
High School & Above	749	66.8	33.2	522	90.5	9.5	725	91.7	8.3

(Contd.)

(Contd. Table 6.3)

Variable & Category	High			Medium			Low		
	N	*Availed*	*Not Availed*	*N*	*Availed*	*Not Availed*	*N*	*Availed*	*Not Availed*
Religion									
Hindu	16818	29.3	70.7	9716	58.4	41.6	4822	76.0	24.0
Muslim	2785	20.8	79.2	1535	50.7	49.3	708	69.4	30.6
Christian	142	30.7	69.3	179	61.2	38.8	365	64.0	36.0
Sikh	28	40.3	59.7	105	51.5	48.5	518	71.3	28.7
Buddhist	5	15.4	84.6	7	55.2	44.8	161	80.3	19.7
Jain	15	100.0	-	21	94.8	5.2	3	82.6	17.4
Others	69	25.9	74.1	62	60.8	39.2	64	50.0	50.0
Caste									
Scheduled Caste	2716	23.0	77.0	1764	50.5	49.5	963	74.1	25.9
Scheduled Tribe	2301	29.2	70.8	1390	47.6	52.4	617	55.0	45.0
Others	14845	29.0	71.0	8470	60.5	39.5	5061	76.5	23.5
Total	**19862**	**28.2**	**71.8**	**11624**	**57.4**	**42.6**	**6642**	**74.1**	**25.9**

the proportion of women who had availed iron and folic acid tablets was 28 per cent in high, 57 per cent in medium and 74 per cent in low mortality groups. Proportion of women availed iron and folic acid tablets tend to decrease with increase in age and birth order. Variation due to educational attainment of women was substantial in all mortality groups.

In the high mortality group, the proportion of women who had availed iron and folic acid tablets decreased from 78 per cent for women aged 20 years or less to 17 per cent for women aged 35 years or more. In the medium mortality group, it has decreased from 72 per cent to 62 percent. The proportion of women who had availed iron and folic acid decrease with increase in birth order. In the high mortality group, it is observed that the proportion who had availed iron and folic acid tablets decreased from 35 percent for first order births to 18 per cent for 6th order or more. In the medium mortality group, it has decreased from 66 per cent to 41 per cent and in the low mortality group it has decreased from 79 per cent to 56 per cent.

The proportion availed iron and folic acid tablets increased with education in all mortality groups. The proportion varied from 23 per cent for illiterates to 67 per cent for high school and above level of education in the high mortality group whereas in the medium mortality group, it varied from 51 per cent to 91 per cent and in the low mortality group, it varied from 65 per cent to 92 per cent.

Proportion of women availed iron and folic acid tablets was comparatively high among Sikh women (40 per cent) in the high mortality group, Christian women (61 per cent) in the medium mortality group and Hindu women (76 per cent) in the low mortality group. A comparatively high proportion of Scheduled Tribe women in the high mortality group and other caste women in the medium and low mortality groups had availed iron and folic acid tablets.

6.4 Place of Delivery

The per cent distribution of live births during the four years preceding the survey by place of delivery is presented in Table 6.4.

A majority of deliveries in all mortality groups took place at home. The proportion of home deliveries in low mortality group (62 per cent) was comparatively lower than the proportion in medium (81 per cent) and high (92 per cent) mortality groups. (See Figure 6.2.).

Table [illegible] Percent distribution of live births during the four years preceding the survey by place of delivery according to selected background characteristics, Rural India, 1992 - 93.

Background Characteristics of Mother	*High*				*Medium*				*Low*			
	N	*Public Health Facility*	*Private Health Facility*	*Home*	*N*	*Public Health Facility*	*Private Health Facility*	*Home*	*N*	*Public Health Facility*	*Private Health Facility*	*Home*
Age												
< 20	4297	6.3	1.8	91.0	3406	14.8	6.1	78.7	1744	17.6	15.7	66.1
20 – 34	14087	5.3	2.2	92.0	7746	11.8	6.5	81.4	4699	20.9	18.2	60.4
35+	1478	2.7	1.3	95.1	473	6.2	3.7	89.2	199	17.3	11.7	70.9
Birth Order												
1	4622	10.1	3.6	85.6	3328	20.5	10.4	68.8	2063	24.8	25.9	49.0
2 - 3	7417	5.1	2.0	92.5	4934	10.8	5.7	83.2	3149	19.9	16.2	63.3
4 - 5	4439	3.0	1.3	94.9	2195	7.3	3.3	88.8	1050	13.7	8.3	76.9
6+	3384	2.2	1.0	96.2	1167	6.3	2.5	90.6	380	10.3	5.2	84.2
Education												
Illiterate	16140	3.1	1.0	95.2	8517	8.4	2.8	88.3	3475	14.0	6.0	79.2
Literate < Middle Complete	2199	10.7	3.2	85.7	1983	20.2	9.6	70.1	1710	24.3	20.4	54.9
Middle Complete	773	16.4	5.5	78.0	603	30.3	17.6	52.2	735	31.5	34.9	33.5
High School & Above	749	25.1	17.1	57.4	522	28.9	37.1	33.9	725	26.2	46.7	27.0

(Contd.)

(Contd. Table 6.4)

Background Characteristics of Mother	High				Medium				Low			
	N	*Public Health Facility*	*Private Health Facility*	*Home*	*N*	*Public Health Facility*	*Private Health Facility*	*Home*	*N*	*Public Health Facility*	*Private Health Facility*	*Home*
Religion												
Hindu	16818	5.7	2.1	91.5	9716	13.2	6.3	80.1	4822	20.7	16.4	62.3
Muslim	2785	2.8	1.4	95.6	1535	8.2	4.3	87.5	708	18.6	24.9	56.2
Christian	142	3.7	0.6	95.4	179	13.9	8.6	77.5	365	22.5	30.5	46.5
Sikh	28	11.9	7.9	80.1	105	9.2	12.1	78.7	518	11.7	12.4	75.8
Buddhist	5	5.1	0.0	94.9	7	0.0	27.6	72.4	161	24.6	3.9	71.2
Jain	15	35.8	23.0	41.3	21	9.5	63.8	26.7	3	61.4	21.1	17.4
Others	69	3.6	0.0	96.4	62	7.1	4.4	88.5	64	9.0	1.1	89.3
Caste												
Scheduled Caste	2716	3.5	1.1	94.4	1764	9.6	2.6	87.1	963	17.5	8.3	73.2
Scheduled Tribe	2301	2.0	0.4	96.5	1390	7.0	2.6	89.8	617	9.2	2.6	87.6
Others	14845	6.2	2.5	91.0	8470	14.0	7.6	78.2	5061	21.7	20.8	57.1
Antenatal Care Visits												
None	11462	1.9	0.7	97.5	3688	3.4	0.8	95.8	1022	4.5	3.4	92.2
1 – 3 visits	6736	8.1	2.6	89.3	4294	13.5	4.6	81.9	2566	15.9	8.7	75.4
4+ visits	1451	20.4	10.5	69.1	3561	20.9	13.9	65.1	2997	28.9	29.8	41.2
DK,missing	213	1.6	0.0	43.7	81	5.7	1.3	45.6	56	6.5	1.8	34.2
Total	**19862**	**5.3**	**2.0**	**92.0**	**11624**	**12.5**	**6.3**	**80.9**	**6642**	**19.9**	**17.3**	**62.3**

Total percentage not equal to 100 in some categories due to the omission of don't know/missing values in the table.

Figure 6.2
Place of Delivery by Mortality Groups

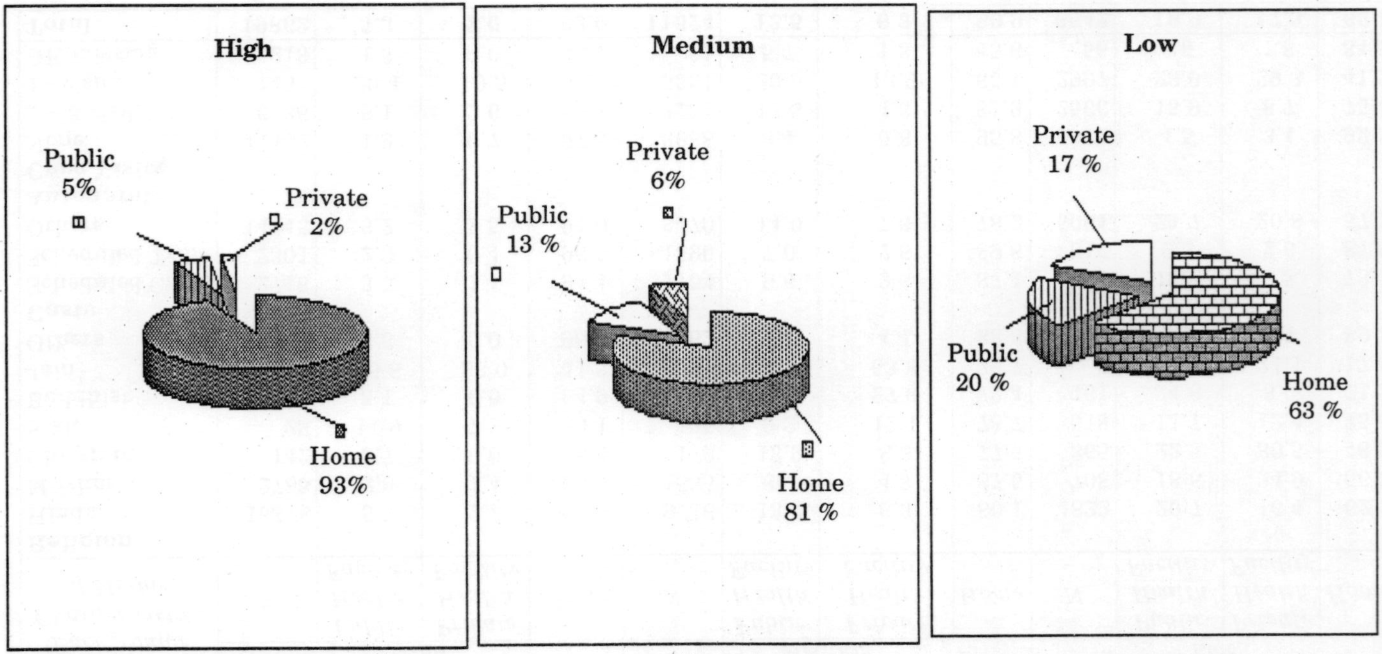

Note : Based on births in the period 1-47 months preceding the Survey

NFHS, Rural India 1992-93

The detailed analysis of the place of delivery by selected background characteristics revealed that home deliveries increased with age of mother and birth order in all mortality groups. In the high mortality group, the proportion of home deliveries increased from 91 per cent for women aged 20 years or less to 95 per cent for women aged 35 or more. In the medium mortality group, it has increased from 79 per cent to 89 per cent and in the high mortality group it has increased from 66 per cent to 71 per cent. Variation in the proportion of home deliveries due to birth order was very substantial in all mortality groups ranging from 86 per cent for first order births to 96 percent for sixth order or more in high mortality group, 69 per cent to 91 per cent in medium mortality group and 49 per cent to 84 percent in low mortality group.

Education of women seemed to play a vital role in reducing home deliveries and increasing institutional deliveries in all mortality groups. It is observed that in the high mortality group, the proportion of home deliveries which was highest at 95 per cent for illiterates had decreased to a level of 57 per cent for women with high school or higher level of education. In the medium mortality group, it has decreased from 88 per cent to 33 per cent and in the low mortality group it has decreased from 79 per cent to 27 per cent.

The proportion of home deliveries varied among different religions in all mortality groups. However, the pattern is not uniform in all mortality groups. It is observed that while the proportion of home deliveries was lowest among Sikh in high mortality groups, it was lowest among Christian in medium and low mortality groups. It is also to be noted that there was not much variation in the proportion of home deliveries in the high mortality group among the three major religious ie., Hindu, Muslim and Christian and it was in the range of 92 to 96 per cent.

Home deliveries observed to be lowest among other caste women in all mortality groups. It is found that 91 per cent of other caste women in high mortality group, 78 per cent in medium mortality group and 57 per cent in low mortality group had home deliveries. There was not much variation in the proportion of home deliveries among the women of different caste groups and it was in the range of 91 per cent for others to 97 per cent for scheduled tribe. In the medium mortality group, the variation was in the range of 78 per cent for others to 90 per cent for scheduled tribe and in low mortality group it was in the range of 57 per cent for others to 88 percent for scheduled tribe. Thus the results indicate that the proportion of home deliveries was observed to be lower among other caste women and higher among scheduled tribe women in all mortality groups.

It is interesting to note that the proportion of home deliveries decreased substantially with increase in the number of antenatal care visits in all mortality groups. It has decreased from 98 per cent for women with no antenatal care visit to 69 per cent for four or more number of visits in the high mortality group (a decline of about 30 per cent). In the case of medium mortality group, it has decreased from 96 per cent to 65 per cent (a decline of about 32 per cent) and in the low mortality group it has decreased from 92 per cent to 41 per cent (a decline of about 55 per cent). The per cent decline of home deliveries was more in the low mortality group as compared to medium and high mortality groups.

6.5 Delivery Assistance

Assistance during delivery or the person attending the delivery is an important factor in deciding the level of infant mortality. Hence, an analysis was made to assess the type of persons attended delivery in all mortality groups. The per cent distribution of live births during four years preceding the survey by type of delivery assistance is presented in Table 6.5.

Substantial variations were observed among the three mortality groups in the proportion of deliveries attended by trained health personnel. The proportion of deliveries attended by trained health personnel was only 15 per cent in high mortality group whereas it was 29 per cent in medium mortality group and 49 per cent in low mortality group (see Figure 6.3).

Deliveries attended by trained health personnel decreased with age of mother in all mortality groups. It is observed that in the high mortality group, the proportion of deliveries attended by trained health personnel varied from a high of 17 per cent for women aged less than 20 years to just 10 per cent for women aged 35 years or more. In the medium mortality group, it varied from a high of

Figure 6.3
Assistance during delivery by mortality groups

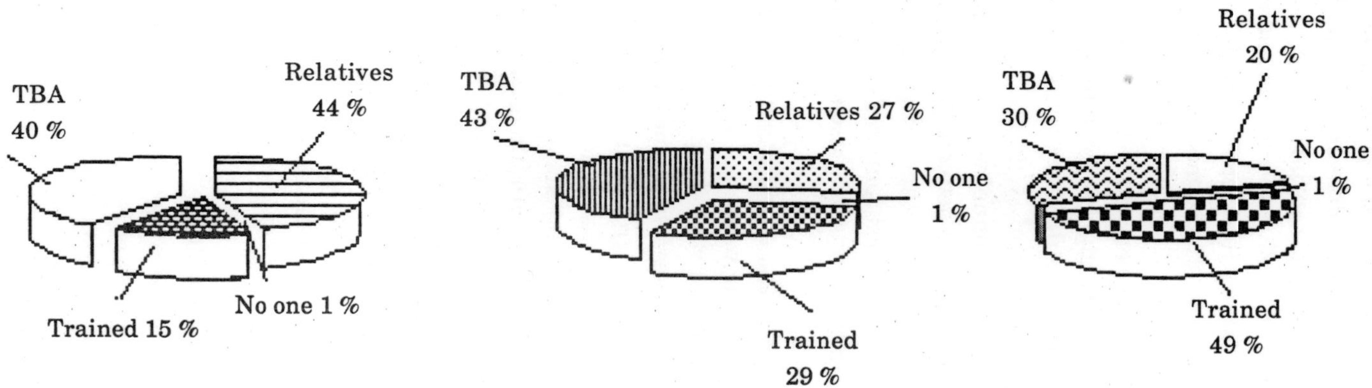

Note : Based on births in the period 1 - 47 months preceding the Survey NFHS, Rural India 1992 - 93.

34 per cent to the low of 14 per cent and in the low mortality group, it varied from a high of 44 per cent to the low of 39 per cent. In the case of birth order, the proportion of deliveries attended by health personnel decreased with increase in birth order. In the high mortality group, the proportion of deliveries attended by health personnel decreased from 23 per cent for first birth order to 8 per cent for birth order of 6 or more. In the medium mortality group it has decreased from 44 per cent to 14 per cent and in the low mortality group, it has decreased from 62 per cent to 25 per cent.

Education seemed to have significant role in increasing the use of trained health personnel for delivery in all mortality groups. It is found that in the high mortality group, the proportion of deliveries attended by health personnel was lowest at just 10 per cent for illiterates and highest at 54 per cent for women with high school or higher level of education. In the medium mortality group, it has increased from a low of 21 per cent to a high of 78 per cent and in the low mortality group it has increased from 32 per cent to 83 per cent.

Substantial variation in the use of trained health personnel for delivery was observed among women of different religion in all mortality groups. It is observed that the proportion of deliveries attended by trained health personnel was highest among Sikh women in the high and medium mortality groups and among the Christian women in low mortality group. It was highest at 35 per cent among Sikh women and lowest at 8 per cent among Christian women in the high mortality group. In the medium mortality group, it was highest at 41 per cent among sikh women and lowest at 19 per cent among muslims. In the low mortality group, it was highest at 61 per cent among Christians and lowest at 47 per cent among sikh women.

Other caste women seemed to have higher proportion of deliveries attended by trained health personnel in all mortality groups. It was highest at 16 per cent among other caste women and was nearly same at 11 per cent among SC and ST women in the high mortality group. In the medium mortality group, it was highest at 35 per cent among other caste women and lowest at 17 per cent among ST women and in the low mortality group, it was highest at 54 per cent among other caste women and lowest at 21 per cent among ST women.

Table 6.5 Percent distribution of live births during the four years period preceding the survey by type of assistance during delivery according to selected background characteristics, Rural India, 1992 - 93.

Background characteristics of mother	*High*				
	N	*Trained* Health Personnel*	*Traditional Birth Attendant*	*Relatives / Others*	*No one*
Age					
< 20	4297	16.5	40.0	42.2	0.4
20 - 34	14087	14.4	39.8	44.4	0.7
35+	1478	9.5	41.5	46.9	0.9
Birth Order					
1	4622	23.4	36.3	39.2	0.2
2 - 3	7417	14.3	39.9	44.7	0.5
4 - 5	4439	10.2	41.7	46.3	1.0
6+	3384	8.4	42.7	46.7	1.3
Education					
Illiterate	16140	10.3	41.5	46.5	0.7
Literate < Middle Complete	2199	24.5	38.3	36.3	0.6
Middle Complete	773	34.6	29.0	35.9	0.0
High School & Above	749	53.9	21.8	23.6	0.5

(Contd.)

(Contd. Table 6.5)

Background characteristics of mother	*Medium*				
	N	*Trained* Health Personnel*	*Traditional Birth Attendant*	*Relatives/ Others*	*No one*
Age					
< 20	3406	34.3	40.5	24.5	0.5
20 - 34	7746	28.0	43.6	27.2	0.7
35+	473	13.9	47.7	36.4	1.1
Birth Order					
1	3328	43.5	36.6	19.3	0.4
2 - 3	4934	28.1	43.0	27.9	0.8
4 - 5	2195	18.7	48.2	31.6	0.9
6+	1167	14.1	50.2	34.2	0.9
Education					
Illiterate	8517	21.1	47.2	30.3	0.7
Literate < Middle Complete	1983	42.1	35.6	21.5	0.7
Middle Complete	603	60.9	27.2	11.9	0.0
High School & Above	522	77.7	16.9	5.3	0.1

(Contd.)

(Contd. Table 6.5)

Background characteristics of mother	*Low*				
	N	*Trained* Health Personnel*	*Traditional Birth Attendant*	*Relatives / Others*	*No one*
Age					
< 20	1744	44.4	27.4	27.7	0.2
20 - 34	4699	50.9	30.9	17.2	0.6
35+	199	39.3	39.9	19.6	1.1
Birth Order					
1	2063	61.6	23.7	14.5	0.1
2 - 3	3149	48.2	30.9	20.0	0.5
4 - 5	1050	34.6	37.5	26.4	0.9
6+	380	24.5	40.8	32.4	1.8
Education					
Illiterate	3475	32.1	37.9	28.9	0.7
Literate < Middle Complete	1710	56.7	27.4	15.2	0.5
Middle Complete	732	76.7	16.5	6.6	0.1
High School & Above	725	83.0	14.4	2.5	0.0

(Contd.)

(Contd. Table 6.5)

Background characteristics of mother	High				
	N	*Trained* Health Personnel*	*Traditional Birth Attendant*	*Relatives / Others*	*No one*
Religion					
Hindu	16818	15.3	39.6	43.6	0.7
Muslim	2785	9.5	42.0	47.7	0.5
Christian	142	7.9	32.8	58.3	0.8
Sikh	28	35.2	38.4	26.3	0.0
Buddhist	5	5.1	84.6	10.3	0.0
Jain	15	94.5	5.5	0.0	0.0
Others	69	16.4	52.9	29.3	1.3
Caste					
Scheduled Caste	2716	11.1	37.5	49.0	1.0
Scheduled Tribe	2301	11.2	41.8	44.9	1.0
Others	14845	15.6	40.1	43.1	0.6
Antenatal Visits					
None	11462	6.7	44.6	47.9	0.6
1 - 3 visits	6736	21.1	35.8	42.2	0.8
4+ visits	1451	47.1	26.1	26.4	0.4
DK,missing	213	6.3	13.4	26.4	3.0
Total	**19862**	**14.5**	**39.9**	**44.1**	**0.7**

(Contd.)

(Contd. Table 6.5)

Background characteristics of mother	*Medium*				
	N	*Trained* Health Personnel*	*Traditional Birth Attendant*	*Relatives / Others*	*No one*
Religion					
Hindu	9716	30.5	43.1	25.3	0.6
Muslim	1535	18.9	43.8	35.9	1.4
Christian	179	38.9	26.6	34.2	0.3
Sikh	105	40.9	43.3	15.8	0.0
Buddhist	7	27.6	44.8	27.6	0.0
Jain	21	89.3	10.6	0.0	0.0
Others	62	20.4	46.6	33.0	0.0
Caste					
Scheduled Caste	1764	22.9	46.7	29.0	0.7
Scheduled Tribe	1390	17.0	48.3	33.8	0.3
Others	8470	32.7	41.2	25.1	0.7
Antenatal Visits					
None	3688	9.6	48.9	39.9	1.1
1 - 3 visits	4294	28.5	46.8	24.1	0.6
4+ visits	3561	51.0	32.2	16.6	0.3
DK,missing	81	11.9	27.3	13.3	2.0
Total	**11624**	**29.3**	**42.9**	**26.9**	**0.7**

(Contd.)

(Contd. Table 6.5)

Background characteristics of mother	*Low*				
	N	*Trained* Health Personnel*	*Traditional Birth Attendant*	*Relatives / Others*	*No one*
Religion					
Hindu	4822	48.8	28.6	21.8	0.4
Muslim	708	49.6	34.6	15.3	0.3
Christian	365	60.7	17.3	19.9	1.6
Sikh	518	46.7	50.5	2.8	0.0
Buddhist	161	40.5	24.7	34.7	0.0
Jain	3	82.6	7.0	10.5	0.0
Others	64	18.1	36.8	41.7	3.5
Caste					
Scheduled Caste	963	39.2	39.4	20.4	0.0
Scheduled Tribe	617	21.0	34.9	42.1	1.7
Others	5061	54.1	28.0	17.3	0.4
Antenatal Visits					
None	1022	15.1	40.0	43.2	1.7
1 - 3 visits	2566	37.9	37.9	24.0	0.3
4+ visits	2997	70.3	20.9	8.6	0.1
DK,missing	56	21.6	6.1	27.2	7.4
Total	**6642**	**48.9**	**30.3**	**20.0**	**0.5**

Note : Total percentage not equal to 100 in some categories due to the omission of don't know/missing values in the table.

* Trained Health personnel include Doctor, Nurse and midwife.

Antenatal care visits during pregnancy is an important factor in influencing the use of trained health personnel for delivery. It is observed that the proportion of deliveries attended by trained health personnel increased from just 7 per cent for women who had no antenatal care visits to a high of 47 per cent for women who had four or more number of antenatal care visits in the high mortality group. In the medium mortality group, it has increased from a low level of just 10 per cent for no antenatal visits to 51 per cent for those who had four or more antenatal visits. In the low mortality group, the proportion of deliveries attended by trained health personnel increased from just 15 per cent for no antenatal visits to a high of 70 per cent for four or more visits.

Deliveries attended by trained health personnel decreased with increase in age of mother and birth order in all mortality groups. On the other hand, it increased with education and number of antenatal care visits in all mortality groups. Among the Hindus, Muslims and Christians, a higher proportion of Hindu women in the high mortality group, Christian women in the medium and low mortality groups tend to have their deliveries attended by trained health personnel. A comparatively higher proportion of other caste women in all mortality groups had their deliveries attended by trained health personnel.

6.6 Summary

The comparative analysis of the utilisation of maternal care services showed substantial variations in the utilisation of maternal care services among the three mortality groups. The proportion of women who had received antenatal care at home was more or less same (32 per cent) for medium and low mortality groups where as it was only 18 per cent in high mortality group. The proportion who had made outside visits for antenatal care was high in the low mortality group (70 per cent) which was followed by medium (51 per cent) and high (27 per cent) mortality groups. Among those who had received antenatal care, the median number of antenatal care visits of both the types (home and outside) was slightly higher in the low mortality group as compared to medium and high mortality groups. There was not much difference in the median months of gestation at first antenatal care visit among the three mortality groups.

Nearly 40 per cent of women in the high mortality group, 65 per cent in the medium and 83 per cent in the low mortality groups had availed a minimum of one dose of TT vaccine during pregnancy. Substantial variations were also observed in the proportion who have availed iron and folic acid tablets during pregnancy among the three mortality groups. The proportion varied from 74 per cent for low mortality group to 28 per cent for high mortality group. Similarly, the proportion of women assisted by trained health personnel at the time of delivery varied from 49 per cent for low mortality group to 15 per cent for high mortality group. Proportion of institutional deliveries also showed considerable variation among the three mortality groups, reaching a high of 37 per cent for low mortality group and a low of just 7 per cent for high mortality group.

It is observed that home deliveries increased with age of mother and birth order in all mortality groups. On the other hand, institutional deliveries tend to increase with education of women in all mortality groups. Among the three major religious groups i.e Hindus, Muslims and Christians, the proportion of home deliveries was more among Muslim and Christian women in the high mortality group, Christian women in the medium mortality group and Hindu women in the low mortality group. Home deliveries were more common among Scheduled Tribe women than others in all mortality groups.

The findings revealed substantial variation in the utilisation of maternal care services among the three mortality groups. The level of utilisation of maternal care services was highest among women in the low mortality group which was followed by medium and high mortality groups. Most important of the findings is that the high mortality group is in a highly disadvantaged position in all aspects of the maternal health care.

7

Immunization and Breast Feeding Practices

Infant feeding practices have significant effects on the health of both mothers and children. Proper infant feeding starting from the time of birth, is important for the physical and mental development of the child.

Under the Reproductive and Child Health Programme, the Government of India recommends that infants should be exclusively breast-fed from birth to age of four months (Ministry of Health and Family Welfare, New Delhi). Most babies do not require any other foods or liquids during this period. By age seven months, adequate and appropriate complementary foods should be added to the infant's diet in order to provide sufficient nutrients for operational growth. It is recommended that breast feeding should continue, along with complementary foods, through the second year of life or beyond (BPNI, 2000).

Besides breast feeding, immunization is one of the major important factor in reducing infant and child mortality and improving child survival. WHO, USAID, UNICEF and other major groups in collaboration with the local governments are taking ambitious efforts to achieve universal immunization against six common childhood diseases viz., measles, diphtheria, pertussis, tetanus, poliomyelitis and tuberculosis. A child who is not immunized is more likely to become undernourished, to become disabled and to die. Hence immunization is urgent, and all immunizations should be completed in the first year of the child's life.

In India, the universal immunization programme was launched in 1985-86 with the aim of covering at least 85 percent of infants against all six vaccine preventable diseases by 1990 and to achieve self sufficiency on vaccine production and the manufacture of cold chain equipment, (Ministry of Health and Family Welfare, 1991). Now the target is to achieve 100 percent immunization coverage. In NFHS-I, data on immunization coverage was collected from mothers who had children aged 12-23 months at the time of survey in order to assess the immunization coverage of children against the six vaccine preventable diseases. The results of the survey are presented in the following sections.

7.1 IMMUNIZATION COVERAGE

The estimates of immunization coverage for children aged 12-23 months presented in Table 7.1 revealed substantial differences in the immunization coverage of children in the three mortality

Table 7.1 Percent distribution of children aged 12 - 23 months who had received specific vaccine at any time before the survey by mortality groups, rural India, 1992-93.

Vaccinations	*High (N= 4847)*	*Medium (N=2644)*	*Low (N= 1647)*
BCG	44.6	65	84.2
Polio (O)	1.8	3.9	8.4
DPT -1	49.8	68.7	87.7
DPT -2	41	61.1	83.8
DPT -3	32.5	52.8	78.5
Polio -1	50.6	70.1	87.6
Polio -2	43.8	63.2	83.3
polio -3	35	54.9	77.6
Measles	24.1	44.5	66.6
All*	17.9	36.5	60.1
None	45.9	26.9	10.3

* Children who have received three doses of DPT and polio and one dose each of BCG and measles vaccines

Fig 7.1 Immunisation coverage of children aged 12-23, months Rural India, 1992-93

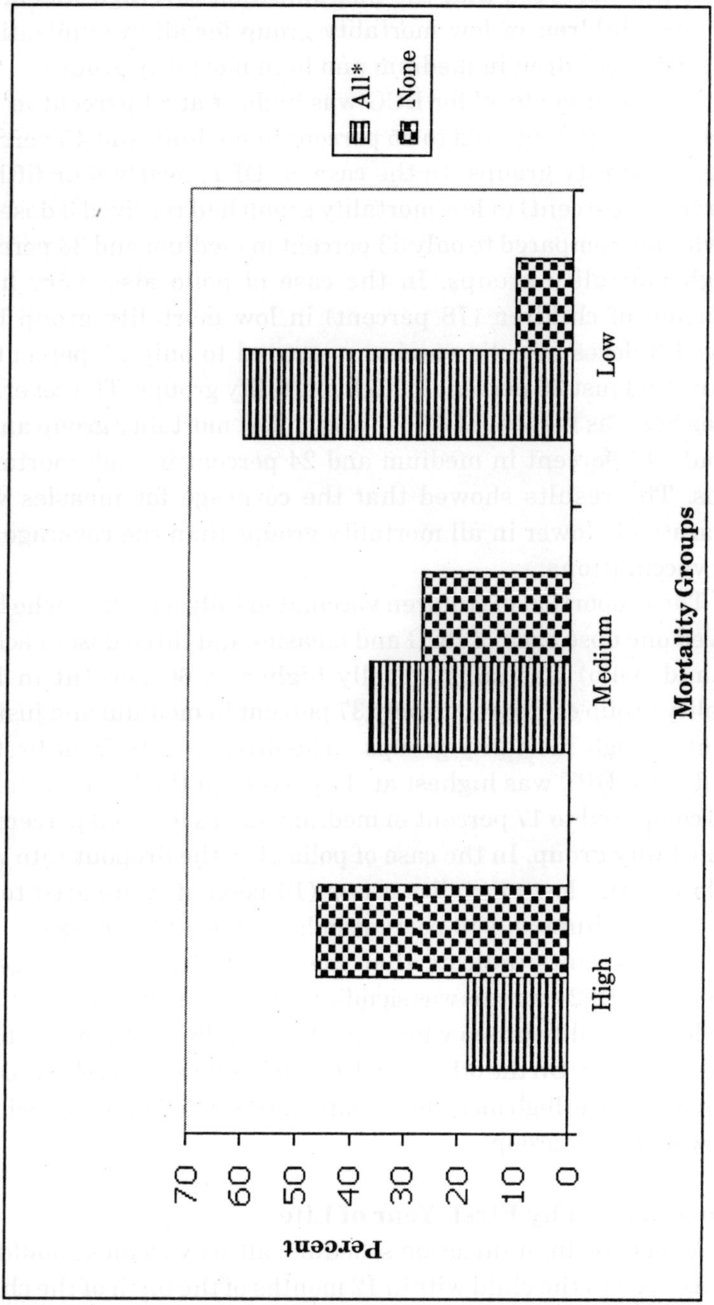

* Children who have received three doses each of DPT and Polio and one dose each of BCG and measles vaccines.

groups. It is observed that the immunization coverage was much higher for children in low mortality group for all immunizations compared to children in medium and high mortality groups.

The coverage level for BCG was highest at 84 percent in low mortality group compared to 65 percent in medium and 45 percent in high mortality groups. In the case of DPT, nearly four fifth of children (79 percent) in low mortality group had received 3 doses of DPT vaccine compared to only 53 percent in medium and 33 percent in high mortality groups. In the case of polio also, very high proportion of children (78 percent) in low mortality group had received 3 doses of polio vaccine compared to only 55 percent in medium and just 35 percent in high mortality groups. The coverage for measles was highest at 67 per cent in low mortality group and it was only 45 percent in medium and 24 percent in high mortality groups. The results showed that the coverage for measles was comparatively lower in all mortality groups than the coverage for other vaccinations.

The proportion of children vaccinated fully (children who had received one dose each of BCG and measles and three doses each of DPT and polio) was substantially higher at 60 percent in low mortality group compared to only 37 percent in medium and just 18 percent in high mortality groups. The dropout rate from first to third dose of DPT was highest at 17 percent in the high mortality group compared to 17 percent in medium and as low as 9 percent in low mortality group. In the case of polio also, the dropout rate was very low in the low mortality group (10 percent) compared to 15 percent in medium and 16 percent in high mortality groups.

The results indicate that the immunization coverage of children aged 12-23 months was significantly high for all immunizations in the low mortality group which was followed by medium and high mortality groups. On the other hand, the dropout rate was observed to be high among the high mortality group which was followed by medium and low mortality group.

7.2 Vaccination by First Year of Life

As per the immunization schedule, all six vaccines should be administered to the child within 12 months of the birth of the child. In order to assess the immunization status of the children by the end of 12 months of age, mothers of all children in the age group of

Table 7.2 : Percentage of children aged 1-3 years immunized against specific vaccine preventable diseases in the first year of life by current age of the child and mortality groups, Rural India, 1992 93

Vaccinations	*High*			
	Child's Age (months)			
	12-23	*24-35*	*36-47*	*All*
	N=4847	*N = 4019*	*N = 4371*	*N =13237*
BCG	40.3	32.8	22.8	32.2
Polio (O)	1.7	1.9	1.9	1.8
DPT –1	44.8	36.1	26.9	36.3
DPT –2	36.1	29.4	20.6	29.0
DPT –3	27.6	22.2	16.2	22.2
Polio –1	45.6	36.6	27.7	37.0
Polio –2	38.7	31.2	22.6	31.1
Polio –3	29.8	23.8	17.6	23.9
Measles	17.1	13.7	9.5	13.5
All*	12.8	10.2	6.4	9.9
None	51.0	60.0	69.8	60.0

(Contd.)

(Contd. Table 7.2)

Vaccinations	*Medium*			
	child's Age (months)			
	12-23	24-35	36-47	*All*
	N = 2644	*N* = 2514	*N* =2724	*N*=7882
BCG	61.1	50.1	36.5	49.1
Polio (O)	3.9	3.0	3.2	3.4
DPT –1	64.2	52.4	36.6	50.9
DPT –2	56.4	48.4	33.9	46.1
DPT –3	47.0	39.9	29.2	38.6
Polio –1	65.3	53.3	38.7	52.3
Polio –2	58.2	49.6	35.9	47.8
Polio –3	48.0	42.1	30.1	39.9
Measles	33.4	25.6	19.1	26.0
All*	27.3	21.4	16.3	21.6
None	31.2	43.9	58.2	44.6

(Contd.)

(Contd. Table 7.2)

Vaccinations	*Low*			
	child's Age (months)			
	12-23	*24-35*	*36-47*	*All*
	N=1647	*N=1583*	*N=1544*	*N=4773*
BCG	82.7	77.1	72.6	77.6
Polio (O)	7.7	8.0	8.6	8.1
DPT –1	86.8	80.2	74.9	80.8
DPT –2	82.3	77.3	70.7	76.9
DPT –3	75.9	72.2	65.2	71.2
Polio –1	86.7	81.2	75.2	81.2
Polio –2	81.7	77.8	70.2	76.7
Polio –3	75.0	71.5	63.9	70.3
Measles	55.9	51.2	45.6	51.0
All*	49.3	44.7	38.5	44.3
None	11.1	17.3	21.7	16.6

* children who have received three doses each of DPT and polio and one dose each of polio(o) and of BCG and measles vaccines

1-3 years were asked information on the age of the child at the time of receiving each immunization.

The results presented in Table 7.2 revealed that higher proportion of children (44 percent) in the low mortality group had received all vaccines in the first year of life compared to only 22 percent in medium and just 10 percent in high mortality group. The proportion of children not availed any vaccine during the first year of life was comparatively low at 17 percent in low mortality group where as it was 45 percent in medium and 60 percent in high mortality group. Proportion of children received all six vaccines during the first year of life was observed to be higher for children of recent births (12-23 moths of age) compared to children aged 24-35 months and 36-47 months in all mortality groups. In the high mortality group, proportion received all six vaccines was 13 percent for children aged 12-23 months where as it was 10 percent for children aged 24-35 months and just 6 percent for children aged 36-47 months. In the medium mortality group, proportion of children fully vaccinated in the first year life was observed to be highest at 27 percent for children aged 12.-23 months compared to 21 percent and 16 percent for children aged 24-35 months and 36-47 months respectively. In the low mortality group of states also, the proportion who had received full vaccination during the first year of life was highest at 49 percent for younger children aged 12-23 months compared to 45 percent and 39 percent for children aged 24-35 months and 36-47 months respectively.

With regard to vaccine specific information, it is observed that nearly one third of children in high mortality group (32 percent), about half of the children in medium mortality group (49 percent) and more than three fourth of children in low mortality group (78 percent) had availed BCG vaccine in the first year of life. Proportion received BCG vaccine in the first year of life was higher among the younger children (aged 12-23 months) compared to those aged 24-35 months and 36-47 months. In the case of DPT, those who had received three doses of DPT in the first year of life was only 22 percent in high mortality group, 39 percent in medium mortality group and 71 percent in low mortality group. Those who had received three doses of polio was also very low at 24 percent in high mortality group compared to 40 percent in medium and as high as 70 percent in low mortality

Figure 7.2
Immunisation coverage of children aged 1-3 years, Rural India, 1992-93

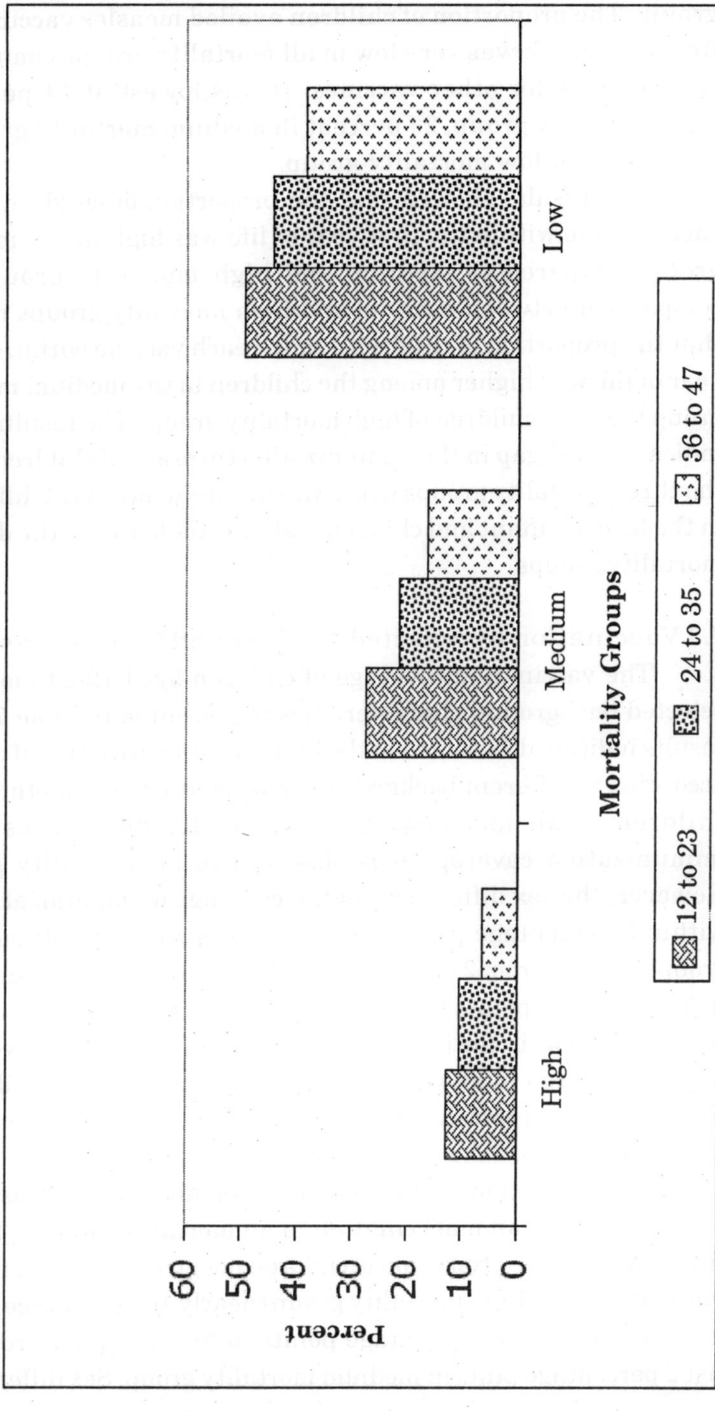

group. The proportion of children availed measles vaccine in the first year of life was very low in all mortality groups compared to the coverage for other vaccines. It was lowest at 14 percent in high mortality group, 26 percent in medium mortality group and 51 percent in low mortality group.

The results showed that the proportion of children availed each vaccine within the first year of life was high in low mortality group compared to medium and high mortality groups. The comparison between medium and high mortality groups revealed that the proportion of children availed each vaccine within the first year of life was higher among the children in the medium mortality group than the children of high mortality group. The results clearly indicate a vast gap in the immunization coverage of children among the three mortality groups which in turn influences vast differences in the level of infant and child mortality rates between the different mortality groups.

7.3 Vaccination by Selected Background Characteristics

The vaccination coverage of children aged 12-23 months by selected background characteristics is presented in table 7.3. The results indicate differences in the immunization coverage of children according to different background characteristics of mothers and children in all mortality groups. Gender differences in the immunization coverage was observed in all mortality groups. However, the sex differences in the coverage of immunization was within 5 percentage points for full immunization in all mortality groups ranging from 2 percentage points for medium mortality group to 5 percentage points for both high and low mortality groups. The sex differentials in the immunization coverage was more favourable to male children in all mortality groups for all vaccines indicating slightly more importance for male than female children in all the mortality groups.

The proportion of children not given any vaccine was higher among female than male children in all mortality groups. The sex differentials in the proportion of children not given any immunization was very high in high mortality group (nearly 10 percentage points) compared to only 5 percentage points in low mortality group and just 2 percentage pints in medium mortality group. Sex differentials

Table 7.3 Percentage of children aged 12- 23 months who had received specific vaccine by selected background characteristics and mortality groups, Rural India 1992-93

Characteristics	*High*						
	N	*BCG*	*DPT*	*Polio**	*Measles**	*All*	*None*
Sex							
Male	2748	48.1	35.6	38.0	26.7	20.2	41.2
Female	2370	40.9	29.2	31.8	21.4	15.1	50.9
Birth order							
1	1122	51.1	39.2	42.1	31.7	24.2	39.6
2-3	1839	47.4	35.3	36.8	24.6	19.0	43.1
4-5	1125	42.0	29.6	32.6	19.8	14.5	49.0
6+	761	31.9	19.9	23.6	17.8	10.9	57.6
Education							
Illiterate	3904	38.3	25.8	28.4	19.2	13.3	51.9
Literate- primary	536	61.3	52.6	56.1	35.6	28.8	28.7
Middle-complete	207	81.5	69.2	68.2	52.6	47.3	11.9
High school &above	200	84.4	69.7	73.6	58.9	48.9	10.9

(Contd.)

(*Contd. Table 7.3*)

Characteristics	*Medium*						
	N	*BCG*	*DPT**	*Polio**	*Measles**	*All*	*None*
Sex							
Male	1347	66.5	54.9	56.2	46.2	37.5	25.8
Female	1297	63.5	50.6	53.4	42.7	35.6	28.1
Birth order							
1	776	70.6	60.9	62.7	51.2	42.9	20.4
2-3	1137	68.3	54.8	56.4	46.3	37.8	25.7
4-5	505	58.7	44.2	47.0	38.8	30.4	30.2
6+	226	43.6	34.5	37.7	25.1	22.3	48.1
Education							
Illiterate	1888	57.9	45.4	47.5	38.0	29.7	33.2
Literate- primary	461	77.9	63.5	66.4	53.1	46.6	15.5
Middle-complete	157	86.5	80.6	81.0	65.7	58.4	7.7
High school & above	137	95.3	86.6	87.9	81.1	72.1	0.6

(*Contd.*)

(Contd. Table 7.3)

Characteristics	Low						
	N	*BCG*	*DPT**	*Polio **	*Measles**	*All*	*None*
Sex							
Male	810	85.9	80.9	79.9	69.0	62.7	8.0
Female	837	82.5	76.2	75.3	64.4	57.5	12.5
Birth order							
1	547	90.7	84.5	85.7	77.6	70.6	4.6
2-3	765	85.3	79.9	78.4	65.6	59.6	9.6
4-5	250	75.0	72.8	68.9	56.0	50.8	18.1
6+	85	59.2	43.2	43.2	33.6	23.9	29.6
Education							
Illiterate	846	78.9	72.7	71.5	59.0	52.2	13.6
Literate- primary	439	85.5	80.0	79.9	68.9	61.7	9.5
Middle-complete	179	92.4	87.2	83.4	79.0	71.0	4.4
High school &above	183	97.2	93.0	94.2	84.5	81.9	2.3

(Contd.)

(Contd. Table 7.3)

Characteristics	High						
	N	*BCG*	*DPT*	*Polio**	*Measles**	*All*	*None*
Religion							
Hindu	4140	46.7	34.4	36.7	25.4	19.1	43.6
Muslim	643	31.4	19.1	23.5	15.1	9.9	61.3
Christian	30	21.3	24.6	24.6	10.1	6.1	63.2
Others	36	61.1	54.4	57.8	43.6	38.9	40.7
Caste							
Scheduled Caste	707	34.9	24.7	25.0	15.1	9.5	54.3
Scheduled Tribe	545	40.4	26.6	27.4	23.4	15.5	50.6
Others	3595	47.1	34.9	38.1	26.0	19.9	43.6
All	**4847**	**44.6**	**32.5**	**35.0**	**24.1**	**17.9**	**45.9**

(Contd.)

(Contd. Table 7.3)

Characteristics	*Medium*						
	N	*BCG*	*DPT**	*Polio**	*Measles**	*All*	*None*
Religion							
Hindu	2224	66.4	54.9	56.9	46.0	38.1	25.7
Muslim	342	54.8	39.2	41.1	34.1	26.2	35.2
Christian	32	68.6	49.5	48.9	46.2	30.4	30.9
Others	46	69.6	58.3	62.2	49.1	41.5	22.2
Caste							
Scheduled Caste	368	58.3	48.2	50.6	39.5	30.1	29.0
Scheduled Tribe	307	52.3	34.7	35.9	34.5	26.0	42.7
Others	1969	68.2	56.5	58.6	47.0	39.4	24.1
All	**2644**	**65.0**	**52.8**	**54.9**	**44.5**	**36.5**	**26.9**

(Contd.)

(Contd. Table 7.3)

Characteristics	*Low*						
	N	*BCG*	*DPT**	*Polio **	*Measles**	*All*	*None*
Religion		88.4	84.4	82.8	70.5	63.6	6.0
Hindu	1190	67.4	87.4	58.2	51.6	44.2	25.9
Muslim	176	72.3	60.8	61.1	53.2	44.8	19.7
Christian	97	79.6	69.9	71.0	63.2	60.3	17.7
Others	183						
Caste		83.9	74.1	75.6	64.7	57.7	11.1
Scheduled Caste	233	67.4	64.1	64.0	53.1	48.1	22.2
Scheduled Tribe	161	86.4	81.1	79.7	68.7	62.1	8.6
Others	1253						
All	**1647**	**84.2**	**78.5**	**77.6**	**66.6**	**60.1**	**10.3**

* DPT and Polio referred to those who had received three doses.

Figure 7.3

Immunisation of children aged 12-23 months by education of mother, Rural India 1992-93

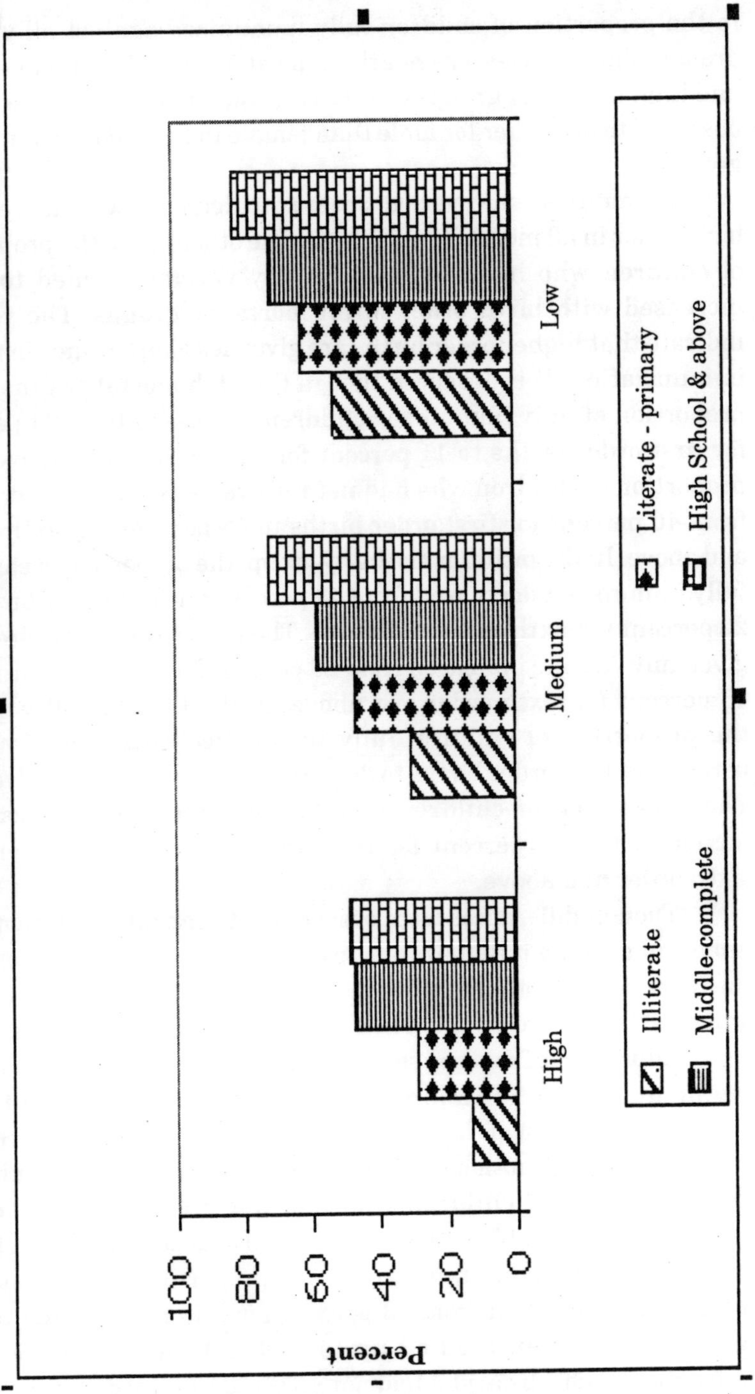

in the proportion of children fully immunized against all vaccine preventable diseases was nearly same at 5 percentage points in low and high mortality groups compared to only two percentage points observed to be higher for male than female in the medium mortality group.

Immunization coverage seemed to decrease with increase in birth order in all mortality groups. On the other hand, the proportion of children who had not received any vaccine seemed to have increased with birth order in all mortality groups. The results indicate that higher order births are given less importance in giving immunization. It is observed that in the high mortality group, the proportion of fully immunized children decreased from 24 percent for first order births to 11 percent for sixth order and above. The proportion of children who had not received any vaccine increased from 40 percent for first order births to 58 percent for sixth order and above. In the medium mortality group, the proportion of children fully immunized decreased from 43 percent for first order births to 22 percent for sixth order and above. The proportion of children not given any vaccine increased from 20 percent for first order births to 48 percent for sixth order and above. In the low mortality group, the proportion of children fully immunized decreased from 71 percent for first order births to 24 percent for sixth order and above. The proportion of children who had not received any vaccine increased from 5 percent for first order births to 30 percent for sixth order and above.

Though differences were observed between different mortality groups in availing immunization to children of different birth orders, the tendency of mothers to give less importance to children of higher order births is more common in all the three mortality groups.

Education of mother seemed to have significant influence on the immunization of children in all mortality groups (see figure 7.3). The proportion of children received full immunization increased with education of mother in all mortality groups. On the other hand, the proportion of children who had not received any vaccine decreased considerably with the increase in education in all mortality groups. In the high mortality group, the proportion of children fully immunized increased from 13 percent for illiterate women to 49 percent for women studied up to high school and above. The proportion of children who had not received any vaccine decreased from 52 percent for illiterates to just 11 percent for women studied up to high school and above. In the medium mortality group, the proportion of children fully immunized increased from 30 percent for illiterates to 72 percent for women studied up to high school and above. On the other hand, the proportion of children who had not received any vaccine decreased from 33 percent for illiterate mothers to just about one percent for mothers studied up to high school and above. In the low mortality group, the proportion of children who had received full immunization has increased from 52 percent for illiterates to 82 percent for mothers studied up to high school and above. On the other hand, the proportion of children who had not received any vaccine decreased from 14 percent for illiterates to just 2 percent for mothers studied up to high school and above.

The achievement of 49 percent of full immunization coverage for children of women who have studied up to high school and above in the high mortality group is well below the achievement of 52 percent coverage made in respect of children whose mothers were illiterate in low mortality group. The results indicate that though education is having a significant influence on the immunization coverage of children, the achievement of 52 percent of full immunization coverage observed for the children of illiterate mothers in low mortality group suggest that even without formal education, it is possible to improve the immunization coverage through the effective implementation of immunization programme with strong communication back up.

The analysis of data related to the religion of mothers revealed that the immunization coverage of both vaccine specific as well as full immunization of children aged 12-23 months was higher among Hindus than Muslims in all mortality groups. Due to small number of children covered among Christians and other religious groups, comparison could not be made possible. The comparison of Hindu and Muslims revealed that the full immunization coverage was highest at 19 percent among Hindus compared to only 10 per cent among Muslims in high mortality group. In the medium mortality group, the proportion of children fully immunized was substantially higher at 38 percent among Hindus compared to 26 percent among Muslims. In the low mortality group, the proportion of children fully immunized was 64 percent among Hindus and 44 percent among Muslims. In all the mortality groups, the proportion of children fully immunized was substantially higher among Hindus than Muslims.

The comparison of full immunization coverage between various caste groups revealed that the coverage was very low among children of scheduled caste compared to the children of scheduled tribe and other caste groups in the high mortality group. In the medium and low mortality groups, the immunization coverage was low among the children of scheduled tribe compared to the children of scheduled caste and other caste groups. In the high mortality group, the proportion of children fully immunized was lowest at 10 per cent for schedule caste compared to 16 per cent and 20 per cent observed for scheduled tribe and other caste groups respectively. In the medium mortality group, the proportion of children fully immunised was lowest at 26 per cent for scheduled tribe compared to 30 per cent and 39 per cent observed for the scheduled caste and other caste groups respectively. In the low mortality group also the proportion of children fully immunised was lowest at 48 per cent for scheduled tribe compared to 58 per cent and 62 per cent observed for scheduled caste and other caste groups respectively. The proportion of children not received any immunization was substantially lower among the children of other caste mothers than the children of SC/ST mothers in all mortality groups. It is observed that the proportion of children not received any vaccine in high mortality group was lowest at 44 per cent for other caste groups compared to 54 per cent and 51 per cent observed for SC and ST respectively. In the medium mortality group, the proportion of children not given any vaccine was lowest at 24 per cent for other caste groups compared to 29 per cent 43 percent observed for SC and ST respectively. In the low mortality group, the proportion of children not immunized against any of the vaccine preventable disease was lowest at 9 percent for children of other caste groups compared to 11 percent and 22 percent observed for SC and ST respectively.

In general, the full immunization coverage among the children of scheduled caste and scheduled tribe was lower than the immunization coverage of children among other caste groups in all mortality groups. The results indicate that the immunization coverage was comparatively low among female children, children of higher order birth, children of illiterate mothers, children of Muslim religious group and children belonging to SC & ST in all mortality groups. Though differences were observed in the immunization coverage of children due to different background characteristics of the mothers, a comparatively higher proportion of coverage was observed for all categories of children in low mortality group than those in other two mortality groups. Thus it is evident that the implementation of immunization programme was more effective in the low mortality group of states than the states grouped under medium and high.

7.4 Breast Feeding Practice

The proportion of children ever breast fed by selected background characteristics of mothers/children for births in the four years preceding the survey are presented in table 7.4. The results showed that most of the children (95 to 96 percent) born in the four years preceding the survey were breast fed at least once in all mortality groups. No variations were observed between different mortality groups in the proportion of children ever breast fed. It is also observed that the proportion of children ever breast fed did not vary much by background characteristics of mothers/children. Thus the results indicate that breast feeding is nearly universal in all mortality groups.

7.5 Duration of Breast Feeding

The median duration of breast feeding for children under four years of age by selected background characteristics is presented in table 7.5. It is observed that the median duration of any breast feeding was 26.5 months for high mortality group 25.4 months for medium mortality group and 22.7 months for low mortality group. In the high mortality group, the median duration of exclusive breast feeding was 2.1 months and full breast feeding (breast milk and water) was 6.0 months. In the medium mortality group, the median duration of exclusive breast feeding was 2.1 months and the full breast feeding was 4.6 months. In the case of low mortality group, the median duration of exclusive breast feeding was 0.7 months and full breast feeding was 3.9 months. The results indicate that the median duration of all types of breast feeding was high in high mortality group which was followed by medium and low mortality groups.

The analysis of median duration of breast feeding by selected background characteristics of mothers/children revealed that there was not much difference in the median duration of breast feeding

Table : 7.4 Percent distribution of children born in the four years period preceding the survey who were ever breast fed by selected background characteristics and mortality groups, Rural India, 1992-93.

Background Characteristic	*High*		*Medium*		*Low*	
	N	*Percent*	*N*	*Percent*	*N*	*Percent*
Sex						
Male	10276	94.9	6032	95.6	3427	95.5
Female	9873	95.3	5747	95.9	3287	96.6
Education						
Illiterate	16389	95.0	8621	95.9	3512	95.3
Literate< middle completed	2221	95.3	2015	95.3	1736	96.6
Middle completed	783	96.4	611	95.1	735	97.8
High school and above	756	94.5	532	94.7	732	96.5

(Contd.)

(Contd. Table 7.4)

Background Characteristic	*High*		*Medium*		*Low*	
	N	*Percent*	*N*	*Percent*	*N*	*Percent*
Religion						
Hindu	17063	95.0	9851	95.8	4867	95.9
Muslim	2824	95.5	1549	95.0	717	96.7
Christian	144	97.1	182	96.0	376	95.6
Sikh	28	98.6	105	99.3	526	96.3
Others	89	93.3	92	93.5	228	97.4
Caste						
Scheduled caste	2765	94.3	1792	95.4	976	94.8
Scheduled tribes	2330	95.4	1417	96.2	622	95.2
Others	15054	95.1	8570	95.7	5116	96.4

(Contd.)

(Contd . Table 7.4)

Background Characteristic	High		Medium		Low	
	N	*Percent*	*N*	*Percent*	*N*	*Percent*
Assistance at Delivery						
Health professional	2935	93.9	3483	94.8	3288	96.7
Trad birth Attendant	8053	96.3	5041	96.6	2036	96.3
Others/none	9015	95.5	3203	96.4	1368	95.4
Missing	147	22.4	52	28.6	22	6.7
Place of Delivery						
Public Health facility	1070	92.1	1470	94.5	1338	97.2
Private health facility	490	95.9	734	94.8	1161	96.5
Own home	16557	95.7	7313	96.9	3002	96.5
Parents home	1888	97.4	2163	95.0	1138	95.8
Others	106	92.9	58	85.6	40	95.0
DK missing	120	0.3	40	4.1	35	8.5
Total	**20149**	**95.1**	**11779**	**95.7**	**6714**	**96**

Table:7.5 Median duration (months) of breast feeding among children under four years of age by selected background characteristics and mortality groups, Rural India, 1992-93.

Background characteristics	*High*			
	N	*Any BF*	*Excl BF*	*Full BF*
Sex				
Male	10276	27.2	2.0	5.7
Female	9873	25.6	2.1	6.3
Education				
Literate	16389	26.4	2.3	6.5
Literate< middle completed	2221	27.9	1.4	4.3
Middle completed	783	21.7	2.6	4.2
High school and above	756	22.5	0.6	2.4
Religion				
Hindu	17063	26.8	2.0	5.8
Muslim	2824	23.8	2.3	7.3
Christian	144	22.4	2.8	5.4
Others	117	22.9	5.9	6.4

(Contd.)

(Contd. Table 7.5)

Background characteristics	*Medium*			
	N	*Any BF*	*Excl BF*	*Full BF*
Sex				
Male	6032	27.0	1.8	4.1
Female	5747	24.3	2.3	5.0
Education				
Literate	8621	26.3	2.7	5.2
Literate< middle completed	2015	23.9	0.7	3.3
Middle completed	611	25.1	1.6	1.9
High school and above	532	17.8	0.5	0.7
Religion				
Hindu	9851	25.5	2.2	4.8
Muslim	1549	26.9	0.7	2.9
Christian	182	22.0	0.7	0.8
Others	197	19.2	2.5	5.6

(Contd.)

(Contd. Table 7.5)

Background characteristics	*Low*			
	N	*Any BF*	*Excl BF*	*Full BF*
Sex				
Male	3427	22.5	8.8	2.9
Female	3287	22.8	0.7	4.8
Education				
Literate	3512	25.2	1.3	5.1
Literate< middle completed	1736	22.4	0.9	3.7
Middle completed	735	21.3	0.6	1.6
High school and above	732	19.3	0.5	1.8
Religion				
Hindu	4867	23.0	1.2	3.7
Muslim	717	22.2	1.0	4.8
Christian	376	19.4	1.2	3.1
Others	754	21.5	0.9	3.8

(Contd.)

(Contd. Table 7.5)

Background characteristics	*High*			
	N	*Any BF*	*Excl BF*	*Full BF*
Caste				
Scheduled caste	2765	25.3	2.8	7.2
Scheduled tribes	2330	32.1	1.4	7.0
Others	15054	26.4	2.0	5.6
Mother work status				
Not working	15875	26.0	2.1	5.9
Working for family	1929	29.9	1.6	5.5
Employed by others	1892	32.7	0.7	7.4
self Employed	454	27.6	2.7	4.2
Assistance at Delivery				
Health professional	2935	25.2	1.6	4.2
Traditional birth Attendants	8053	26.4	2.1	6.6
others or none	9015	27.2	2.3	6.1
Missing	147	0.5	0.5	0.5
Total	**20149**	**26.5**	**2.1**	**6.0**

(Contd.)

(Contd. Table 7.5)

Background characteristics	*Medium*			
	N	*Any BF*	*Excl BF*	*Full BF*
Scheduled caste	1792	24.7	2.7	4.5
Scheduled tribes	1417	23.1	2.9	6.8
Others	8570	26.2	1.6	4.2
Mother work status				
Not working	6876	24.7	1.8	4.1
Working for family	2365	26.9	2.5	5.3
Employed by others	2233	25.9	2.4	5.2
self Employed	305	22.7	0.6	0.7
Assistance at Delivery				
Health professional	3483	23.3	0.7	3.5
Traditional birth Attendants	5041	26.0	2.3	4.5
others or none	3203	26.4	2.9	5.7
Missing	52	2.4	1.9	2.4
Total	**1177**	**25.4**	**2.1**	**4.6**

(Contd.)

(Contd. Table 7.5)

Background characteristics	*Low*			
	N	*Any BF*	*Excl BF*	*Full BF*
Caste				
Scheduled caste	976	23.7	0.6	4.5
Scheduled tribes	622	24.8	1.6	6.7
Others	5116	22.4	0.7	3.6
Mother work status				
Not working	3818	20.6	0.7	3.4
Working for family	1241	26.0	1.2	4.7
Employed by others	1501	26.1	2.3	5.4
self Employed	154	27.7	0.7	1.7
Assistance at Delivery				
Health professional	3288	21.3	0.7	2.5
Traditional birth Attendants	2036	23.6	0.7	1.3
others or none	1368	25.1	2.8	6.7
Missing	22	0.4	0.4	0.4
Total	**671**	**22.7**	**0.7**	**3.9**

Medians are based on the current status of breast feeding ; BF - Breast feeding; Excl- Exclusive between male and female children in all mortality groups. However, education seemed to have negative effect on the breast feeding behaviour of mothers. It is observed that in the high mortality group, the median duration of any breast feeding decreased from 26 months for illiterates to 23 months for mothers with high school education or more. In the medium mortality group, the median duration decreased from 26 months for illiterates to 18 months for mothers with high school education or more. In the case of low mortality group, the median duration decreased from 25 months for illiterates to 19 months for mothers with high school or higher education. Thus the median duration of breast feeding of any kind tend to decrease with the increase in education in all mortality groups. There was very little variation in the median duration of breast feeding of any kind between various religious groups in all mortality groups. It is observed that in the high mortality group, the median duration of any breast feeding was 27 months for Hindu, 24 months for Muslim and 22 months for Christian. In the Medium mortality group, the median duration of any breast feeding was highest at 27 months for Muslim which was followed by Hindu (26 months) and Christian (22 months). In the low mortality group, it was highest at 23 months for Hindu compared to 22 months for Muslim and 19 months for Christian.

The median duration of any breast feeding was higher among the children of scheduled tribe mothers (32 months) than the children of other caste mothers (26 months) and scheduled caste mothers (25 months) in the high mortality group. However, in the case of medium and low mortality groups, not much differences were observed in the median duration of any breast feeding between various caste groups.

The work status of mother showed little variation in the median duration breast feeding. It is observed that the median duration of any breast feeding was lowest for the children of non-working women compared to the children of working women in high and low mortality groups. In the case of medium mortality group, not much differences were observed in the median duration of breast feeding among the children of mothers with various work status. The examination of the influence of delivery attendant on the duration of breast feeding revealed that there was not much difference in the median duration of breast feeding of any kind in all mortality groups.

The results indicate that the breast feeding pattern was more or less same in all mortality groups. However improvement in education seemed to have negative effect on the median duration of breast feeding among women in all mortality groups.

7.6 Timing of Breast Feeding

The timing of breast feeding after the birth of child by selected background characteristics is presented in table 7.6. It is observed that the proportion of children breast fed within one hour was nearly same at 11 per cent in low and medium mortality groups compared to only 7 per cent observed in high mortality group. The proportion of children who were breast fed within a day was very low at 19 percent in high mortality group compared to 28 percent in medium mortality group and 37 percent in low mortality group. No sex differentials were observed in the timing of breast feeding in all mortality groups. However, differences due to selected background characteristics of mothers were observed in all mortality groups. In the high mortality group, the proportion of children who were given breast feeding with in one hour was high for children of mothers with middle school education (8 percent), children of Christian mothers (20 percent) children of scheduled tribe mothers (20 percent), children of mothers whose delivery was attended by relatives/others (9 percent) and children of mothers whose delivery took place at home (8 percent). The proportion of children who were given breast feeding within a day was comparatively high for children of mothers with middle school education (27 percent), children of Christian mothers (53 percent), children of scheduled tribe mothers (39 percent) children of mothers whose delivery was assisted by relatives/others (19 percent) and children of mothers whose delivery took place at public health facilities (20 percent).

In the medium mortality group, the proportion of children who were given breast feeding with in one hour of birth was observed to be high among children of mothers with middle school education (13 percent), children of Christian mothers (11 percent), children of scheduled tribe mothers (12 percent), children of mothers whose delivery was attended by persons other than health personnel and traditional birth attendants (13 percent) and children of mothers whose delivery took place at parents home (12 percent). The proportion of children who were given breast feeding within a day

Table 7.6 : Percent distribution of last born children in the four years period preceding the survey who were given breast feeding with in one hour and one day of birth by selected background characteristics and mortality groups, Rural India, 1992-93.

Background characteristics	*High*			*Medium*			*Low*		
	N	*With-in one hour*	*With in a day**	*N*	*With- in one hour*	*With in a day**	*N*	*With-in one hour*	*With in a day**
Sex of child	7975	7.4	18.5	4714	10.6	28.1	2657	10.5	35.9
Male	7413	7.0	18.6	4371	10.8	28.2	2524	12.4	37.5
Female									
Education	12531	7.1	17.3	6594	10.8	27.1	2659	10.1	28.2
literate	1679	7.4	24.2	1576	9.5	30.2	1343	12.6	40.6
Literate < Mid Complete	591	8.4	27.1	480	13.3	31.7	576	15.5	55.4
Middle completed	588	7.5	21.6	434	10.4	32.8	604	10.6	47.3
high school & above									

(Contd.)

(Contd. Table 7.6)

Background characteristics	*High*			*Medium*			*Low*		
	N	*With-in one hour*	*With in a day**	*N*	*With- in one hour*	*With in a day**	*N*	*With- in one hour*	*With in a day**
Religion									
Hindu	13086	7.6	18.8	7631	10.9	28.0	3772	10.7	34.0
Muslim	2102	3.9	15.3	1167	10.1	26.0	540	12.8	49.3
Christian	107	20.4	53.0	139	11.3	46.2	298	22.8	65.6
Others	93	7.8	20.2	148	8.3	35.9	572	9.1	26.7
Caste									
Scheduled caste	2089	4.9	12.0	1346	11.0	27.2	730	12.916	35.5
Scheduled Tribe	1788	19.8	38.6	1089	12.4	32.9	461	.8	36.1
Others	11511	5.7	16.6	6650	10.4	27.6	3991	10.6	36.9

(Contd.)

(Contd. Table 7.6)

Background characteristics	*High*			*Medium*			*Low*		
	N	*With-in one hour*	*With in a day**	*N*	*With- in one hour*	*With in a day**	*N*	*With- in one hour*	*With in a day**
Assistance at Delivery									
Health Professional	2310	6.8	21.9	2749	11.6	28.2	2631	13.1	47.8
Trad. Birth Attendants	6185	5.9	17.3	3845	8.9	26.8	1526	9.7	28.9
Others or None	6821	8.6	18.7	2468	12.5	30.5	1017	9.7	19.6
Missing	72	5.8	5.8	22	0.0	0.0	8	0.0	0.0
Place of Delivery									
Public Health Facilities	842	5.9	20.0	1152	11.3	31.0	1069	14.2	51.9
Private Health Facilities	312	5.6	18.7	597	9.9	28.2	944	12.7	54.5
Own Home	12621	7.5	18.8	5615	10.4	28.9	2258	11.4	28.5
Parents Home	1487	6.0	15.7	1657	11.9	24.3	872	6.9	19.8
Others	78	5.7	19.1	49	0.0	14.0	30	10.9	34.3
DK/Missing	48	0.6	0.6	14	12.1	12.1	9	0.0	17.2
Total	**15388**	**7.2**	**18.5**	**9084**	**10.7**	**28.2**	**5182**	**11.4**	**36.6**

* Include Children who were given breast feeding with in one hour.

Fig 7.4 Timing of first breast feeding

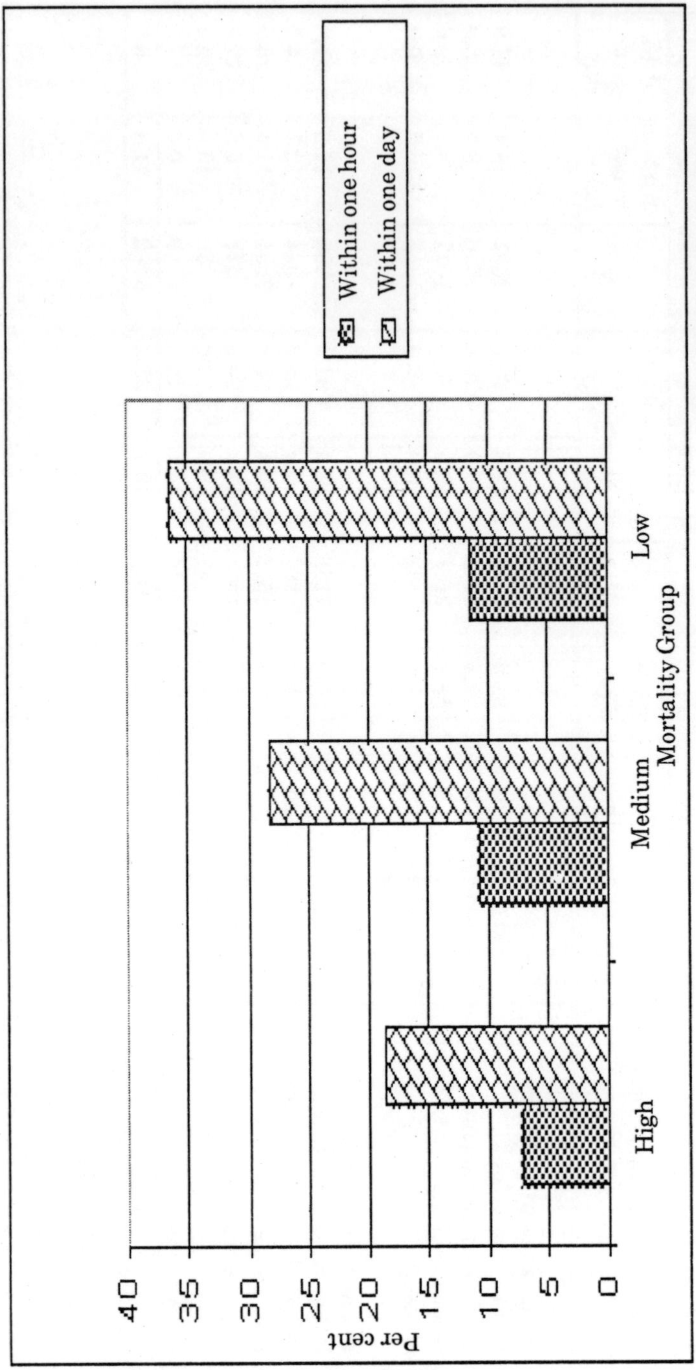

NFHS Rural India 1992-93.

was high for children of mothers with high school education (33 percent), children of Christian mothers (46 percent), children of scheduled tribe mothers (33 percent), children of mothers whose delivery was attended by person other than health personnel and traditional birth attendants (31 percent) and children of mothers whose delivery took place at own home (29 percent).

In the low mortality group, proportion of children who were given breast feeding within one hour and within a day was high for children of mothers with middle school education (16 percent and 55 percent), children of Christian mothers (23 percent and 66 percent), children of scheduled tribe mothers (17 percent and 36 percent) and children of mothers whose delivery was attended by health personnel (13 percent and 48 percent). In the case of place of delivery, the proportion of children who were given breast feeding with in one hour was high for children of mothers whose delivery took place at public health facilities (14 percent) and the proportion who were given breast feeding with in a day was high among children of mothers whose delivery took place at private health facilities (55 per cent).

In general, the timing of breast feeding by background characteristics of mother indicate a nearly similar pattern in all mortality groups except for place of delivery for which the proportion of children who were given breast feeding with in one hour and within a day was high for mothers whose delivery took place at home in high and medium mortality groups where as it was high for children of mothers whose delivery took place at institution in low mortality group.

7.7 Squeezed Out the First Milk

Due to ignorance, illiteracy and cultural taboos, squeezing out first milk from breast before breast feeding the child is more prevalent in many parts of India and it is believed to be widespread in rural areas. In order to assess the extent of the practice of squeezing out the first milk from breast, mothers who had children in the four years preceding the survey were asked whether they squeezed out the milk from breast before breast feeding. The results of the survey presented in table 7.7 revealed that the practice of squeezing out first milk before breast feeding was more common in low mortality group (73 percent) compared to high and medium mortality groups where the proportion of mothers squeezing out first milk from breast lingering around 61-63 percent.

Sex of the child did not make much difference in the proportion of mothers squeezing out the first milk. However, education of mothers seemed to reduce the practice of squeezing out the first milk in all mortality groups. It is observed that the practice had decreased from 63 percent for illiterates to 55 percent for those who had studied up to high school and above in high mortality group where as in medium and low mortality groups the decrease was from 62 to 53 percent and from 80 to 58 percent respectively. In the case of religion and caste, no uniform pattern was observed among the three different mortality groups. While the practice of squeezing out the first milk was very high (75 percent) among Christians in high mortality group, it is high among Muslims in medium mortality group (65 percent) and among Hindu in low mortality group (75 percent). The practice of squeezing out first milk before breast feeding was observed to be high among scheduled tribe mothers in high mortality group (68 percent) and among scheduled caste mothers both in medium (64 percent) and low (87.5 per cent) mortality groups. In general, the practice was more among SC/ST mothers than others.

Births attended by traditional dais played a major role in the practice of squeezing out first milk in all mortality groups. In the high mortality group, the practice was prevalent among 68 percent of mothers whose delivery attended by traditional birth attendants compared to 63 percent observed among mothers whose delivery attended by health personnel. In the medium mortality group, the practice was highest at 63 percent among mothers whose delivery attended by traditional birth attendents compared to 59 percent observed among mothers whose delivery attended by health personnel. In the low mortality group, the practice was highest at 81 percent among mothers whose birth was attended by traditional birth attendents compared to 66 percent observed among mothers whose birth was attended by health personnel. Home deliveries (own home/parents home) seems to increase the practice of squeezing out first milk before breast feeding in all mortality groups. The proportion of mothers following the practice of squeezing out first milk before breast feeding was higher among mothers whose delivery took place in home than among mothers whose delivery took place at institutions (both private & public).

Table 7.7 Percent distribution of mothers who squeezed out the milk before first put the child to the breast for children born during the four years preceding the survey, according to selected background characteristics, Rural India, 1992-93.

Characteristics	*High*		*Medium*		*Low*	
	N	*Percent*	*N*	*Percent*	*N*	*Percent*
All	12359	63.2	4786	61.3	3583	72.9
Sex						
Male	6357	63.1	2507	61.3	1864	73.0
Female	6002	63.4	2279	61.2	1719	72.7
Education of mother						
Illiterate	9951	63.1	3646	61.9	1742	80.0
Lit., <middle school	1417	66.8	666	63.1	960	70.1
Middle school	488	65.4	203	54.7	424	65.2
High school & above	503	54.7	271	52.6	457	58.4

(Contd.)

(Contd. Table 7.7)

Characteristics	High		Medium		Low	
	N	Percent	N	Percent	N	Percent
Religion						
Hindu	10230	63.7	4277	60.9	2309	74.9
Muslim	1973	60.1	331	65.3	497	61.3
Christian	96	74.9	76	61.7	227	54.6
Others	62	72.6	102	62.7	550	82.3
Caste						
Scheduled caste	1815	63.7	746	63.8	329	87.2
Scheduled tribe	909	67.6	756	61.2	427	66.5
Others	9635	62.7	3284	60.7	2827	72.2

(Contd.)

(Contd. Table 7.7)

Characteristics	*High*		*Medium*		*Low*	
	N	*Percent*	*N*	*Percent*	*N*	*Percent*
Assistant at delivery						
Health professional	1654	62.8	1381	59.1	1741	66.0
Traditional birth attendant	5183	68.1	2115	63.1	1006	80.6
Others or none	5501	58.8	1280	60.5	836	77.9
Missing	21	51.0	10	64.5	-	-
Place of delivery						
Public health facilities	633	55.5	479	58.1	662	63.7
Private health facilities	278	53.9	335	57.2	643	58.7
Own home	10265	64.3	3107	60.3	1610	80.5
Parents home	1118	60.2	846	67.6	648	77.6
Others	65	62.8	19	88.0	20	59.9
Total	**12359**	**63.2**	**4786**	**61.3**	**3583**	**72.9**

7.8 Frequency of Breast Feeding

Frequency of breast feeding is considered to be an important factor in determining the growth and development of the child particularly when the child mainly depends on breast milk during the first six months. Hence in this survey, mothers who had children aged less than 6 months at the time of survey were asked whether they had breast fed their child atleast six times during the last 24 hours before the survey. The results of the survey presented in table 7.8 revealed that the proportion of mothers who had breast fed their child 6 times or more in the past 24 hours was observed to be highest at 94 percent among mothers in the high mortality group compared to 93 percent in medium and 88 percent in low mortality groups.

Sex of the child did not make much difference in the frequency of breast feeding among mothers in all mortality groups. Proportion of children who were breast fed six or more times was comparatively low among children of mothers who had high school and above level of education than others in high and medium mortality groups. However, in the low mortality group, it was high among children of mothers who had high school and above level of education than others. Proportion of children who were breast fed six or more times was comparatively low among children of Hindu mothers in high and low mortality groups where as it was low among children of Muslim mothers in medium mortality group.

Children of Scheduled Caste mothers seemed to have less frequency of breast feeding compared to the children of mothers of other caste groups both in the medium and low mortality groups where as it was low among the children scheduled tribe in high mortality group. In the case of work status of mothers, it is observed that the frequency of breast feeding was more among self employed women in high and low mortality groups while it was more among working women (working for family business and for others) in the medium mortality group.

Exposure to mass media did not show any consistent relationship with the frequency of breast feeding in all mortality groups. Children whose delivery attended by health personnel seemed to receive less frequency of breast feeding in high and low mortality groups where as it was low among children whose delivery attended by others in medium mortality group.

Table 7.8 Percent children under six months of age who were breast fed six or moretimes in the 24 hours preceding the survey according to selected background characteristics, Rural India 1992 - 93.

Characteristics	*High*		*Medium*		*Low*	
	N	*Percent*	*N*	*Percent*	*N*	*Percent*
Sex of the child						
Male	1336	94.0	685	92.9	411	88.6
Female	1336	94.8	728	92.3	398	88.1
Education of mother						
Illiterate	2247	94.7	1018	92.6	386	89.4
Literate < middle school	282	92.6	252	93.7	230	84.9
Middle school	117	95.7	67	91.5	86	89.1
High school & above	86	91.4	76	89.4	107	91.6
Religion						
Hindu	2263	94.0	1188	93.7	565	86.7
Muslim	434	95.8	174	85.2	91	91.3
Christian	25	100.0	24	88.1	51	90.3
Others	10	100.0	27	96.3	102	93.1

(Contd.)

(Contd. Table 7.8)

Characteristics	*High*		*Medium*		*Low*	
	N	*Percent*	*N*	*Percent*	*N*	*Percent*
Caste						
Scheduled caste	402	95.5	240	90.6	121	84.4
Scheduled tribe	300	90.8	181	96.2	70	95.5
Others	2030	94.7	992	92.4	618	88.4
Mothers work status						
Not working	2281	94.6	941	91.9	559	87.7
Working family business	211	91.6	220	94.2	126	88.0
Employed by others	188	93.2	223	94.1	108	90.9
self-employed	52	99.1	29	89.7	16	98.2

(Contd.)

(Contd. Table 7.8)

Characteristics	High		Medium		Low	
	N	Percent	N	Percent	N	Percent
Exposure to mass media						
Exposed to any media	677	94.5	660	94.3	496	87.0
Watch T.V. weekly	217	94.3	255	92.6	298	87.0
Listen to radio weekly	596	94.2	573	94.9	412	85.3
visit cinema monthly	63	86.9	245	92.8	127	83.9
Not exposed to any media	2055	94.4	753	91.0	313	90.7
Assistance at Delivery						
Health professional	375	89.7	435	93.8	419	87.3
Traditional birth attendant	1084	95.1	626	92.6	218	87.9
Others or none	1270	95.2	350	90.9	172	91.7
Total	**2732**	**94.4**	**1413**	**92.6**	**809**	**88.4**

Note: Total include 3 and 2 children with missing information on assistance at delivery in high and medium mortality groups respectively which are not shown separately.

7.9 Type of Supplementation

In order to assess the timing and type of supplement food given to breast feeding children under 12 months of age, mothers of breast feeding children under 12 months of age were asked about the type of food given to the child in the previous day or night.

The results presented in table 7.9 revealed that in the high mortality group, the proportion of children received infant formula increased from less than one percent for children aged one month or less to 4 percent for children aged 3 months. For children aged 4-5 months, the use of infant formula had decreased to 2 percent and thereafter slowly increased with age up to 6 percent for children aged 8 months. Again there was a decline in the use of infant formula for children aged up to 10 months of age and a sudden increase in the use of infant formula was observed for children aged 11 months and there after showed a declining trend.

Supplementation with other milk (cow's milk or buffalo's milk) increased with the age of children. The use of other milk increased from 8.2 percent for children aged 9 months and there after the proportion of children given other milk was lingering between 38 to 42 percent as it is quite natural to reduce other milk supplementation as the children would be supplemented with other solid/mushy food at these ages. Supplementation by other liquids (juice, tea, ricewater etc.,) increased consistently with the age of children. It has increased from 8 percent for children aged less than one month to 57 percent for children aged 12 months of age. The supplementation by solid/ mushy food has also increased consistently with the age of the child from third month onwards. About two third of children (66.3 per cent) were given solid/mushy food by the age of 12 months.

In the medium mortality group, about 5 to 9 percent in the age range of 4-12 months were given supplementation by infant formula. Supplementation by other milk has increased consistently from 7 percent for children aged less than one month to 46 percent for children aged 12 months. Supplementation by other liquids also increased with age of children. It has increased from 11 percent for children aged less than one month to 53 percent for children aged 12 months. It is also observed that 70 percent of children had received supplementation of solid/mushy food by the age of 12 months.

In the low mortality group, comparatively higher percentage of children were given supplementation by infant formula compared to high and medium mortality groups at almost all ages.

Supplementation by other milk has increased from 5 percent for children aged less than one month to 61 percent for children aged 8 months. After a decrease in the use of other milk at the age of 9 to 11 months, it has again increased to the level of 76 percent by the age of 12 months. Supplementation with other liquid has also increased with age upto 9 months and after that an up and down trend was observed for children aged between 10-12 months.

Table 7.9 Percent distribution of last born breast feeding children by type of supplementation during the 24 hours before the survey in different mortality groups, Rural India 1992-93.

Age in Months	*Type of supplementation*				
	N	*Infant formula*	*Other milk*	*Other liquid*	*Solid / Mushy food*
			High		
<1	266	0.5	8.2	7.6	0.9
1	465	0.3	12.8	7.5	0.4
2	513	1.6	12.1	7.5	1.0
3	502	3.8	19.3	10.5	2.1
4	486	1.5	22.5	13.1	3.7
5	458	1.5	24.7	16.0	5.1
6	442	2.7	30.7	16.8	10.8
7	387	2.6	35.0	31.0	17.6
8	328	5.5	36.0	38.5	28.4
9	338	4.9	41.7	40.0	35.8
10	317	3.5	38.1	53.9	43.8
11	226	7.4	42.2	51.7	50.5
12	390	4.6	40.7	57.4	66.3
			Medium		
<1	131	0.0	6.9	11.4	0.1
1	225	0.0	11.9	14.7	2.2
2	213	2.2	17.0	16.9	1.9
3	292	1.7	16.4	15.0	1.0
4	263	4.5	24.9	21.7	6.2
5	257	4.5	26.2	25.7	12.3
6	287	6.8	28.0	34.3	17.6
7	318	8.3	34.5	33.7	35.9
8	258	6.2	42.4	45.2	45.8
9	251	7.0	34.6	45.1	55.9
10	201	7.0	40.8	43.9	65.4
11	201	9.5	45.7	47.7	76.2
12	174	7.8	45.8	52.9	69.7

(Contd.)

(Contd. Table 7.9)

Age in Months	*Type of supplementation*				
	N	*Infant formula*	*Other milk*	*Other liquid*	*Solid / Mushy food*
			Low		
<1	69	0.0	4.6	19.7	0.0
1	137	2.3	9.9	18.0	0.0
2	155	2.8	11.7	18.7	2.8
3	143	4.6	26.0	18.1	3.7
4	168	7.7	30.8	15.8	11.5
5	123	5.2	39.4	32.7	15.4
6	130	6.4	41.2	41.2	28.5
7	128	8.4	48.0	47.3	37.4
8	130	13.0	61.4	50.0	47.2
9	114	16.7	56.1	69.3	66.9
10	91	9.5	50.0	65.7	67.5
11	95	5.7	59.7	80.2	66.6
12	93	8.8	76.4	71.6	79.1

Supplementation by solid/mushy food increased consistently with the age of the child and it is observed that 79 percent of the children were given supplementation of solid/mushy food by the age of 12 months.

7.10 Summary

The results of the immunization coverage for children 12-23 months of age indicate appreciable differences in the coverage for different immunizations among the three mortality groups. The coverage for BCG varied from 84 percent for children of low mortality group to 45 percent for children of high mortality group. The coverage for DPT (3 doses) varied from 79 percent for the children of low mortality group to 33 percent for the children of high mortality group. Similar variations were also observed in the coverage for polio and measles vaccines.

The variations in the proportion of fully immunized children varied from 60 percent in low mortality group to just 18 percent for children of high mortality group. Substantial differences were also observed in the proportion of children immunized against all vaccine preventable diseases in the first year of life. In the low mortality group, 44 percent of children were fully immunized in the first year of life where as it was only 22 percent in the medium mortality group and just 10 percent in the high mortality group.

Sex differentials in the immunization coverage were observed in all mortality groups. Higher proportion of male children were vaccinated in all mortality groups. In all, female children, children of higher order births, children of illiterate mothers, children of Muslim mothers and children of SC/ST mothers seemed to have very less immunization coverage than others. The achievement of 52 percent of immunization coverage for the children of illiterate mothers in the low mortality group was higher than the immunization coverage among the children of mothers who had studied high school and above in high mortality group (49 percent). The results indicate the effectiveness of information, education and communication (IEC) activities of the programme personnel in the low mortality group. Improvement in the health infrastructure facilities and the effective implementation of IEC activities will help to improve the immunization coverage even in places where the formal education of mothers is at a very low level.

The analysis of data on the breast feeding practices of women revealed that breast feeding was near universal in all mortality groups. Not much variations were observed in the breast feeding practice and duration of breast feeding among the mothers in the three mortality groups. It is also observed that the duration of breast feeding by background characteristics of the mothers and children did not vary much in all mortality groups. Since the data related to rural areas and breast feeding is universal in rural India, not much variations were observed among the three mortality groups with regard to the breast feeding practice.

8

Differentials in the Nutritional Status of Children

In order to assess the nutritional status of children, anthropometric measurements were taken for two most recent births in the three years period preceeding the survey. Data collected on age, weight and height of the children were used to calculate the following indices of nutritional status.

(i) Weight for height

(ii) Weight for age

(iii) Height for age

The nutritional status of children measured based on these indices are compared with the nutritional status of an international reference population recommended by the world health organization. (Dipley et.al., 1987a, 1987b) to assess the level of undernourished.

8.1 Weight for Height

The weight for height index helps to assess the nutritional status of children by examining the body mass in relation to body length. Children who are more than two standard deviations below the median of the reference population in terms of weight for height are considered as malnourished and children who are more than three standard deviation below the median of the reference population are considered severely malnourished.

The weight for height index presented in table 8.1 indicates that the level of malnutrition among children in the three mortality groups did not vary much. The percentage of malnourished children was lingering around 17-19 percent in all mortality groups and the percentage of severely malnourished children was observed to be very low at about three percent in all mortality groups.

In the high mortality group, the percentage of malnourished children presented according to age of the child indicates that the percentage of malnourished children increased with age up to 23 months and after that there was a declining trend. It has increased from a low of nine percent among children aged less than 6 months to 29 percent for children aged 12-23 months and after that it has decreased to 12 percent for children aged 36-47 months. A similar trend was observed for severely malnourished children. The percentage of severely malnourished children increased from a low level of just two percent among children aged less than six months to six percent for children aged 12-23 months and then declined to a low level of about two percent for children aged 36-47 months. A similar trend was observed for both medium and low mortality groups where the percentage of malnourished and severely malnourished children increased with age up to 12-23 months and then showed a declining trend. It is observed that in the medium mortality group, the percentage of malnourished children increased from eight percent for children aged less than 6 months to 27 percent for children aged 12-23 months. The percentage of severely malnourished also, increased to from just one percent 6 percent for those aged 12-23 months and then declined to a level of 3 percent for children aged 36-47 months. In the low mortality group, the percentage of malnourished increased from just 91 percent for children aged less than six months to 31 percent for children aged 12-23 months and then declined to a lower level of 11 percent for children aged 36-47 months. The percentage of severely malnourished also increased from just two percent for children aged less than six months to 5 percent for children aged 12-23 months and then declined to a lowest level of 2 percent for children aged 36-47 months.

Differentials by sex of the child is more pronounced in high mortality group than in other two groups. In all the three groups, percentage of both malnourished and severely malnourished is

Table 8. 1 Percent distribution of children under four years of age classified as malnourished based on anthropometric indices of nutritional status (weight for height) presented according to selected background characteristics by mortality groups, Rural India, 1992 – 93.

Background characteristics	*Anthropometric indices (Weight for Height)*								
	High			*Medium*			*Low*		
	below -3SD	*Below -2SD*	*Number of children*	*below -3SD*	*below -2SD*	*Number of children*	*below -3SD*	*below -2SD*	*Number of children*
Child's Age									
<6 months	2.1	8.7	1562	1.1	8.1	514	2.4	11.1	492
6-11 months	3.5	6.7	1326	2.1	14.3	611	3.4	15.0	424
12-23 months	5.8	28.6	3294	5.9	27.1	1159	5.2	31.3	936
24-35 months	2.1	18.5	2655	2.9	14.1	1069	3.2	18.5	909
36-47 months	1.5	12.0	2783	2.6	13.2	1122	2.1	11.5	844
Sex									
Male	3.9	20.7	5860	3.8	16.8	2317	3.7	19.3	1864
Female	2.5	15.8	5760	2.8	16.3	2158	3.0	18.2	1741
Birth order									
1	2.8	17.9	2518	2.6	16.0	1229	3.9	16.7	1095
2-3	3.3	18.2	4401	3.8	16.4	1889	2.7	19.4	1727
4-5	3.5	19.4	2654	3.3	18.8	890	3.8	18.8	574
6+	2.9	17.7	2047	2.9	14.4	467	5.3	24.7	209

(Contd.)

(Contd. Table 8.1)

Background characteristics	Anthropometric indices (Weight for Height)								
	High			*Medium*			*Low*		
	below -3SD	*Below -2SD*	*Number of children*	*below -3SD*	*below -2SD*	*Number of children*	*below -3SD*	*below -2SD*	*Number of children*
Birth Interval									
First birth	2.8	17.9	2525	2.6	16.1	1232	3.9	16.6	1102
under 24 months	3.2	16.0	2001	4.6	16.4	828	3.3	18.2	655
24-47 months	3.1	18.5	5179	3.0	16.4	1859	3.1	21.2	1444
48+ months	3.9	20.6	1915	4.0	16.4	556	3.3	17.2	404
Education of mother									
illiterate	3.2	18.9	9235	3.7	17.9	3295	4.4	22.4	1704
lit < mid complete	3.2	16.5	1370	2.4	14.0	700	2.9	18.1	994
middle complete	2.9	15.2	520	1.0	10.2	206	2.9	13.4	445
high school & above	3.5	15.9	495	2.4	12.5	273	1.2	11.9	462
Caste									
Scheduled caste	3.2	19.4	1731	3.3	13.7	701	3.7	24.8	360
Scheduled tribe	3.4	19.6	829	6.3	24.5	635	2.5	22.6	432
Others	3.2	18.0	9060	2.7	15.6	3139	2.5	17.4	2813
Total	**3.2**	**18.3**	**11620**	**3.3**	**16.6**	**4475**	**3.4**	**18.8**	**3605**

Fig 8.1 Malnourished Children Aged 1-4 years (weight for height), Rural India- 1992-93

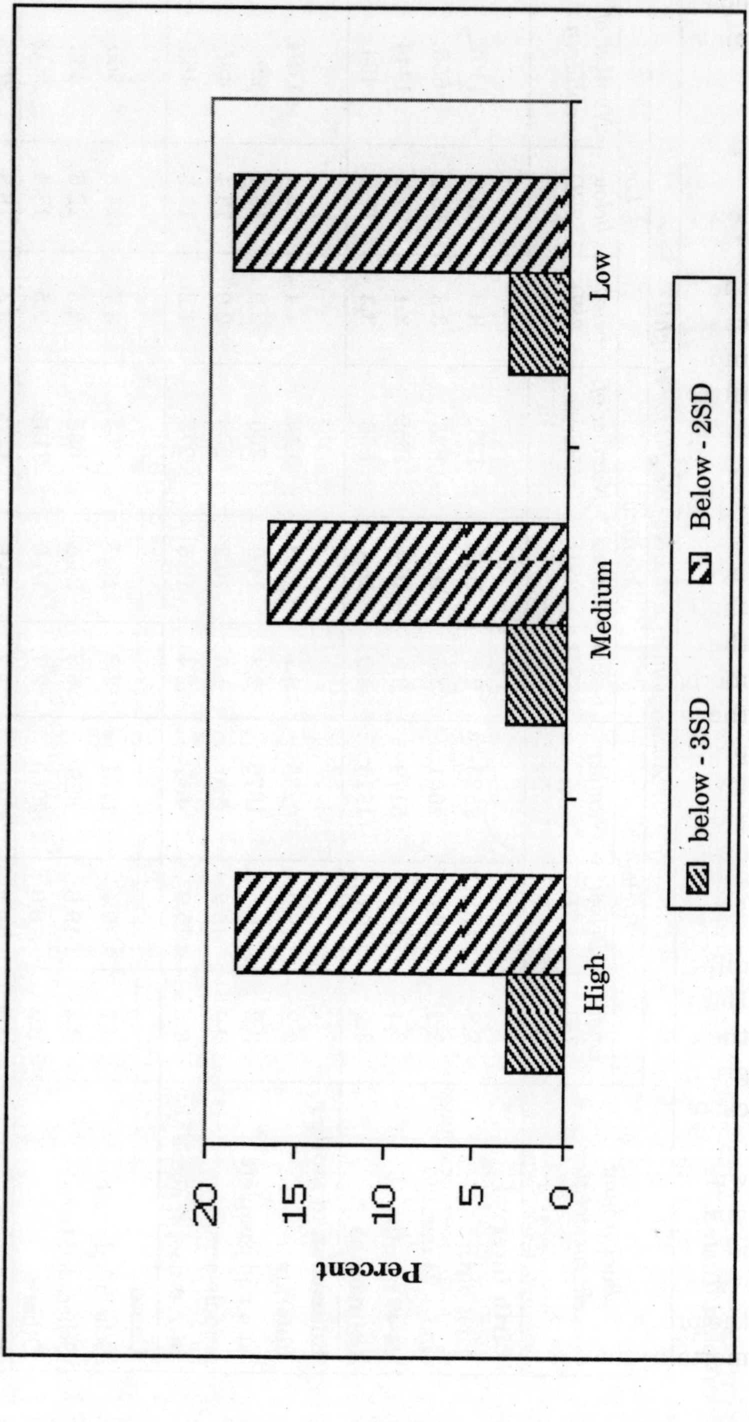

observed to be higher among male than female. Birth order did not make much difference in the prevalence of malnutrition in the high mortality group. The percentage of malnourished children was around 17-19 percent for children of all birth orders. No consistant relationship has been observed in the prevalence of malnutrition among the children of different birth orders both in medium and low mortality groups.

Increase in birth interval is generally expected to improve the nutritional status of children. However this is not true in the case of nutritional status measured based on weight for height index in all the mortality groups. In the high mortality group, birth interval did not make much difference in the prevalence of malnutrition. The percentage of malnutrition was lingering around 16-21 percent and the prevalence of severely malnourised was around 3-4 percent for all categories of children.

Education of mother is expected to make notable difference in the prevalence of malnutrition among children. It is observed that the prevalence of malnutrition was comparatively lower among the children of literate mothers than among the children of illiterate mothers in all mortality groups. However, within the literate group, the increase in education did not make a consistent decrease in the prevalence and even it has showed a increasing trend at a higher level of education (high school and above) in high and medium mortality groups. In the case of low mortality group, the percentage of both malnourished and severely malnourished children has decreased consistently with the increase in education.

The prevalence of malnutrition did not differ much due to different caste affiliations of the mothers in the high mortality group. However in medium mortality group, the prevalence was high among the children of scheduled tribe mothers and in the low mortality group the prevalence was high among the children of scheduled caste mothers.

Overall, the nutritional status of children as measured by the weight for height index revealed that the proportion of malnourished children was in the same level around 17-19 percent in all mortality groups. The proportion of severely malnourished was also nearly same around 3 percent in all mortality groups. Thus the prevalence of malnutrition did not vary much among the three mortality groups. The percentage of both malnourished and severely malnourished children was observed to be more among male than female children in all mortality groups. Birth order and birth interval did not make much difference in the prevalence of malnutrition among children in all mortality groups. Education of mothers seemed to have substantial effect on the reduction of malnutrition among children in all mortality groups.

8.2 Weight for Age

The nutritional status of children measured based on the weight for age index presented in table 8.2 revealed that a substantially large proportion of children in all mortality groups were malnourished. It is observed that about three fifth of children (60 percent) in high mortality group and a little more than half of the children in both medium (52 per cent) and low (51 per cent) mortality groups were malnourished (-2 SD). The proportion of children severely malnourished (-3 SD) was found to be comparatively higher among the children of high mortality group (27 percent) compared to 19 percent observed among the children of medium mortality group and 17 percent observed among the children of low mortality group.

The proportion of malnourished and severely malnourished children classified according to the background characteristics of the mother revealed that the percentage of both the malnourished and severely malnourished children increased with age of children up to 12-23 months of age and then showed a declining trend with the increase in age in all mortality groups. It is observed that in the high mortality group, the percentage of malnourished children increased from 20 percent among children under 6 months of age to 71 percent among children aged 12-23 months and then started declining to the level of 63 percent by the age of 36-47 months. In the medium mortality group, the percentage of malnourished children increased from 14 percent among children aged less than 6 months to 62 percent among children aged 12-23 months and then started declining and reached a level of 59 per cent by the age of 36-47 months. In the high mortality group, the proportion of malnourished children increased from 11 percent among children aged less than 6 months to 61 per cent for children aged 12-23 months and then started declining and reached a level of 57 per cent for

Table 8.2 Percent distribution of children under four years of age classified as malnourished based on anthropometric indices of nutritional status (weight for age) presented according to selected background characteristics by mortality groups, Rural India, 1992 – 93.

Background characteristics	Anthropometric indices (Weight for age)								
	High			Medium			Low		
	below –3SD	*below –2SD*	*No of children*	*Below – 3SD*	*below –2SD*	*No of children*	*below –3SD*	*below –2SD*	*No of children*
Child's Age									
< 6 months	3.5	20.0	1879	2.3	14.0	960	2.0	10.9	621
6 - 11 months	21.6	54.0	1,700	10.2	39.8	1,275	10.9	37.6	619
12 - 23 months	33.7	71.2	3,899	24.5	62.2	2,105	21.1	60.9	1,311
24 - 35 months	32.7	69.7	3,160	23.3	60.8	2,010	23.2	60.3	1,242
36 - 47 months	27.6	63.2	3,302	20.2	59.2	2,098	18.5	56.6	1,163
Sex									
Male	27.1	62.1	7,072	16.7	50.2	4,350	16.1	48.5	2,502
Female	25.8	57.7	6,868	20.3	54.4	4,098	18.7	52.7	2,453
Birth order									
1	24.1	56.9	3,131	16.5	50.6	2,392	14.0	47.6	1,544
2-3	25.5	59.2	5,311	17.8	51.9	3,688	18.2	50.5	2,388
4-5	27.9	60.7	3,124	22.0.	56.2	1,576	18.4	55.8	771
6+	29.8	64.6	2,374	20.8	51.4	792	26.2	54.1	253

(Contd.)

(Contd. Table 8.2)

Background characteristics	*Anthropometric indices (Weight for age)*								
	High			*Medium*			*Low*		
	below −3SD	*below −2SD*	*No of children*	*Below − 3SD*	*below −2SD*	*No of children*	*below −3SD*	*below −2SD*	*No of children*
Birth Interval									
First birth	24.2	56.9	3,138	16.6	50.7	2,397	14.0	47.6	1,554
< 24 months	28.1	61.4	2,333	22.2	56.7	1,374	21.5	53.7	888
24-47 months	26.4	61.1	6,199	18.6	52.5	3,498	19.7	53.8	1,937
48+ months	28.1	59.5	2,270	17.5	49.6	1,179	12.1	42.7	575
Education of mother									
illiterate	28.2	62.0	11,181	20.4	54.4	6,016	22.7	60.3	2,435
lit<mid complete	21.9	55.2	1,596	16.2	52.0	1,536	14.5	48.0	1,335
middle complete	16.7	51.4	607	13.2	45.5	469	13.0	38.0	595
high school & above	14.8	40.6	556	5.6	30.5	427	6.3	29.4	594
Caste									
Scheduled caste	28.1	62.4	1,932	19.2	52.4	1,259	22.2	58.0	670
Scheduled tribe	26.7	58.8	1,546	24.2	54.5	922	28.0	59.2	449
Others	26.1	59.7	10,462	17.5	51.9	6,266	15.3	48.3	3,836
Total	**26.5**	**59.9**	**13,940**	**18.5**	**52.3**	**8448**	**17.4**	**50.6**	**4,955**

Fig 8.2 Malnourished Children aged 1-4 years (weight for age), Rural India 1992-93

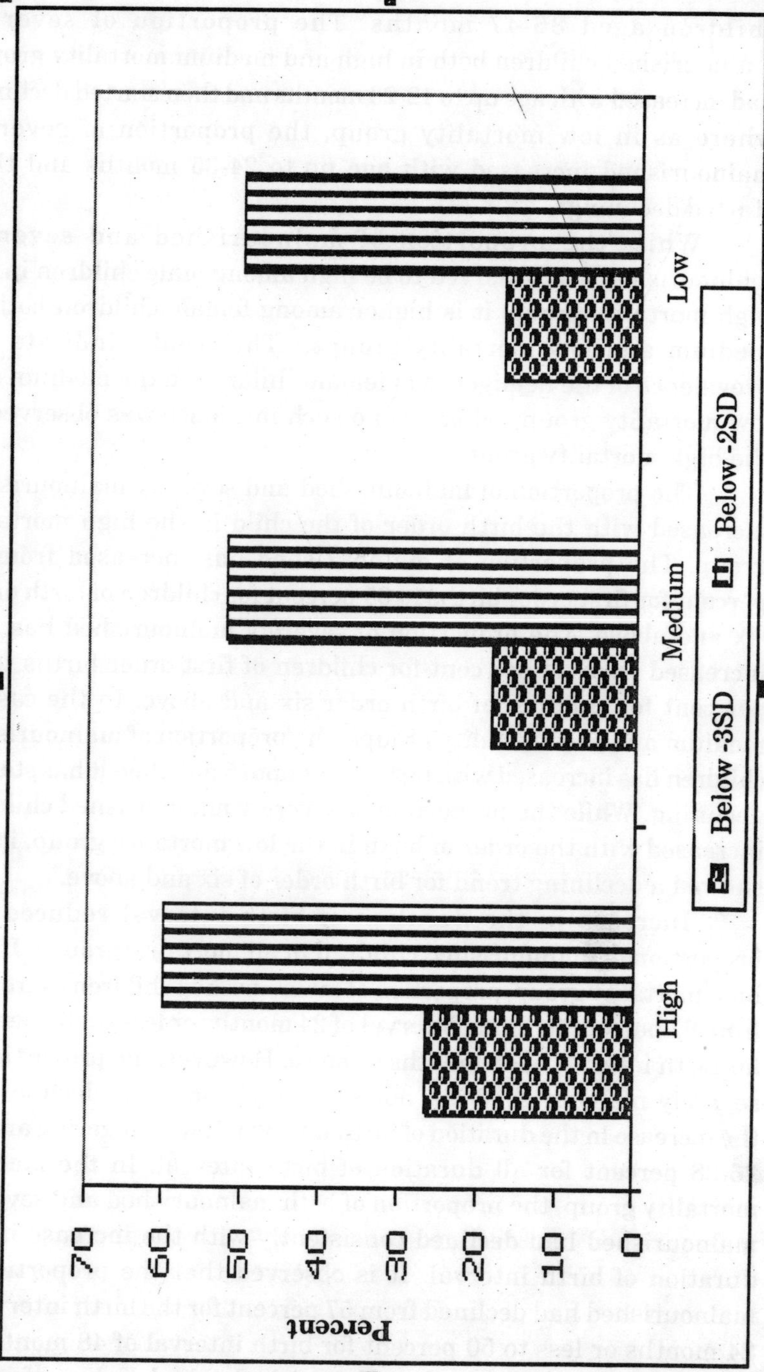

children aged 36-47 months. The proportion of severely malnourished children both in high and medium mortality groups had increased with age up to 12-23 months and then started declining where as in low mortality group, the proportion of severely malnourished increased with age up to 24-35 months and then started declining.

While the proportion of malnourished and severely malnourished was observed to be high among male children in the high mortality group, it is higher among female children both in medium and low mortality groups. The results indicate the prevalence of the negligence of female children in the medium and low mortality groups where as no such incidence was observed in the high mortality group.

The proportion of malnourished and severely malnourished increased with the birth order of the child in the high mortality group. The proportion of malnourished has increased from 57 percent for first order births to 65 percent for children of birth order six and above. The proportion of severely malnourished has also increased from 24 per cent for children of first order births to 30 per cent for children of birth order six and above. In the case of medium and low mortality groups, the proportion of malnourished children has increased with birth order upto 5 and then it has started declining. While the proportion of severely malnourished children increased with the order of birth in the low mortality group, it has showed a declining trend for birth order of six and above.

Increase in the duration of birth interval reduced the proportion of malnourished children in all mortality groups. In the high mortality group, proportion of malnourished children decreased from 61 percent for birth interval of 24 months or less to 60 percent for birth interval of 48 months or more. However, the proportion of severely malnourished did not show any consistent decline with the increase in the duration of birth interval. It was lingering around 26-28 percent for all duration of birth interval. In the medium mortality group, the proportion of both malnourished and severely malnourished had declined consistently with the increase in the duration of birth interval. It is observed that the proportion of malnourished had declined from 57 percent for the birth interval of 24 months or less to 50 percent for birth interval of 48 months or more. In the case of severely malnourished, it had declined from 22 percent for a birth interval of 24 months or less to 18 percent for a birth interval of 48 months or more. In the low mortality group also the duration of birth interval indicates a substantial differences in the level of malnutrition among the children under four years of age. It is observed that the proportion of malnourished children has decreased with the increase in the duration of birth interval. It has decreased from 54 percent for a birth interval of 24 months or less to 43 percent for a birth interval of 48 months or more. Similarly, the proportion of severely malnourished had declined from 22 percent for a birth interval of 24 moths or less to 12 percent for a birth interval of 48 months or more. Thus the results indicate that the duration of birth interval played a major role in reducing malnutrition among children under four years of age in all mortality groups.

It is generally believed that education helps mothers to acquire more knowledge on child rearing practices and reduces the level of malnutrition among children. The results of the survey indicate that in the high mortality group, the proportion of malnourished children had declined from 62 percent among children of illiterate mothers to 41 percent among children of mothers who had high school and higher level of education. The proportion of severely malnourished children had also declined substantially from 28 percent among the children of illiterate mothers to 15 percent among the children of mothers who had high school and higher level of education.

In the medium mortality group, the proportion of malnourished children had declined from 54 percent among the children of illiterate mothers to 31 percent among the children of mothers who had high school or higher level of education. The proportion of severely malnourished had also indicated a substantial decline from 20 percent among the children of illiterate mothers to just 6 percent among the children of mothers who had high school or higher level of education. In the low mortality group, the proportion of malnourished children had declined substantially from a high of 60 percent among the children of illiterate mothers to as low as 29 percent among the children of mothers who had high school or higher level of education.

The proportion of severely malnourished children had also declined substantially with the increase in education. It is observed that the proportion of severely malnourished children had declined from 23 percent among the children of illiterate mothers to just 6 percent among the children of mothers who had high school or higher level of education. Thus the results indicate that education of mother has an independent and substantial effect in reducing malnutrition in all mortality groups.

It is expected that the cultural practices and the food fads and taboos prevailed in different caste groups influence the nutritional status of children which in turn affect the infant and child mortality. The results of the present analysis presented in table 8.2 revealed that in the high mortality group the proportion of malnourished children did not vary much among different caste groups and was lingering around 59 to 62 percent. The proportion of severely malnourished children was also not varied much among the children of different caste groups. It was around 26 to 28 percent for all caste groups. In the medium mortality group, the proportion of malnourished children was ranging from 52 percent for the children of other than SC/ST groups to 55 percent for the children of scheduled tribe. The proportion of severely malnourished children was observed to be highest at 24 percent for the children of scheduled tribe families and lowest at 18 percent for the children from other than SC/ST families. In the low mortality group, the proportion of malnourished children was observed to be lowest at 48 percent for children from other than SC/ST families and it was nearly same at 58-59 percent for the children of both SC/ST families. The proportion of severely malnourished children was also observed to be lowest at 15 percent for children from other than SC/ST families and it was 22 percent for the children of scheduled caste and 28 percent for the children of scheduled tribe.

Overall, the results of the nutritional status of children under 4 years of age measured using weight for age index revealed that the proportion malnourished and severely malnourished children increased with the age of the child up to 12-23 months of age and showed a declining trend at higher ages of 24 months or more in all mortality groups. While a high prevalence of malnutrition was observed among male children in high mortality group it was higher among female children in the medium and low mortality groups. Increase in birth order seemed to increase the prevalence of malnourished and severely malnourished in high mortality group. However in medium and low mortality groups, though the proportion of malnourished increased with birth order upto 4-5, it has showed a declining trend for the birth order of 6 and above. While the proportion of severely malnourished increased with birth order in medium mortality group, it has showed a declining trend for the birth orders of 6 and above in low mortality group. The increase in birth interval seemed to reduce the prevalence of malnutrition among the children under four years of age in all mortality groups. Similarly, education of mother seemed to have substantial impact on the nutritional status of children in all mortality groups. While the prevalence of malnutrition is observed to be highest among the children of scheduled tribes in medium and low mortality groups, it was highest among the children of schedule caste in high mortality group. Overall the prevalence of malnutrition was comparatively lower among the children of low mortality group compared to children in high and medium mortality groups.

8.3 Height for Age

The nutritional status of children measured using height for age index presented in table 8.3 revealed that the prevalence of malnutrition was observed to be highest among children in high mortality group and lowest among children in low mortality group. It is observed that the proportion of malnourished children was highest at 59 per cent among the children in high mortality group compared to 48 per cent observed among children in medium and 45 per cent observed among children in low mortality group. The proportion of severely malnourished children was also observed to be highest at 36 per cent among children in high mortality group compared to 25 per cent in medium and 22 per cent in low mortality group.

The analysis of the nutritional status of children by their background characteristics revealed that the proportion of malnourished and severely malnourished children increased with the age of the child in all mortality groups. In the high mortality group, the proportion of malnourished increased from 20 per cent among children aged less than six months to 75 per cent among children aged 36-47 months. The proportion of severely malnourished increased from 5 per cent for children aged less than six months to 36 per cent for children aged 36-47 months. In the medium mortality group, the proportion of malnourished children increased from 14 percent for children aged less than six months to

Table 8.3 Percent distribution of children under age four years classified as malnourished based on anthropometric indices of nutritional status (height for age) presented according to selected background characteristics by mortality groups. Rural India, 1992-93.

Background characteristics	*Anthropometric indices (Height for age)*								
	High			*Medium*			*Low*		
	below -3SD	*below -2SD*	*Number of children*	*below -3SD*	*below -2SD*	*Number of children*	*Below -3SD*	*below -2SD*	*Number of children*
Child's Age									
<6 months	7.7	19.9	1562	4.6	13.9	514	3.0	10.2	492
6-11 months	21.1	43.5	1326	10.9	28.9	611	7.0	25.5	424
12-23 months	38.8	64.6	3294	25.1	53.6	1159	21.7	47.0	937
24-35 months	41.4	67.9	2655	31.7	54.3	1069	29.3	56.1	909
36-47 months	50.2	74.9	2782	36.1	61.2	1222	32.3	61.2	844
Sex									
Male	36.1	60.8	5860	23.4	47.2	2317	20.5	43.3	1864
Female	35.8	58.0	5760	27.1	48.3	2158	23.3	47.0	1741
Birth order									
1	33.3	58.7	2518	23.5	45.7	1229	17.8	40.7	1095
2-3	34.8	57.2	4402	24.3	46.9	1889	21.8	44.3	1727
4-5	36.8	61.1	2654	28.2	50.2	890	27.5	51.1	574
6+	40.9	62.7	2045	27.2	51.8	467	27.4	57.7	209

(Contd.)

(Contd. Table 8.3)

Background characteristics	Anthropometric indices (Height for age)								
	High			Medium			Low		
	below -3SD	below -2SD	Number of children	below -3SD	below -2SD	Number of children	Below -3SD	below -2SD	Number of children
Birth Interval									
First birth	33.3	58.7	2525	23.7	45.9	1232	17.8	40.7	1102
< 24 months	39.8	62.2	2001	28.6	52.1	828	28.2	54.5	655
24 - 47 months	36.9	60.3	5179	25.0	48.3	1859	23.6	46.5	144
48+ months	32.7	54.8	1914	24.1	43.3	556	16.2	36.7	404
Education of mother									
Illiterate	38.1	62.0	9235	27.9	50.7	3296	30.2	55.2	1704
Literate <mid complete	29.7	52.7	1370	20.8	44.0	700	18.2	42.6	994
middle complete	27.3	47.4	520	15.1	38.2	206	13.1	33.4	445
high school & above	21.5	42.0	495	11.0	29.2	273	7.1	24.3	462
Caste									
Scheduled caste	38.7	61.5	1731	27.5	53.2	701	25.4	50.9	360
Scheduled tribe	30.6	56.3	828.5	27.8	48.9	635	31.3	55.3	432
Others	35.9	59.3	9060	24.1	46.3	3139	19.9	42.8	2813
Total	**35.9**	**59.4**	**11619**	**25.2**	**47.7**	**44751**	**21.8**	**45.1**	**36057**

Figure 8.3 : Malnourished Children aged 1-4 years (Height for age), Rural India, 1992-93.

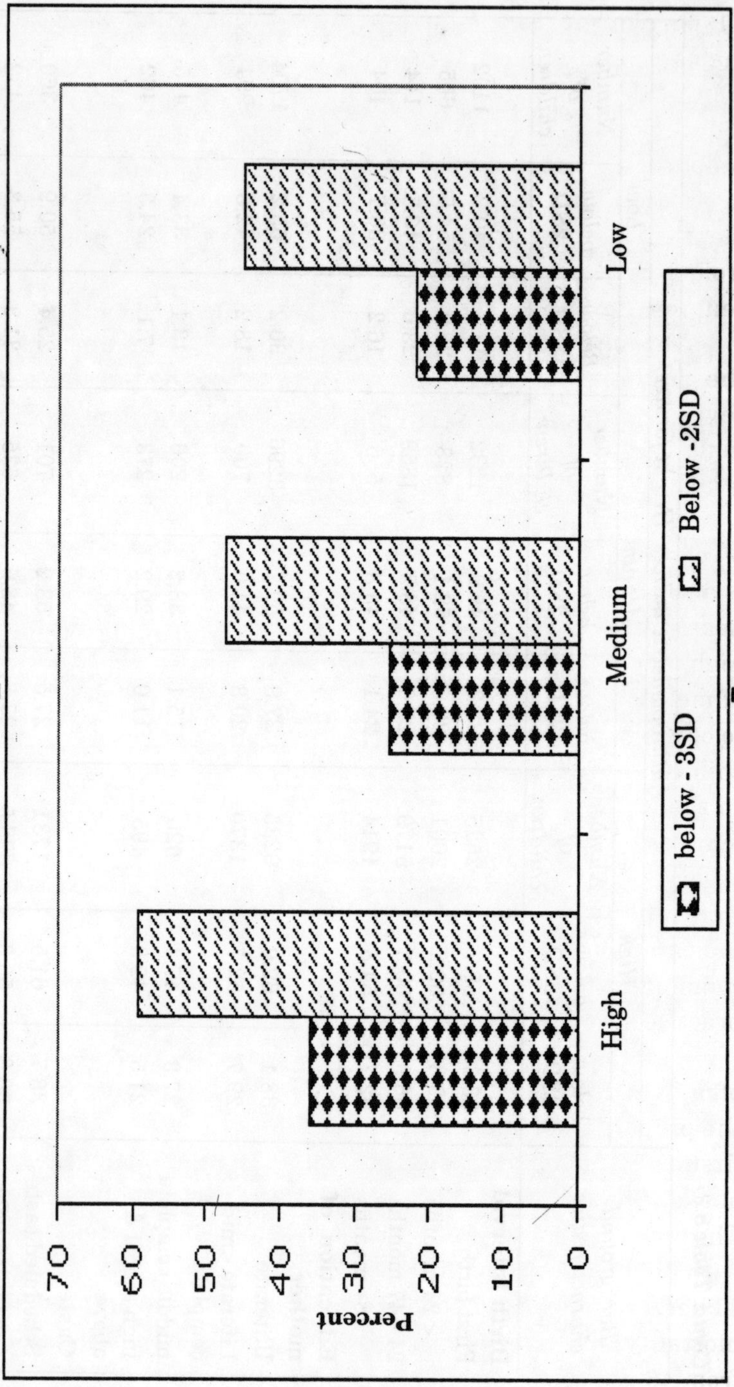

61 percent for children aged 36-47 months. The severely malnourished children had also increased with age. It has increased from 5 percent for children aged less than six months to 36 percent for children aged 36-47 months. In the low mortality group, the proportion of malnourished increased from 10 per cent for children aged less than six months to 61 per cent for children aged 36-47 months. The proportion of severely malnourished had increased from 3 per cent for children aged less than six months to 32 per cent for children aged 36 - 47 months.

The prevalence of malnutrition presented according to sex of the child revealed that while the prevalence of malnourished and severely malnourished children was observed to be higher among male children in high mortality group it was higher among the female children both in medium and low mortality groups.

In the high mortality group, 61 per cent of male children and 58 per cent of female children were reported to be malnourished. It is also observed that the proportion of severely malnourished was nearly same at 36 per cent for both male and female children in the high mortality group. In the medium mortality group, 47 per cent of male children and 48 per cent of female children were reported to be malnourished and 23 percent of male and 27 per cent of female children were reported to have suffered with severe malnutrition. In the low mortality group, 43 per cent of male and 47 per cent of female children were reported to be malnourished and it was also observed that 21 per cent of male and 23 per cent of female children were reported to have suffered with severe malnutrition. The results indicate that the practice of neglecting female children was more common in medium and low mortality groups, where as no such practice seemed to exist in high mortality group.

Increase in the birth order seemed to increase the prevalence of malnutrition in all mortality groups. In the high mortality group, the proportion of malnourished had increased from 59 per cent for first order births to 63 per cent for children of birth order six and above with a slight decline observed for children of birth order 2-3. The proportion of severely malnourished had increased consistently with birth order from 33 per cent for children of first order birth to 41 per cent for children of birth order six and above. In the medium mortality group, the proportion of malnourished children increased from 46 per cent for children of first birth order to 52 per cent for children of birth order six and above. The percentage of severely malnourished children had increased from 24 per cent for first birth order to 28 per cent for children of birth order 4-5 and then showed a declining trend for children of higher birth orders.

In the low mortality group, the percentage of severely malnourished had increased from 41 per cent for first order birth to 58 per cent for children of birth order six and above. The per centage of severely malnourished had increased from 18 per cent for first order birth to 27 per cent for children of birth order six and above.

Increase in the inter birth interval seemed to decrease the prevalence of malnutrition among children in all mortality groups. In the high mortality group, the percentage of malnourished children had decreased from 63 per cent for children of birth interval less than 24 months to 55 per cent for children of birth interval 48 months or more. The percentage of severely malnourished had decreased from 40 per cent for children of birth interval less than 24 months to 33 per cent for children of birth interval 48 months or more.

In the medium mortality group, the percentage of malnourished has decreased from 52 per cent for children of birth interval less than 24 months to 43 per cent for children of birth interval 48 months or more. The percentage of severely malnourished had decreased from 29 percent for children of birth interval 24 months or less to 24 per cent for children of birth interval 48 months or more. In the low mortality group, the percent of malnourished children had declined from 55 per cent for children of birth interval 24 months or less to 31 per cent for children of birth interval 48 months or more. The percentage of severely malnourished had decreased from a high level of 28 per cent for children of birth interval 24 months or less to 16 per cent for children of birth interval 48 months or more.

Education of mother seemed to have substantial impact on the prevalence of malnutrition among children in all mortality groups. It is observed that the prevalence of malnutrition decreased consistently with the increase in the level of education in all mortality groups. In the high mortality group, the percentage of malnourished children had decreased substantially from 62 per cent for children of illiterate mothers to 42 percent for children of mothers with higher level of education (high school or above). Similarly, the percent of severely malnourished had also decreased from 38 per cent for children of illiterate mothers to 22 per cent for children of mothers with higher level of educations (high school or above). In the medium mortality group, the percent of malnourished had decreased from a high of 51 per cent for children of illiterate mothers to 29 per cent for children of mothers with higher level of education. Similarly, the percent of severely malnourished children had decreased from 28 per cent for children of illiterate mothers to 11 per cent for children of mothers with higher level of education. In the low mortality group, the percentage of malnourished children had decreased substantially from a high level of 55 per cent for children of illiterate mothers to 24 per cent for children of mothers with higher level of education (high school or above). The percentage severely malnourished had also dropped substantially from a high of 30 per cent for children of illiterate mothers to just 7 per cent for children of mothers with higher level of education.

The influence of caste on the prevalence of malnutrition among children seemed to be very little as the prevalence was not uniform for all mortality groups. It is observed that while the prevalence of malnutrition was high among the children of scheduled caste in high and medium mortality groups, it was high among the children of scheduled tribe in low mortality group. In the high mortality group, the prevalence of malnutrition was 62 per cent for the children of scheduled caste, 56 per cent for scheduled tribe and 60 per cent for others. The percentage of severely malnourished also showed a similar trend with 39 per cent observed among scheduled caste 31 per cent observed among of scheduled tribe and 36 per cent observed among others.

In the medium mortality group, the percentage of malnourished was 53 per cent for the children of scheduled caste, 49 per cent for scheduled tribe and 46 per cent for others. The prevalence of severely malnourished was observed to be nearly similar at 28 per cent for both scheduled caste and scheduled tribe while it was observed to be comparatively low at 24 per cent for others.

In the low mortality group, the prevalence of malnutrition was observed to be highest at 55 percent for the children of scheduled tribe compared to 51 per cent for scheduled caste and 43 percent for others. The prevalence severely malnourished also showed a similar trend with a high prevalence of 31 per cent observed among the children of scheduled tribe which was followed by the children of scheduled caste with 25 percent and others with 20 per cent.

Overall, the prevalence of malnutrition among children in the three mortality groups as measured by height for age index was varying substantially with the observation of high prevalence among the children of high mortality group which was followed by medium and low mortality groups. The proportion of malnourished children increased with age and birth order in all mortality groups. While the prevalence of malnutrition was higher among male children in high mortality groups, it was higher among female children in medium and low mortality groups. Increase in birth interval decrease the prevalence of malnutrition in all mortality groups. The increase in the education of mother resulted in the substantial reduction of malnutrition among children in all mortality groups.

9

Levels, Trends and Differentials of Infant and Child Mortality

This Chapter provides information on the levels, trends and differentials in neonatal, post-neonatal, infant and child mortality in the three mortality groups. The mortality estimates were derived from the mother's birth history data. The trends in infant and child mortality rates were derived for the three quinquennial period preceding the survey. The mortality estimates by socio-economic, demographic and mass media variables were derived for 10 years period preceding the survey and the mortality estimates by maternal care variables were derived for four years period preceding the survey. The univariate analysis of mortality estimate was made to see the intragroup and intergroup variations in the infant and child mortality rates according to selected background characteristics of the mother and child.

9.1 Levels and Trends

9.1.1 Infant, Child and under - five mortality rates

Infant and child mortality rates for the three quinquennial period preceding the survey for the three mortality groups are presented in Table 9.1. The infant and child mortality rates that prevailed during the five years preceding thc survey (approximately 1988-92) as estimated from the birth history data revealed that the variation in the levels of infant and child mortality rates among the three mortality groups was very large. In the low mortality group, the infant mortality rate was only 57 per 1000 live births and the child mortality rate was only 21 per 1000 live births. These rates are very low when compared to the infant and child mortality rates of 73 and 32 respectively, estimated for the medium mortality group and 101 and 48 respectively, estimated for the high mortality group. The proportion of neonatal deaths to infant deaths was 61 per cent in the high mortality group, 63 per cent in the medium mortality group and 68 per cent in the low mortality group (see Figure 9.2). The results indicate that more than 60 per cent of infants died before reaching their first month of life in all mortality groups.

Infant and child mortality rates declined considerably over the fifteen years period preceding the survey in all mortality groups. In the high mortality group, the infant mortality rate declined from 140 per 1000 live births during 10-14 years preceding the survey (approximately 1978-82) to 101 during 0-4 years preceding the survey (approximately 1988-92), a decline of about 28 per cent. During the same period, the child mortality rate declined from 68 per 1000 live births to 48, a decline of about 30 per cent. On an average there was a decline of two per cent per year in infant as well as child mortality during 1978-92. In the medium mortality group, the infant mortality rate declined from 92 per 1000 live births during 1978-82 to 73 during 1988-92, a decline of about 20 per cent. The child mortality rate during the same period declined from 46 per 1000 live births to 32, a decline of about 31 per cent. In the low mortality group, the infant mortality rate declined from 69 per 1000 live births during 1978-82 to 57 during 1988-92, a decline of about 18 per cent. The child mortality rate during the same period declined from 42 per 1000 live births to 21, a decline of about 50 per cent.

Infant and child mortality declined considerably during the 15 years period preceding the survey in all mortality groups. The per cent decline of infant mortality was high in the high mortality group (28 per cent) as compared to medium (20 per cent) and low (18 per cent) mortality groups (see Figure 9.1). This is so because, the mortality levels were comparatively at lower level during the reference period in the medium and low mortality groups than in the high mortality group. In the case of child mortality, the per cent decline was high in the low mortality group (about 50 per cent) which was followed by medium mortality group (about 31 per cent) and low mortality group (about 30 per cent). The fast decline of child mortality rate in the low mortality group indicate the

Table 9.1 Infant, Child and under - five mortality rates for five years periods preceding the survey, Rural India, 1992 - 93.

Years before	*High*					*Medium*					*Low*				
Survey	*NNM*	*PNM**	*IM*	*CM*	*U5M*	*NNM*	*PNM**	*IM*	*CM*	*U5M*	*NNM*	*PNM**	*IM*	*CM*	*U5M*
0 - 4	61.4	39.9	101.3	47.6	144.1	46.2	27.0	73.2	31.5	102.4	38.9	18.2	57.1	20.5	76.4
5 - 9	74.1	52.4	126.5	55.5	175.0	55.3	31.1	86.4	35.3	118.7	39.9	24.1	63.9	25.9	88.1
10 - 14	79.1	61.2	140.3	67.7	198.6	56.1	36.0	92.0	45.8	133.6	44.1	25.3	69.4	41.8	108.3

* Computed as the difference between infant and Neonatal mortality ratesNNM - Neonatal mortality / PNM - Postneonatal mortality / IM - Infant mortality ($1q_0$) / CM - Child mortality ($4q_1$) / U5M - Under - five mortality ($5q_0$)

Figure 9.1

Infant Mortality Rates for Five Year periods by Mortality Groups, Rural India 1992-93

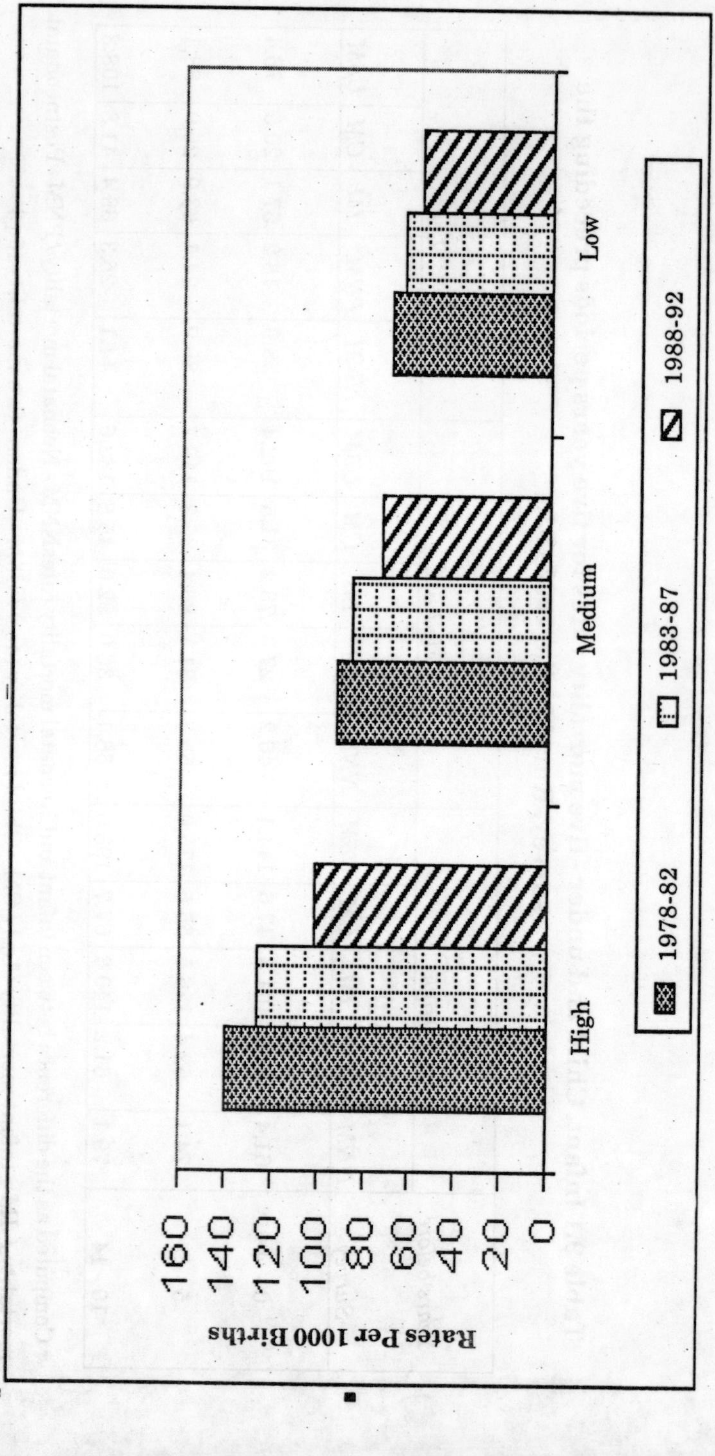

Figure 9.2
Infant, Neonatal and Post Neonatal Mortality Rates by Mortality Groups
Rural India (1988-92)

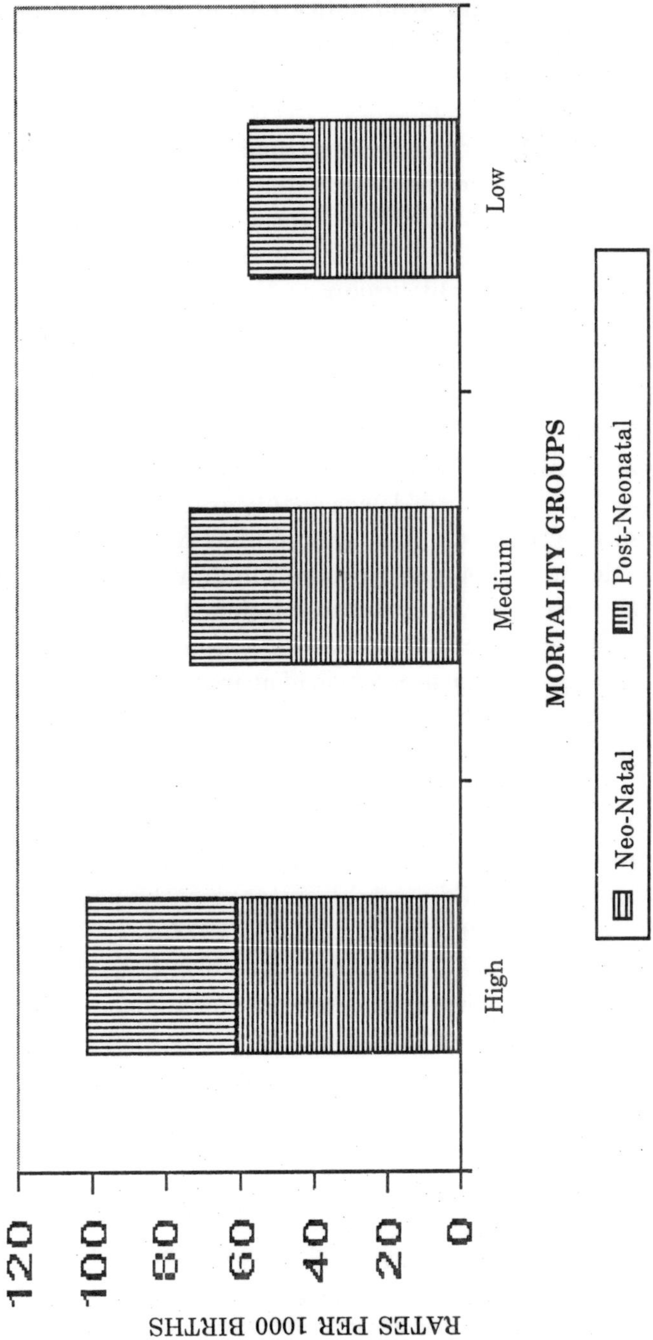

Note : Rates are for five year period preceding the survey (1988 – 92).

improvement in the availability and utilisation of health care services in the low mortality group of states.

9.1.2 Summary

The current levels, recent trends and differentials of infant and child mortality rates derived from the birth history data of ever married women, revealed that deaths to children under the age of five have declined over the fifteen years period preceding the survey (1978-92) in all mortality groups.

Though unequal between the mortality groups, the declines have been substantial in all mortality groups. The infant mortality decline was 28 per cent in high mortality group, 20 per cent in medium mortality group and 18 per cent in low mortality group. The pace of decline was very fast in the high mortality group as compared to medium and low mortality groups. There was not much difference between the medium and low mortality groups in the pace of decline. Though the decline of infant mortality was high in the high mortality group, the infant mortality rate continued to be high in the high mortality group as compared to medium and low mortality groups. The proportion of neonatal deaths was more than 60 per cent in all mortality groups.

While the decline of infant mortality rate was high in the high mortality group, the decline of child mortality rate was high in the low mortality group. It is also to be noted that there was not much difference between the medium and high mortality groups, in the decline of child mortality rates over the period of 15 years preceding the survey (approximately 1978-92). The fast decline observed in the child mortality rate among the children of low mortality group indicate the improvements in the delivery of health care services and the adoption of appropriate health care measures by mothers in the low mortality group.

9.2 Socio-economic differentials of infant and child mortality

Infant and child mortality rates for births ten years period preceding the survey by selected socio-economic characteristics of the mother are presented in Table 9.2. The socio-economic variables examined in the study are : 1. Religion; 2. Caste; 3. Parent's education; 4. Work status of mother and 5. Standard of living index. The extent of the influences of these variable on infant and child mortality are discussed in the following sections.

9.2.1 Religion

Comparison of the infant and child mortality rates among the three major religious groups (Hindu, Muslim, Christian) revealed that infant mortality rate was higher among the children of Hindu than the children of other religions in all mortality groups. However, in the medium mortality group, the infant mortality rate for Muslim was nearly same as that of Hindu. Among the Hindu, the infant mortality rate was higher among the children of high mortality group (116 per 1000 live births) as compared to medium (81) and low (66) mortality groups. In the case of Muslims, the infant mortality rate was more than two and half times higher among the children of high mortality group (107) and nearly two times higher among the children of medium mortality group (81) than the infant mortality in the low mortality group (41). Among Christian, there was not much difference in the infant mortality rate between the high and medium mortality groups. However, the infant mortality rates observed among these two groups (71 and 73 respectively) were much higher than the infant mortality rate of 40 observed for the low mortality group. The results showed that for all religions, the infant mortality rate was lower among the children of low mortality group than the medium and high mortality groups. While the child mortality rate was relatively high among the children of Hindu in high and low mortality groups, it was high among the children of Muslim in medium mortality group. For all religions, the child mortality rate was lowest among the children of low mortality group as compared to high and medium mortality groups.

9.2.2 Caste

Comparatively, high infant mortality rate was observed among the children of Scheduled Caste in all mortality groups. The rate was 137 for high mortality group, 96 for medium mortality group and 81 per 1000 live births for the low mortality group. The infant mortality rate observed for the Scheduled caste children of high mortality group was more than three and half times higher than the rate observed for the low mortality group. In the case of medium mortality group the rate was more than two and half a times higher than the rate observed for low mortality group. In the case Scheduled Tribe and others also, the infant mortality rate was lower among children of low mortality group than the medium and high mortality groups.

The child mortality rate was observed to be high among children of scheduled caste in the high and low mortality groups. In the case of medium mortality group, children of Scheduled Tribe families experienced higher mortality than others. In general, for all caste groups, both the infant and child mortality rates were much lower among the children of low mortality group than the medium and high mortality groups.

9.2.3 Parents Education

Virtually in all the three mortality groups, both the infant and child mortality rates decreased consistently with increase in education. In the high mortality group, the infant mortality rate decreased from 122 per 1000 live births for children of illiterate mothers to 59 for high school education and above. The child mortality rate decreased from 57 per 1000 live births for illiterates to just 9 for high school education and above.

In the medium mortality group, the infant mortality rate decreased from 86 per 1000 live births for children of illiterate mothers to 46 for high school education and above. The child mortality rate decreased from 37 per 1000 live births for illiterates to just 7 for middle school education and then the rate slightly increased to a level of 8 for high school education and above. In the low mortality group, the infant mortality rate decreased from 73 per 1000 live births for children of illiterate mothers to 37 for high school education and above. The child mortality rate decreased from 30 per 1000 live births for illiterates to just 7 for high school education and above.

The results indicate that both infant and child mortality rates were the lowest for the low mortality group at all levels of education as compared to the medium and high mortality groups. However, it is very interesting to note that the differences in the infant and child mortality rates between the high and low mortality groups as well as the medium and low mortality groups narrowed down significantly with the increase in education of mothers.

A similar results were observed for the education of father. However, education of mothers have more influence on infant and child mortality than the education of father in all mortality groups.

Table 9.2 Infant and child mortality rates for the ten years period preceding the survey by selected socio-economic characteristics, Rural India,1992-93.

Socio – economic Characteristics	*High*			
	NNM	*PNM**	*IM*	*CM*
Religion				
Hindu	68.6	47.2	115.8	51.9
Muslim	65.7	41.2	106.9	47.3
Christian	25.0	45.5	70.5	60.1
Sikh	53.6	23.4	77.0	52.3
Jain	-	-	-	-
Buddhist	0.0	64.6	64.6	125.1
Others	96.4	37.3	133.7	61.7
Caste				
Scheduled Caste	76.5	60.5	137.0	65.7
Scheduled Tribe	60.5	46.9	107.4	62.1
Others	67.5	43.6	111.1	47.3
Education (Mother)				
Illeterate	71.6	49.9	121.5	56.9
Literate & Primary	52.4	31.4	83.7	30.1
Middle Complete	51.4	23.7	75.0	12.9
High School & Above	38.0	21.1	59.1	9.2

(Contd.)

(Contd. Table 9.2)

Socio – economic Characteristics	*Medium*			
	NNM	*PNM**	*IM*	*CM*
Religion				
Hindu	51.0	29.9	80.9	33.5
Muslim	52.8	28.0	80.8	35.6
Christian	57.6	15.2	72.8	10.6
Sikh	29.8	11.3	41.0	24.1
Jain	16.9	0.0	16.9	52.9
Buddhist	43.9	0.0	43.9	36.9
Others	41.5	27.6	69.2	17.8
Caste				
Scheduled Caste	60.5	35.1	95.6	37.2
Scheduled Tribe	57.1	29.4	86.5	44.7
Others	48.0	27.9	75.9	30.6
Education (Mother)				
Illeterate	53.9	31.7	85.6	37.0
Literate & Primary	43.3	23.1	66.4	26.6
Middle Complete	43.1	17.3	60.4	6.9
High School & Above	32.2	14.1	46.4	7.8

(Contd.)

(Contd. Table 9.2)

Socio – economic Characteristics	*Low*			
	NNM	*PNM**	*IM*	*CM*
Religion				
Hindu	43.0	22.8	65.8	23.9
Muslim	28.4	12.2	40.6	14.9
Christian	25.6	14.5	40.1	17.1
Sikh	31.1	19.5	50.7	21.0
Jain	-	-	-	-
Buddhist	38.6	27.4	66.0	37.2
Others		38.2	78.8	80.1
Caste				
Scheduled Caste	53.1	27.5	80.6	35.4
Scheduled Tribe	34.5	26.5	61.0	31.8
Others	37.3	19.3	56.6	19.7
Education (Mother)				
Illeterate	48.1	24.4	72.5	30.4
Literate & Primary	30.9	19.2	50.1	16.7
Middle Complete	27.8	12.1	39.9	8.5
High School & Above	21.3	15.5	36.8	7.2

(Contd.)

(*Contd. Table 9.2*)

Socio – economic Characteristics	*High*			
	NNM	*PNM**	*IM*	*CM*
Education (Father)				
Illeterate	78.0	51.9	129.9	67.1
Literate & Primary	63.5	47.2	110.7	48.0
Middle Complete	65.2	48.3	113.5	42.2
High School & Above	52.5	31.4	83.9	25.3
Working Status (Mother)				
Not working	61.6	44.1	105.7	48.9
Working for family	61.3	54.2	115.4	69.7
Working for some-one else	58.4	53.2	111.5	72.4
Self employed	45.1	21.0	66.1	39.6
Standard of living index (SLI)				
Low	64.8	40.4	105.3	49.9
Medium	58.9	38.9	97.8	46.1
High	55.5	41.7	97.2	42.8
Total	**67.2**	**46.3**	**114.2**	**51.4**

(*Contd.*)

(Contd. Table 9.2)

Socio – economic Characteristics	*Medium*			
	NNM	*PNM**	*IM*	*CM*
Education (Father)				
Illeterate	56.5	33.2	89.6	39.7
Literate & Primary	48.4	27.9	76.3	33.3
Middle Complete	42.4	29.0	71.4	26.5
High School & Above	44.2	19.2	63.4	16.7
Working Status (Mother)				
Not working	46.1	29.6	75.7	32.9
Working for family	41.8	31.2	73.1	37.2
Working for some-one else	49.5	28.2	77.8	39.4
Self employed	41.7	22.0	63.6	31.8
Standard of living index (SLI)				
Low	48.0	24.9	73.0	33.9
Medium	46.6	29.1	75.7	28.5
High	37.6	28.9	66.5	30.6
Total	**51.0**	**29.2**	**80.2**	**33.3**

(Contd.)

(Contd. Table 9.2)

Socio – economic Characteristics	*Low*			
	NNM	*PNM**	*IM*	*CM*
Education (Father)				
Illeterate	53.7	27.7	81.4	32.2
Literate & Primary	41.1	19.7	60.8	21.1
Middle Complete	26.2	21.2	47.4	20.6
High School & Above	23.7	13.3	36.9	13.9
Working Status (Mother)				
Not working	30.7	19.6	50.3	17.1
Working for family	35.7	26.8	62.5	25.1
Working for some-one else	46.4	25.4	71.7	39.6
Self employed	24.1	7.6	31.6	43.3
Standard of living index (SLI)				
Low	44.0	19.8	63.8	25.9
Medium	35.6	16.4	52.0	15.9
High	32.2	17.8	49.9	15.6
Total	**39.4**	**21.2**	**60.6**	**23.2**

NNM - Neonatal mortality / PNM - Postneonatal mortality / IM - Infant mortality ($1q_0$) / CM - Child mortality ($4q_1$)

* Computed as the difference between the infant and neonatal mortality rates.

Infant and Child Mortality Rates by Mother's Education, Rural India 1992-93

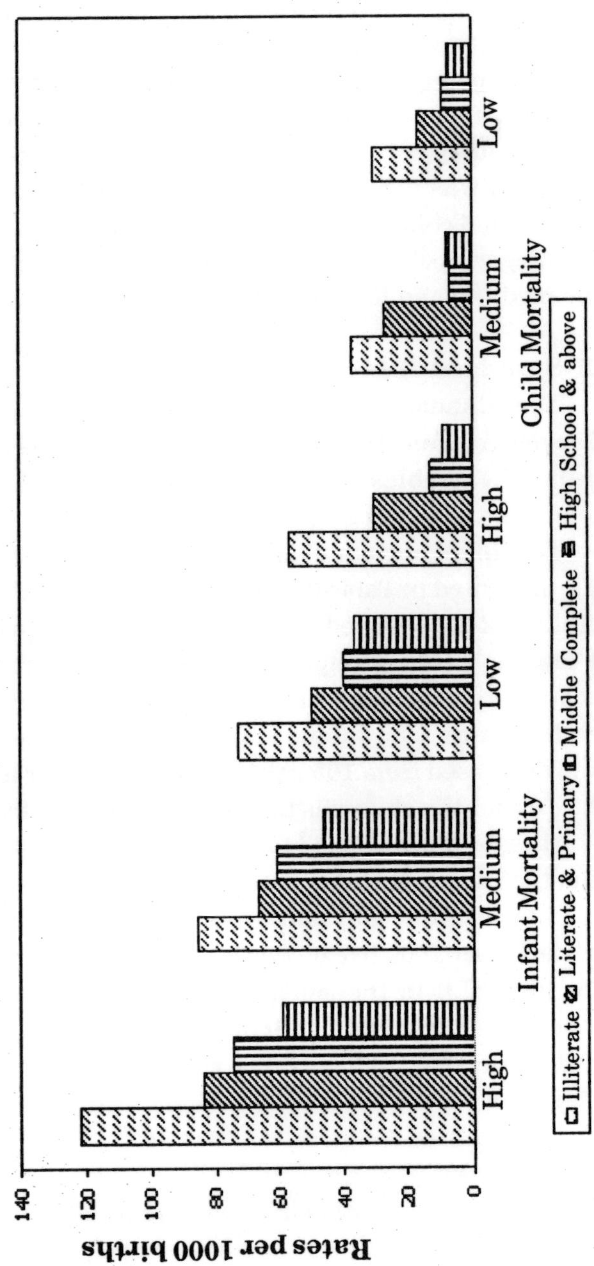

9.2.4 Work Status of Mother

Children of self employed mothers have experienced lower infant mortality risk than others in all mortality groups. The child mortality rate was comparatively low among the children of self employed mothers of high mortality group and non-working mothers of medium and low mortality groups. Though infant and child mortality rates were varying depending on the work status of mother, the pattern was not uniform for all mortality groups. In general, the infant and child mortality rates were lowest among the children of all categories of mothers in the low mortality group as compared to the medium and high mortality groups.

9.2.5 Standard of Living Index

The Standard of Living Index (SLI) developed by T.K. Roy and Jeyachandran (1996) is used here for the present analysis. The details of variables and the scoring procedure used for the development of SLI is given in the appendix.

The infant and child mortality rates by the standard of living index presented in Table 9.2 indicate that both the infant and child mortality rates decreased with increase in standard of living in high and low mortality groups. In the medium mortality group, no consistent relationship was observed for both infant and child mortality rates. The infant mortality rate in the high mortality group, decreased from 105 per 1000 live births for low SLI to 97 for high SLI and the child mortality rate decreased from 50 per 1000 live births for low SLI to 43 for high SLI. In the medium mortality group, the infant mortality rate was 73 per 1000 live births for low SLI, 76 for medium SLI and 67 for high SLI. The child mortality rate was 34 per 1000 live births for low SLI, 29 for medium SLI and 31 for high SLI. In the low mortality group, the infant mortality rate decreased from 64 per 1000 live births for low SLI to 50 for high SLI and the child mortality rate decreased from 26 per 1000 live birth for low SLI to just 16 for high SLI.

9.2.6 Summary

Substantial variation in infant and child mortality rates were observed among the three mortality groups for all religious groups. Both the infant and child mortality risks were much higher among the children of Hindu than other religions in all mortality groups. Irrespective of the religion, both the infant and child mortality rates were observed to be very low among the children of low mortality group as compared to medium and high mortality groups.

Both infant and child mortality rates were observed to be high among the children of Scheduled Caste in all mortality groups except for child mortality in the medium mortality group where it was high among children of Scheduled Tribe. The castewise comparison of infant and child mortality rates among the three mortality groups revealed that both infant and child mortality rates were lower among the children of low mortality group than high and medium mortality groups for all caste groups. Both infant and child mortality rates decreased with increase in education of parents in all mortality groups. The variations observed among the three mortality groups narrowed down at higher level of education of parents. Infant mortality rate was lower among the children of self employed mothers than others in all mortality groups. While child mortality was low among children of self employed mothers in high mortality group it was low among non-working mothers (house wives) in the medium and low mortality groups.

There was not much variations both in infant and child mortality rates due to the mothers standard of living in all mortality groups. The comparison of infant and child mortality rates among the three mortality groups revealed that even at the same level of standard of living both the infant and child mortality rates were very low among the children of low mortality group as compared to medium and high mortality groups.

9.3 Demographic differentials of infant and child mortality

The infant and child mortality rates by selected demographic variables are presented in Table 9.3. The demographic variables examined are: 1. age of mother; 2. birth order; 3. previous birth interval; 4. sex of the child and 5. birth weight. The influences of these variables on infant and child mortality are discussed in the following sections.

9.3.1 Age of mother

Children born to very young (<20 years) and very old (> 35 years) mothers are more likely to die in infancy. The results

Table 9.3 Infant and child mortality rates for the ten years period preceding the survey by selected demographic characteristics, Rural India,1992-93.

Demographic characteristics	*High*				*Medium*				*Low*			
	NNM	*PNM**	*IM*	*CM*	*NNM*	*PNM**	*IM*	*CM*	*NNM*	*PNM**	*IM*	*CM*
Age of Mother												
< 20	91.2	48.1	139.3	54.7	68.2	31.6	99.8	34.3	53.8	24.6	78.4	23.4
20 – 29	60.4	44.4	104.8	51.2	40.7	26.9	67.6	32.8	32.2	19.7	51.8	23.1
30 – 39	62.7	47.7	110.4	45.8	55.5	31.9	87.4	33.1	43.1	21.0	64.2	23.5
40 – 49	59.3	73.0	132.4	81.7	35.0	54.5	89.4	29.6	48.8	18.1	67.0	5.1
Birth Order												
1	87.7	43.5	131.2	41.2	64.8	28.2	92.9	27.6	45.9	18.4	64.3	15.4
2	65.2	41.5	106.6	47.5	45.6	25.8	71.4	33.4	34.4	20.2	54.5	19.3
3	56.1	38.0	94.1	56.1	40.1	28.1	68.2	33.0	32.4	24.2	56.5	26.4
4	57.3	49.7	107.0	52.5	40.7	29.2	69.9	30.8	39.0	20.1	59.0	35.2
5	58.7	51.5	110.2	60.3	45.5	30.0	75.5	38.5	41.9	31.8	73.7	29.6
6	62.1	50.3	112.4	49.5	55.3	36.5	91.7	33.7	45.0	26.8	71.9	27.1
7+	77.2	62.9	140.0	63.9	70.8	43.0	113.8	54.9	51.5	16.2	67.7	37.0

(Contd.)

(Contd. Table 9.3)

Demographic characteristics	High				Medium				Low			
	NNM	*PNM**	*IM*	*CM*	*NNM*	*PNM**	*IM*	*CM*	*NNM*	*PNM**	*IM*	*CM*
Previous Birth Interval (months)												
< 24	100.2	72.1	172.3	82.3	73.2	43.3	116.5	47.7	55.7	34.6	90.3	31.2
24 – 47	48.3	39.4	87.7	46.7	36.1	25.2	61.3	33.7	28.1	17.5	45.6	26.8
48 +	30.1	19.4	49.5	20.2	22.8	16.3	39.0	13.5	25.5	12.6	38.1	13.2
Sex of Child **												
Male	72.5	43.2	115.6	42.3	54.1	26.5	80.6	27.3	45.5	20.8	66.2	22.2
Female	63.0	49.6	112.6	61.2	47.8	32.0	79.8	39.5	32.9	21.6	54.6	24.2
Birth weight **												
< 2.5 kg.	88.8	42.9	131.7	46.2	44.6	33.4	78.0	20.0	53.0	31.6	84.6	19.3
2.5 kg or More	89.5	54.8	144.3	43.2	35.1	25.6	60.7	19.4	22.0	9.5	31.6	19.6

* Computed as the difference between the infant and neonatal mortality rates.** Rate for the four years period preceding the survey.NNM - Neonatal mortality / PNM - Postneonatal mortality / IM - Infant mortality ($1q_0$) / CM - Child mortality ($4q_1$)

Figure 9.4
Infant and Child Mortality Rates by Previous Bith Internal (Months), Rural India, 1992-93

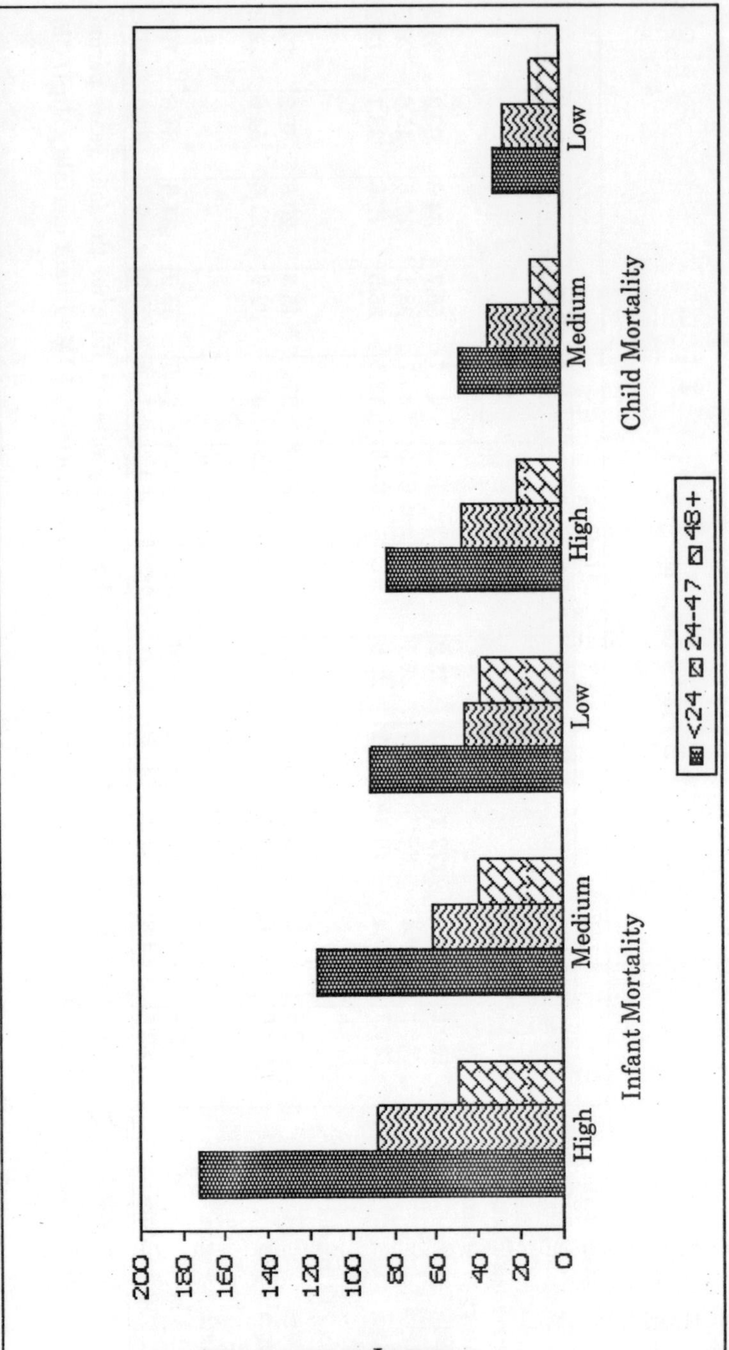

presented in Table 9.3 revealed that infant mortality rate was comparatively low among children born to mothers age 20-29 years and was high among children born to mothers age less than 20 and above 30 years in all mortality groups. A U-Shaped relationship is evident for infant mortality in all mortality groups. The comparison of mortality rates among the three mortality groups at every age group of mothers revealed that both infant and child mortality rates were comparatively low among the children of low mortality group as compared to medium and high mortality groups. In the case of child mortality, the pattern of mortality vary among the three mortality groups. It is observed that the child mortality rate declined with increase in age in the medium mortality group. In the high mortality group, the child mortality rate declined with increase in age up to the age of 40, after that a sharp increase was noticed. In the low mortality group, the child mortality rate was more or less at the same level up to the age of 40, after that a sudden decline was noticed.

9.3.2 Birth order

It is generally believed that mortality among children under-five years of age is closely associated with the order of birth. The chances of dying during infancy and early childhood are more for first and higher order births (usually after three). This is so because, first born children are more likely to be born to a mother who is biologically, mentally, socially and economically unprepared to bear and bring up a child. In the case of children of higher birth orders, they are likely to be born to mothers who are physically weak and older, they will receive very less care as there are more children in the family. As a result, the chances of dying for children of higher birth orders are more. Because of these reasons, we expect the mortality to have a U-shaped relationship. The results of infant and child mortality rates by birth order presented in Table 9.3 indicated a U-shaped relationship for all the three mortality groups.

The infant mortality rate was observed to be higher for first and higher birth orders than others in all mortality groups. In the high mortality group, infant mortality rate decreased form 131 per 1000 live births for first birth order to 94 for the 3rd birth order and then gradually increased to the level of 140 for the birth order of seven and above. In the medium mortality group, the infant mortality rate decreased from 93 for the first birth order to 68 for the third birth order and then gradually increased to the level of 114 for the birth order of seven and above. In the low mortality group, the infant mortality rate decreased from 64 for the first birth order to 55 for the second birth order and then it gradually increased to the level of 74 for the fifth birth order and again it decreased to the level 68 for the birth order of seven and above.

The child mortality rate in the high and medium mortality groups increased with order of birth except for the birth order of four and six, where a sudden decline was observed. In the low mortality group, the child mortality rate increased with birth order except for the fifth and sixth birth order, where the child mortality rate declined before it reached the highest rate for the birth order of seven and above.

The pattern of mortality by birth order was more or less similar in all mortality groups, up to the births order of four.

9.3.3 Previous birth interval

In general, children born less than two years after the preceding birth are much less likely to live until their fifth birth day than those born after two to three years of previous birth. Equally, children born after long intervals (four or more years) have a better chance of survival upto their fifth birth day.

The analysis of the data on infant and child mortality rates by previous birth interval presented in Table 9.3 supported the above notion for all mortality groups. In the high mortality group, both the infant and child mortality rates decreased with increase in birth interval. The infant mortality rate decrease from 172 per 1000 live births for the birth interval of less than 24 months to 50 for the birth interval of 48 months and above and the child mortality rate decreased from 82 to 20 per 1000 live births. In the medium mortality group, the infant mortality rate decreased from 117 per 1000 live births for the birth interval of less than 24 months to 39 for the birth interval of 48 months and above and the child mortality rate decreased from 48 to 14 per 1000 live births. In the low mortality group, the infant mortality rate decreased from 90 per 1000 live births for the birth interval of less than 24 months to 38 per 1000 live births for the birth interval of 48 months and above and the child mortality rate decreased from 31 to 13 per 1000 live births.

The variations in the infant and child mortality rates among the three mortality groups narrowed down with the increase in birth interval. It is observed that the chances of children dying in infancy and at ages 1-4 in the high mortality group was nearly twice to that of low mortality group for the birth interval of less than 24 months and 24-47 months. This difference has narrowed down significantly for the birth interval of 48 months or more. The chances of children dying in the medium mortality group was more or less same to that of the low mortality group for the birth interval of 48 months or more.

9.3.4 Sex of child

It is common that males have higher mortality than female during infancy and childhood. The results presented in Table 9.3 revealed that the male mortality during infancy was higher than the female mortality in all mortality groups. However, in the case of child mortality, the female mortality was observed to be higher than the male, in all mortality groups.

The infant mortality rate for male was 116 per 1000 live births and for female it was 113 in the high mortality group. In the medium mortality group, it was 81 for male and 80 for female. In the low mortality group, it was 66 for male and 55 for female. Though the results indicate excess male mortality during infancy in all mortality groups, the difference was substantial only in the low mortality group.

The child mortality rate was 42 per 1000 live births for male and 61 for female in the high mortality group. In the medium mortality group, it was 27 for male and 40 for female. In the case of low mortality group, it was 22 for male and 24 for female. Though excess female mortality at ages 1-4 was observed in all mortality groups, the differences were substantial only in the high and medium mortality groups. In the low mortality group, there was not much difference between the male and female child mortality rates. The excess female mortality at ages 1-4 was nine times higher for the high mortality group and six times higher for the medium mortality group as compared to the excess female mortality observed for the low mortality group. The results indicate that sex bias during childhood with favoritism for male children was more prevalent in the medium and high mortality groups than in the low mortality group.

9.3.5 Birth weight

It is generally belived that low birth weight (<2500 grams) babies are having more chances of dying during infancy than the babies born with normal weight (2500 grams and above). The infant and child mortality rates by birth weight presented in Table 9.3 showed that the low birth weight babies were having higher chances of dying during infancy in medium and low mortality groups. However, in the high mortality group, the infant mortality rate was higher among the children of normal birth weight than the children of low birth weight. Probably, the care during infancy and other socio-economic and cultural factors might have nullified the effect of birth weight in the high mortality group. This needs further investigation. Birth weight seemed to have no influence on child mortality as there was not much difference in the child mortality rates between the low birth weight and normal birth weight children in all mortality groups.

9.3.6 Summary

Infant mortality rate was higher among mother age less than 20 and over 30 years than others in all mortality groups. Child mortality rate increased with age of mother (up to age 40) both in the high and medium mortality groups. In the case of low mortality group, the child mortality rates were more or less at the same level up to the age 40. Both the infant and child mortality rates were less in the low mortality group than in the medium and high mortality groups at all age groups of mother. Infant mortality was higher among children of first and higher birth orders than others in all mortality groups. The child mortality rates were comparatively high among higher order births in all mortality groups. Both the infant and child mortality rates were observed to be high among the children born less than 2 years following the birth of its preceding sibling in all mortality groups.

Fewer female than male die during infancy in all mortality groups, although the female advantage reversed among children aged 1-4 years. Though excess male infant mortality was observed in all mortality groups, the excess was substantial only in the low mortality group. The excess female mortality observed at ages 1-4 years was 9 times higher for high mortality group and 6 times higher for medium mortality group as compared to the low mortality group. The variations observed in the excess female mortality at ages 1-4 years among the three mortality groups revealed that the sex bias was more prevalent in the high and medium mortality groups than the low mortality group.

Though birth weight is expected to have significant influence on the chances of survival of children during infancy and childhood, the results of the present study indicate a higher infant mortality rate among the children of normal birth weight than the children of low birth weight in the high mortality group. However, in the case of medium and low mortality groups, the infant mortality rates were higher among the low birth weight children than the normal birth weight children. It was also observed that there was not much difference in the child mortality rates between the low birth weight and normal birth weight children in all mortality groups. Variations in the infant mortality rates among the three mortality groups were substantial for both low birth weight and normal birth weight children. Even among children born with normal birth weight, the chances of dying during infancy was more than four times higher in the high mortality group and more than two times higher in the medium mortality group as compared to the low mortality group. In the case of child mortality, there was not much difference between the medium and low mortality groups. However, the chances of normal birth weight children dying during childhood was more than two times higher in the high mortality group as compared to the low mortality group.

9.4 Infant and Child Mortality by Maternal Care Variables

Infant and child mortality rates by selected maternal care variables for births four years preceding the survey are presented in Table 9.4. The maternal care variables examined are: 1) antenatal care visits; 2) medical maternity care; 3) Place of delivery; 4) birth attendant and 5) complications at delivery. The influence of these variables on infant and child mortality are discussed in the following sections.

9.4.1 Antenatal care visits

Both the infant and child mortality rates decreased consistently with the increase in the number of antenatal care visits in all mortality groups. In the high mortality group, the infant mortality rate decreased from 113 per 1000 live births for no antenatal care visits to 65 for more than four visits. In the medium mortality group, the infant mortality rate decreased from 81 per 1000 live births for no visits to 57 for more than four visits. In the case of low mortality group, the infant mortality rate decreased from 78 per 1000 live births for no visits to 42 for more than four visits. Though infant mortality rates exhibit a similar pattern for all mortality groups, the rates were high at all stages of antenatal care visits in the high and medium mortality groups as compared to the low mortality group. However, the differences in the infant mortality rates among the three mortality groups narrowed down with the increase in the number of antenatal care visits.

9.4.2 Medical maternity care

Children of mothers who have received antenatal and delivery care from trained health personnel are expected to have a very less risk of dying during infancy and childhood. The results presented in Table 9.4 revealed that both infant and child mortality rates were higher among children whose mothers had not received any antenatal/delivery care than those who had received antenatal and delivery care.

In the high mortality group, the infant mortality rate decreased from 107 per 1000 live births for children of mothers who had received neither antenatal nor delivery care to 73 for those who had received either antenatal or delivery care and further decreased to 57 for those who had received both antenatal and delivery care. The child mortality rate decreased from 60 per 1000 live births for no antenatal/delivery care to 33 for either antenatal or delivery care and to 12 for both antenatal and delivery care. In the medium mortality group, the infant mortality rate declined from 75 per 1000 live births for no antenatal/delivery care to 72 for either antenatal or delivery care and to 52 for both antenatal and delivery care. The child mortality rate declined from 41 for no antenatal / delivery care to 25 for either antenatal or delivery care and to 24 for both antenatal and delivery care. In the low mortality group, the infant mortality rate declined from 83 per 1000 live births for no antenatal/delivery care to 48 for either antenatal or delivery care and to 44 for both antenatal and delivery care. The child mortality rate declined from 39 per 1000 live births for no antenatal/ delivery care to 17 for either antenatal or delivery care and then it has slightly increased to 18 for both antenatal and delivery care. The results clearly indicate the importance of medical maternity care in reducing the infant and child mortality rates in all mortality groups.

Both infant and child mortality rates were low at all levels of medical maternity care for the low mortality group as compared to the high and medium mortality groups. However, the differences observed between low and medium mortality group as well as low and high mortality groups narrowed down with the increase in medical maternity care. i.e. when the mother availed both antenatal and delivery care from trained health personnel.

The per cent reduction in infant mortality rate in the high mortality group due to the availing of both antenatal and delivery care was same as that of the reduction observed in the low mortality group (47 per cent). The results indicate that increasing the availability and quality of medical maternal care services in the high and medium mortality groups could help for further reduction in the infant and child mortality rates in Rural India.

9.4.3 Place of delivery

Due to the improved care and hygiene at the time of birth, children born in institutions are generally expected to have low risk of death as compared to children born at home. The infant and child mortality rates by place of delivery presented in Table 9.4 showed different picture for high and medium mortality groups. It is observed that the infant mortality rate was lower among births occurred at home than the births occurred at public sector facilities. It is also observed that births occurred at private hospitals tend to have lower risk of death than the births occurred at home and public sector facilities. The results indicate the need for further investigation in to the reasons for high infant mortality among children born in Public sector facilities than the private and home delivery. Probably, most of the cases died in public sector facilities might be of complicated cases and admitted in the hospital at the last minute after exploring all possibilities at home by poor people.

Contrary to the above results, the infant mortality rate in the low mortality group was lower among births occurred at public sector facilities than the births occurred at private sector facilities and home.

While the child mortality rate was high among births occurred at home in the high and medium mortality groups, it was high among births occurred at public sector facilities in the low mortality group. The inconsistent relationship observed between infant and child mortality rates and place of delivery among the three mortality groups require further investigation.

9.4.4 Birth attendants

It is generally expected that the chances of child survival are higher among children whose birth was attended by a trained health personnel than others. The infant and child mortality rates by person assisted during delivery is presented in Table 9.4. The results indicate that both infant and child mortality rates were lower among births attended by trained health personnel (Doctor/Nurse/midwife) than untrained personnel (traditional birth attendants/relative/others) in all mortality groups. Among the trained health personnel, the infant mortality rate was slightly higher among births attended by doctor than Nurse/midwife in all mortality groups. This may be due to the fact that nurse/midwife continued to give follow up services where as it was not so in the case of doctors. It is generally expected that the chances of child survival are higher among children whose birth was attended by a trained health personnel than others. The infant and child mortality rates by person assisted during delivery is presented in Table 9.4. The results indicate that both infant and child mortality rates were lower among births attended by trained health personnel (Doctor/Nurse/midwife) than untrained personnel (traditional birth attendants/relative/others) in all mortality groups. Among the trained health personnel, the infant mortality rate was slightly higher among births attended by doctor than Nurse/midwife in all mortality groups.

The comparison of infant and child mortality rates among the three mortality groups revealed that the rates were low among children of low mortality group for all categories of birth attendants as compared to the medium and high mortality groups.

9.4.5 Complications at delivery

Delivery complications are expected to have more influence on infant and child mortality. The results presented in Table 9.4 revealed that both infant and child mortality rates were observed to be high for births with delivery complications than those without complications in all mortality groups.

Long period of labour was the complication reported by most of the mothers who had experienced complication in all mortality groups. The infant mortality rate among births with complications of delayed labour was 111 per 1000 live births in the high mortality group, 99 in the medium mortality group and 93 in the low mortality group. The results also showed that child mortality was higher among births with delivery complications than those with no complications in the high and low mortality groups. However, not much differences were observed in the medium mortality group.

9.4.6 Summary

Antenatal care visits seemed to have significant influence on infant and child mortality in all mortality groups. Though variations were observed in the infant and child mortality rates among the three mortality groups, the differences were narrowed down significantly with the increase in the number of antenatal care visits. In all mortality groups, both infant and child mortality rates declined considerably when the mother availed both antenatal and delivery care from trained health personnel. The variation observed in the infant and child mortality rates among the three mortality groups was great when the mother did not receive neither antenatal nor delivery care from trained health personnel.

While the infant mortality rate was high among children whose birth took place at home in low mortality group, it was high among children whose birth took place at public sector facilities in the medium and high mortality groups. The results indicate the need for improvements in the quality of services provided by the public sector facilities in the high and medium mortality groups.

In the case of delivery attendants, both the infant and child mortality rates were low among births attended by trained health personnel and was high among births attended by untrained personnel in all mortality groups. It was also observed that both

Table 9.4 Infant and child mortality rates for the four years period preceding the survey by selected maternal care variables, Rural India, 1992 – 93.

Maternal care variables	*High*				*Medium*				*Low*			
	NNM	*PNM**	*IM*	*CM*	*NNM*	*PNM**	*IM*	*CM*	*NNM*	*PNM**	*IM*	*CM*
Antenatal Visit												
None	67.0	46.1	113.1	54.9	49.1	31.5	80.6	39.1	51.8	26.4	78.2	18.4
1 – 3	48.9	28.0	76.9	36.7	45.5	27.8	73.4	31.9	39.1	18.1	57.2	21.3
4 + visits	42.9	22.1	65.0	31.2	39.2	17.5	56.7	21.1	28.1	14.2	42.3	17.6
Medical Maternity Care												
No. Antenatal/ delivery care	62.9	44.4	107.3	60.3	43.1	32.3	75.3	41.3	59.1	23.9	83.0	39.1
Either Antenatal/ delivery care	48.3	24.6	72.9	32.9	46.9	25.2	72.1	24.7	33.4	14.8	48.2	16.8
Both Antenatals/ delivery care	43.5	13.6	57.1	11.6	36.4	15.9	52.3	24.0	26.6	17.1	43.7	17.5
Place of delivery												
Public Sector Facility	82.4	24.1	106.5	13.9	47.1	22.2	69.3	18.2	23.6	16.3	39.9	36.1
Private Sector Facility	24.9	14.6	39.5	8.1	45.5	15.1	60.6	6.7	32.8	14.2	47.0	7.4
Home	54.8	37.4	92.2	50.3	40.5	26.1	66.6	34.5	37.3	18.2	55.6	17.1

(Contd.)

(Contd. Table 9.4)

Maternal care variables	High				Medium				Low			
	NNM	PNM*	IM	CM	NNM	PNM*	IM	CM	NNM	PNM*	IM	CM
Birth Attendant												
Doctor	64.1	26.4	90.5	23.6	44.0	19.5	63.5	19.9	31.0	14.8	45.8	15.8
Nurse/Mid Wife	47.7	31.3	79.0	35.9	36.9	24.3	61.1	23.6	29.1	16.3	45.5	17.6
Traditional Birth/Attendant	54.9	40.5	95.4	49.4	43.8	27.3	71.1	34.5	39.6	17.3	57.0	20.8
Relative/Others	64.5	40.1	104.7	49.4	49.3	27.6	76.9	34.8	46.9	23.3	70.1	24.1
Complications at Delivery												
No Complications	55.4	41.1	96.6	47.6	43.3	26.3	69.6	32.4	36.1	16.6	52.6	21.0
Caesarian	**	**	**	**	**	**	**	**	28.0	26.0	54.0	21.3
Use of forceps	**	**	**	**	**	**	**	**	**	**	**	**
Excessive bleeding	**	**	**	**	**	**	**	**	**	**	**	**
Long period of Labour	86.9	24.1	111.0	41.5	67.6	30.9	98.5	31.8	62.5	30.0	92.5	35.9
Delayed Delivery of placenta	**	**	**	**	**	**	**	**	**	**	**	**
Total	**61.4**	**39.9**	**101.3**	**47.6**	**46.2**	**27.0**	**73.2**	**31.5**	**38.9**	**18.2**	**57.1**	**20.5**

Figure 9.5 Infant and Child Mortality Rates by Number of Antenatal Visits, Rural India, 1992-93

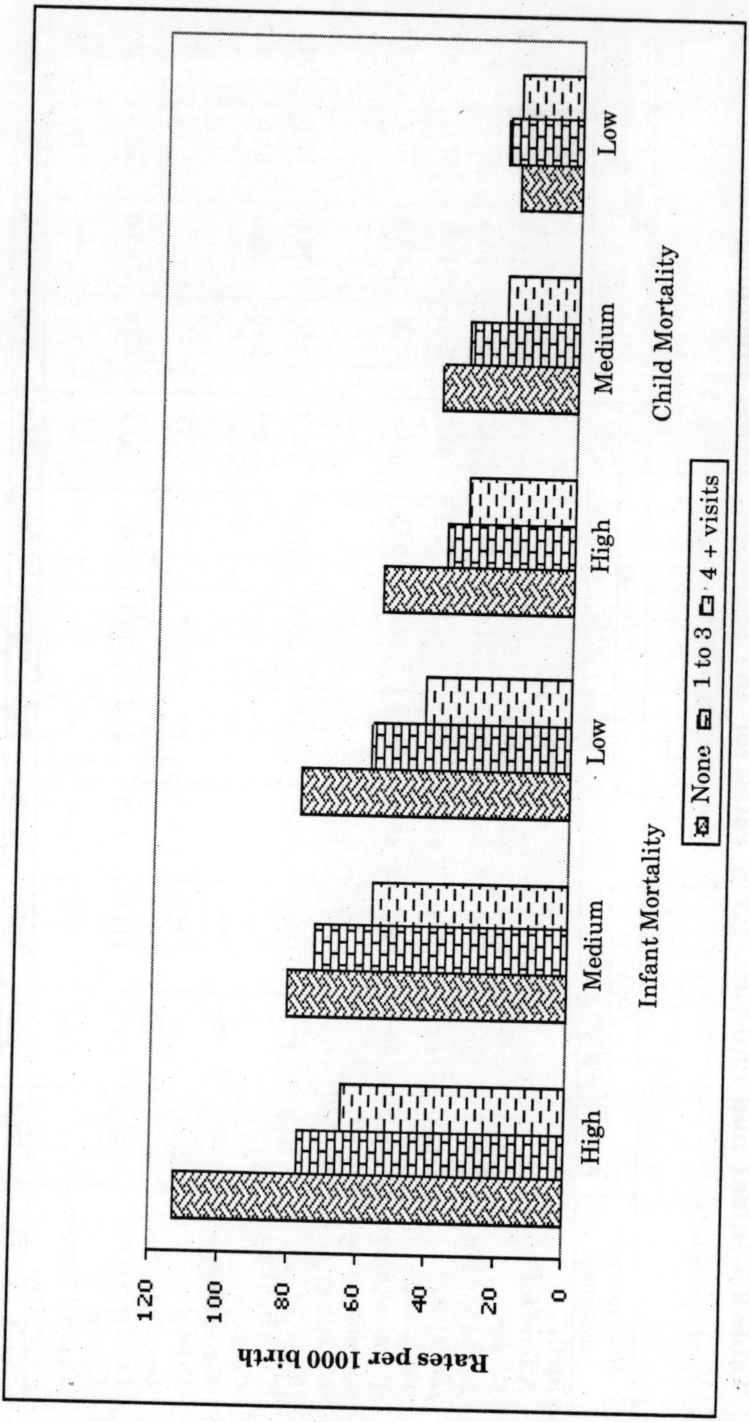

Table 9.5 Infant and child mortality rates for the ten years period preceding the survey by exposure to mass media, Rural India, 1992 – 93.

E4xposure to mass media	*High*				*Medium*				*Low*			
	NNM	*PNM**	*IM*	*CM*	*NNM*	*PNM**	*IM*	*CM*	*NNM*	*PNM**	*IM*	*CM*
Not exposed any media	70.9	48.2	119.1	56.5	52.9	31.6	84.5	37.6	42.5	22.8	65.3	28.0
Exposed to media	59.1	40.5	99.7	36.1	48.8	26.3	75.1	28.0	37.2	20.0	57.2	19.6
Watch TV once a week	49.7	29.0	78.7	24.0	46.7	27.8	74.5	21.9	34.1	18.0	52.1	16.6
Listen Radio once a week	58.5	41.5	100.0	35.3	50.2	26.6	76.7	29.7	35.5	19.7	55.2	18.2
Visit cinema once a month	44.2	31.7	75.9	40.5	43.7	24.5	68.1	24.5	50.7	20.2	70.9	25.1

* Computed as the difference between the infant and neonatal mortality rates.NNM - Neonatal mortality / PNM - Postneonatal mortality / IM - Infant mortality ($1q_0$) / CM - Child mortality ($4q_1$)

Figure 9.6 Infant and Child Mortality Rates by Exposure Mass Media, Rural India, 1992-93

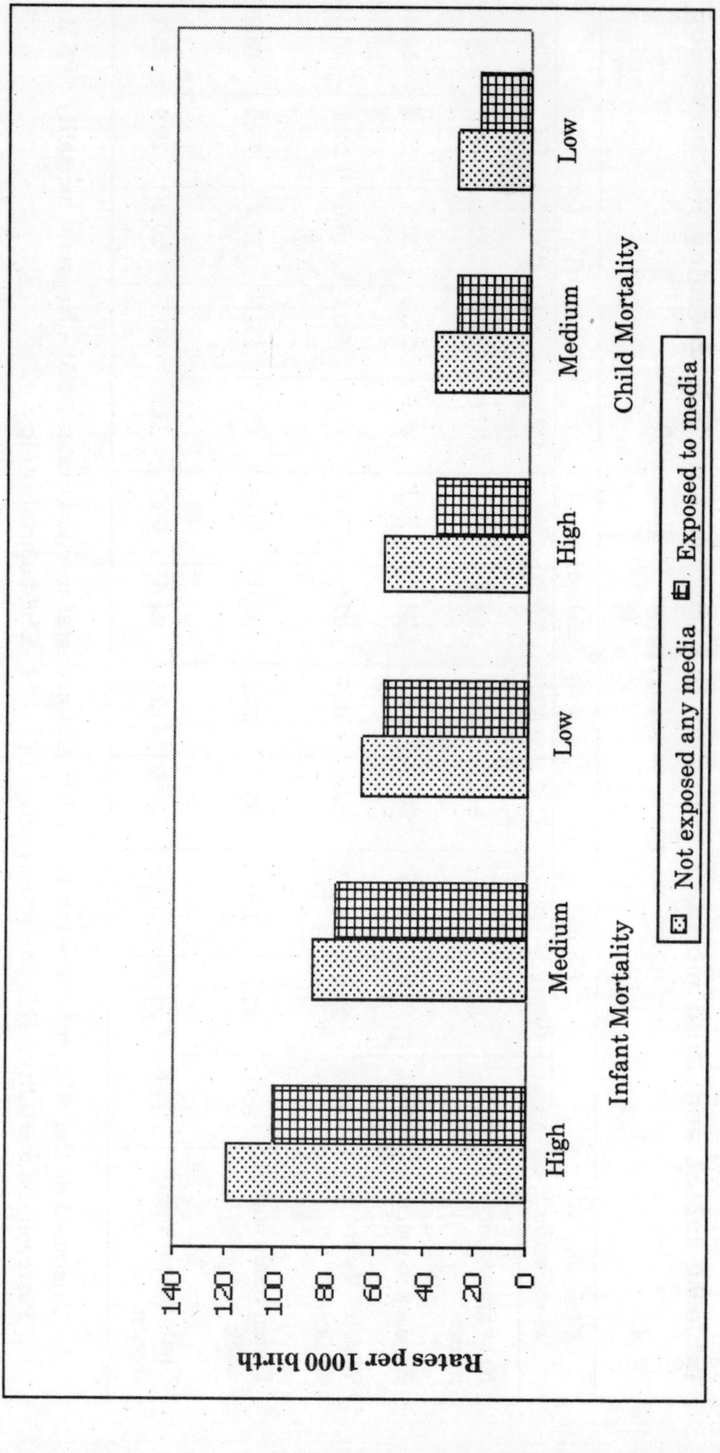

infant and child mortality rates were higher for births with delivery complications than the births with no delivery complications in all mortality groups.

9.5 Infant and child mortality by exposure to mass media

Mass media is playing a vital role in propagating the health care messages to the rural mass. Mothers who have exposed to mass media frequently are expected to acquire more knowledge on appropriate health care measures. As a result, children of mothers who have exposed to mass media are likely to have low risk of infant and child mortality as compared to those who have not exposed to any mass media.

The results presented in Table 9.5 revealed that both infant and child mortality rates were comparatively lower among children of mothers who had exposed to any mass media than those who had not, in all mortality groups. In the high mortality group, the infant mortality rate which was 119 per 1000 live births for those who have not exposed to any mass media declined to 100 for those who had exposed to any media and the child mortality rate which was 57 per 1000 live births for those who had not exposed to any mass media declined to 36 for those who had exposed to any media. In the medium mortality group, the infant mortality rate declined from 85 per 1000 live births to 75 and the child mortality rate declined from 38 per 1000 live births to 28. In the low mortality group, the infant mortality rate declined from 65 per 1000 live births to 57 and the child mortality rate declined from 28 per 1000 live births to 20. The results clearly indicate the influence of mass media in reducing infant and child mortality rates in rural India. Among those who had exposed to mass media, the infant mortality rate was low among the children of mothers who had visited cinema once a month in the high and medium mortality groups where as it was low among children of mothers watching television (TV) once a week in the low mortality group. The child mortality rate was comparatively low among children of mothers watching Television once a week in all mortality groups.

In all, both infant and child mortality declined considerably when the mother exposed to any mass media in all mortality groups.

The results suggest that the effective use of mass media to propagate health and family welfare messages will help to reduce infant and child mortality in rural India.

10

Multivariate Analysis of Infant and Child Mortality

The results of the univariate analysis of infant and child mortality presented in Chapter - IX revealed that the probability of survival through infancy and childhood varied according to different background characteristics of the mothers and children in all the three mortality groups. As many of these variables are closely related to each other, these associations make it difficult to interpret the infant and child mortality differentials observed in the univariate analysis. In order to estimate the independent effects of each variable, while other variables are controlled, the multivariate approach is adopted. The method adopted for the multivariate analysis is proportional hazard models. A brief description of these models are given below.

10.1 A Brief description of hazard models

The dependent variable in the multivariate analysis is a measure of the force of mortality for an individual i, in the age interval t and is given by ëi(t). The hazard in the age interval t, which can be interpreted as the probability of dying between t and delta-t, given that the child has survived at the beginning of the age interval, is assumed to have the following functional form.

In [ëi(t)] = á(t) + xi(t) â(t)

Where ëi(t), is the risk of dying in age interval t for child i, exp (á(t)) is the underlying age specific risk of dying xi(t) is a vector of characteristics for individual i, and

â(t) is the set of associated co-efficients

Estimates of the coefficients â(t), when exponentiated, can be interpreted as the risk associated with a set of characteristics xi(t), related to an omitted reference category.

Coefficients are estimated using maximum likelihood methods and Z- statistics (the estimated coefficient divided by the standard error) is used to assess whether an effect is statistically significant.

Four different proportional hazard models were considered in the multivariate analysis to see the relative risk of dying through ages 0-11 months and 1-4 years for births during the 4 years preceding the survey.

The first model assesses the relative risk of sex of the child, mother's age at the time of child's birth, religion, caste, mother's standard of living index and mother's education on infant and child mortality.

The second model assesses the relative risk of birth order, mothers age at the time of child's birth and mothers education on infant and child mortality.

The third model assesses the relative risk of sex of the child, mother's age at birth, sex composition of older surviving siblings, interaction term between sex of the child and sex composition of older surviving siblings and mother's education on infant and child mortality.

The fourth model assesses the relative risk of antenatal care, Tetanus Toxoid, place of delivery and mother's education on infant and child mortality.

10.2 Results of Multivariate Analysis

The results of the multivariate analysis are presented in Table 10.1 to 10.4. In the tables, exponent of coefficients are presented as the relative risk of dying during infancy and childhood by children of various groups considered under the models.

The results of model 1 presented in Table 10.1 revealed that in the low mortality group, the relative risk of infant mortality was significantly high (about 28 per cent) among male children as compared to female children. No significant difference was observed in the relative risk of infant mortality between the male and female children in the high and medium mortality groups. There was no significant difference in the relative risk of infant mortality among the children of various religions in all mortality groups except the medium mortality group where the relative risk of infant mortality was significantly less among the children of other religion as compared to Muslims.

The children of Scheduled Tribe in the high and low mortality groups and the children of other castes in the high and medium mortality groups have significantly lower risk of infant mortality than Scheduled Caste. Mother's standard of living has a significant effect on infant mortality only at higher level of standard of living in the high and medium mortality groups. The children of mothers from households of high standard of living in the high and low mortality groups have significantly less risk of infant mortality as compared to low standard of living. Education of mother has a significant effect on infant mortality only in the high and low mortality groups. The relative risk of infant mortality among the children of literate mothers was significantly less in the high and low mortality groups as compared to illiterates. In the medium mortality group, though the risk was less among the children of literate mothers, the effect of education on infant mortality was not significant.

The relative risk of selected socio-economic and demographic variables on child mortality (deaths among children age 1-4 years) also presented in Table 10.1, revealed that the relative risk of child mortality was significantly less among male children as compared to female children in all mortality groups. The relative risk of child mortality among male children was as less as about 24 percent in high mortality group whereas it was 32 per cent less in medium mortality group and 19 per cent less in low mortality group as compared to female children.

In the high and low mortality groups, there was no significant differences in the relative risk of child mortality between the children of different religions. However, in the medium mortality group, the relative risk was significantly less among the children of mothers belonging to Hindu and other religions as compared to Muslims. Children of Scheduled Tribe in the medium mortality group seemed to have a high risk of child mortality as compared to Scheduled Caste. Mother's standard of living did not show any significant effect on child mortality in high and medium mortality groups. However, in the low mortality group, the relative risk of child mortality was

Table 10.1 Relative risk of sex of the child, mother's age at the time of child's birth, religion, caste, mother's standard of living index and mother's education on infant and child mortality, estimated by using hazard model for four years period preceding The survey, Rural India, 1992 - 93.

Covariates	*Infant Mortality*			*Child Mortality*		
	High	*Medium*	*Low*	*High*	*Medium*	*Low*
Sex of the Child						
Male	1.04	0.93	1.28***	0.76***	0.68***	0.81*
Mother's age at Birth						
Age at birth	0.85***	0.86***	0.85***	1.04	0.96	1.05
Square term of age at birth	1.00***	1.00***	1.00***	1.00	1.00	1.00
Religion						
Hindu	1.06	0.96	1.09	1.01	0.76*	1.01
Others	0.92	0.70*	1.02	1.35	0.38***	1.40

(Contd.)

(Contd. Table 10.1)

Covariates	*Infant Mortality*			*Child Mortality*		
	High	*Medium*	*Low*	*High*	*Medium*	*Low*
Caste						
Scheduled Tribe	0.84*	0.87	0.62***	0.99	1.39*	0.84
Others	0.88*	0.76***	0.86	0.86	0.99	0.91
Mothers standard of living index (SLI)						
Medium SLI	0.94	0.92	0.83**	0.88	0.97	0.71**
High SLI	0.74*	0.98	0.67***	0.73	0.65	0.87
Mother's Education						
Literate	0.73***	0.96	0.77***	0.76**	0.76*	0.89

* $P < 0.10$ **$P < 0.05$ ***$P < 0.01$ Reference Category : Female Child; Muslims; Scheduled Caste; Low SLI; Illiterate

significantly less among the children of mothers from the households of medium standard of living as compared to low standard of living. The relative risk of child mortality was significantly less among the children of literate mothers in the high and medium mortality groups. In the low mortality group, though the relative risk was less among the children of literate mothers, the effect of education on child mortality was not significant.

The results of the second model presented in Table 10.2 revealed that in the high mortality group, the relative risk of infant mortality was significantly less among children of second and third order births as compared to first order births. In the medium mortality group the relative risk was significantly less among the children of second order births, and in the low mortality group the risk was significantly high among the children of fifth order births as compared to first order births.

Birth order did not show any significant effect on child mortality in the medium and low mortality groups. However, in the high mortality group, the relative risk of child mortality was significantly high for third, fourth and fifth order births as compared to first order births. The introduction of birth order did not alter the effect of education on infant and child mortality as emerged in model- 1.

The results of model-3 presented in Table 10.3 revealed that the sex composition of older surviving siblings did not make any significant effect on infant mortality in all mortality groups. The effect of interaction between sex of the child and sex composition of older surviving siblings was significant in the medium and low mortality groups when the child was male with all older surviving siblings female as compared to male with all older surviving siblings mixed. The consideration of interaction in the model altered the significant effect of sex of the child and mothers education in the low mortality group as emerged in model-1. The significant effect of these variables as emerged in model-1 has become non-significant in model-3 due to the interaction effect. In the medium mortality group, the significant effect of age at birth on infant mortality as emerged in model-1 became non-significant due to interaction effect.

The sex composition of older surviving siblings did not make any significant effect on child mortality in the medium and low mortality groups. However, in the high mortality group, the relative

Table 10.2 Relative risk of birth order, mother's age at birth and mother's education on infant and child mortality estimated by using hazard model for four years period preceding the survey, Rural India, 1992 - 93.

Covariates	*Infant Mortality*			*Child Mortality*		
	High	*Medium*	*Low*	*High*	*Medium*	*Low*
Birth Order						
2	0.81***	0.85*	0.97	1.13	0.86	0.94
3	0.74***	0.91	1.09	1.39**	0.95	0.90
4	0.90	0.86	1.27	1.37*	0.77	1.32
5+	0.99	1.24	1.34*	1.35*	0.83	0.70
Mother's education						
Literate	0.69***	0.90	0.72***	0.73***	0.66***	0.86
Mother's age at birth						
Age at birth	0.87***	0.87***	0.83***	0.98	0.98	1.02
Square term of mother's age at birth	1.00***	1.00***	1.00***	1.00	1.00	1.00

* P < 0.10   ** P < 0.05   *** P < 0.01Reference Category : Birth order 1, illiterate mother

Table 10.3 Relative risk of sex of the child and mother's age at birth, sex combination of older surviving siblings and interaction terms between sex of the child and sex composition of older surviving siblings and mother's education on infant and child mortality estimated by using hazard model for four years period preceding the survey, Rural India, 1992-93.

Covariates	*Infant Mortality*			*Child Mortality*		
	High	*Medium*	*Low*	*High*	*Medium*	*Low*
Sex of the child	1.07	0.87	1.18	0.65***	0.62**	1.06
Male						
Mother's age at birth	0.86***	0.97	0.80***	0.91	0.93	0.94
Age at birth	1.00***	1.00	1.00**	1.00	1.00	1.00
Square term of age at birth						
Sex composition of older surviving siblings						
All sib are brothers	1.13	0.88	0.81	0.84	0.76	0.90
All sib are sisters	1.09	1.23	1.26	0.64**	0.84	1.70
Interaction terms between sex of the child and sex composition of older of older surviving siblings						
Male, all sib, are brothers	0.96	1.04	1.11	1.26	1.66	1.14
Male, all sib, are sisters	0.96	0.68*	0.89**	1.46	1.18	0.35
Mothers Education						
Literate	0.71***	0.89	0.73	0.59***	0.62	0.70

Note : Model includes only birth order of 3 and above* P < 0.10 ** P < 0.05 *** P < 0.01Reference Category : Female Child; Mixed siblings; Male, all siblings are mixed; illiterate mother.

risk of child mortality was significantly less when all older surviving siblings were female as compared to mixed siblings. There was no significant effect of interaction between sex of the child and sex composition of older surviving siblings on child mortality in all mortality groups. Due to the introduction of sex composition variable, the significant effect of sex of the child on child mortality in the low mortality group and the significant effect of education of mother on child mortality in the medium mortality group as emerged in model-1 became non-significant in this model.

The results of model 4 are presented in Table 10.4. It is found that the antenatal care during pregnancy did not make any significant effect on infant mortality in all mortality groups. Hospital delivery has a significant effect on infant mortality in the high and low mortality groups where as in the medium mortality group the effect was not significant. For hospital deliveries, while the relative risk of infant mortality was 20 per cent high in the high mortality group, it was 20 per cent less in the low mortality group as compared to home deliveries.

Immunisation during pregnancy has a significant effect on infant mortality in all mortality groups. The relative risk of infant mortality among children of mothers who had received tetanus toxoid vaccination was as less as 27 per cent in the high mortality group, 18 per cent less in the medium mortality group and 30 per cent less in the low mortality group as compared to the children of mothers who had not received tetanus toxoid vaccine during pregnancy.

Maternal care variables did not show any significant effect on child mortality in all mortality groups except for antenatal care in the low mortality group and tetanus toxoid in the medium mortality group. It is found that in the low mortality group, the relative risk of child mortality was significantly less among the children of mothers who had received antenatal care as compared to those who had not. In the medium mortality group, the relative risk of child mortality was significantly less among the children of mothers who had received tetanus toxoid as compared to those who had not. The significant effect of education on child mortality in the high mortality group as emerged in model-1 became non-significant in this model.

Table 10.4 Relative risk of Antenatal care (ANC), Tetanus Toxoid (TT) place of delivery and mother's education on infant and child mortality estimated by using hazard model for four years period preceding the Survey, Rural India,1992-93.

Covariates	*Infant Mortality*			*Child Mortality*		
	High	*Medium*	*Low*	*High*	*Medium*	*Low*
Antenatal Care (ANC)						
Availed	0.88	0.96	1.23	0.80	1.11	0.58*
Place of Delivery						
Hospital	1.20*	1.03	0.80**	0.81	0.89	0.86
Immunisation (T T)						
Availed	0.73**	0.82*	0.70**	0.93	0.96	1.52
Mother's Education						
Literate	0.80***	1.01	0.76***	0.85	0.70**	0.94

*P < 0.10 **P < 0.05 ***P < 0.01Reference Category : ANC not availed; other than hospital delivery; T T not availed; illiterate mother

10.3 Summary

The effect of various socio-economic, demographic and health care variables on infant and child mortality are estimated using proportional hazard models. The results are summarised and presented in the following sections.

10.3.1 Infant mortality

In the high mortality group, among the various socio-economic variables examined, caste, standard of living and education of mother seemed to have significant effect on infant mortality. It is found that children of Scheduled Tribe and other castes, children of mothers from households of high standard of living and children of literate mothers have significantly less risk of infant mortality. It is very suprising to note that the relative risk of infant mortality was significantly less among the children of Scheduled Tribe as compared to Scheduled Caste. Mother's age at birth, order of birth and immunisation during pregnancy also have significant effect on infant mortality. Contrary to general expectations, hospital delivery has a high risk of infant mortality compared to home delivery. This requires further investigation on the health care seeking behaviour of women during pregnancy and the availability and quality of services in the high mortality group.

In all, infant mortality in the high mortality group is significantly associated with the different cultural practices prevailed among various caste groups, standard of living, educational status of mother, fertility behaviour of women (timing and number) and the use of Tetanus Toxoid during pregnancy.

In the medium mortality group, among the various socio-economic variables examined, only religion and caste seemed to have significant effect on infant mortality. Children of other religion (other than Hindu and Muslim) and other caste (i.e. other than SC/ST) seemed to have significantly less risk of infant mortality. Age of mother at birth, order of birth and sex composition of older surviving siblings were the demographic variables having significant effect on infant mortality. The relative risk of infant mortality was significantly less among male children with all older surviving siblings female as compared to male children with mixed older surviving siblings. Among the maternal care variables, only tetanus toxoid injection has a significant effect on infant mortality.

In all, infant mortality in the medium mortality group is significantly influenced by the cultural practices of various religions and caste groups, fertility behaviour of women (timing and number), sex composition of older surviving siblings and the use of Tetanus Toxoid during pregnancy.

In the low mortality group, caste, standard of living and mother's education emerged as significant socio-economic variables influencing infant mortality. It is observed that children of mothers belonging to ST, children of mothers from households of both medium and high standard of living and children of literate mothers have significantly less risk of infant mortality. Sex of child, age of mother at birth, order of birth and sex composition of older surviving siblings were the demographic variables having significant effect on infant mortality. The significantly high risk of infant mortality observed among the male children became non-significant due to the interaction between sex of the child and sex composition of older surviving siblings. It is observed that the infant mortality risk was significantly less among male children with all older surviving siblings female as compared to male with mixed older surviving siblings. In the case of maternal care variables, hospital delivery and the use of tetanus toxoid during pregnancy seemed to have significant effect on infant mortality.

In all, infant mortality in the low mortality group is significantly influenced by sex of child, sex composition of older surviving siblings, order of birth, caste, standard of living, education of mother, place of delivery and immunisation (Tetanus Toxoid) of mother during pregnancy.

10.3.2 Child mortality

In the high mortality group, education of mother was the only socio-economic variable having significant effect on child mortality. It is found that the children of literate mothers have significantly less risk of child mortality as compared to illiterates. Sex of the child, sex composition of older surviving siblings and order of birth were the demographic variables having significant effect on child mortality. The relative risk was significantly less among male children and it is observed to be higher among higher order births (three and above). None of the maternal care variables seemed to have any significant effect on child mortality in the high mortality group.

In all, child mortality in the high mortality group is significantly associated with education of mother, sex of the child, sex composition of older surviving siblings and order of birth.

In the medium mortality group, among the various socio-economic variables examined, religion, caste and mother's education seemed to have significant effect on child mortality. It is observed that the child mortality risk was significantly less among male children and children of mothers belonging to Hindu and other religions and children of literate mothers. Children of Scheduled Tribe have significantly high risk of child mortality as compared to Scheduled Caste. Sex of the child was the only demographic variable having significant effect on child mortality. It is observed that male children have significantly less risk of child mortality as compared to female. None of the maternal care variables seemed to have any significant effect on child mortality.

In all, child mortality in the medium mortality group is significantly associated with religion, caste, education of mother and sex of the child.

In the low mortality group, male children of mothers from households of medium standard of living and children of mothers who have availed antenatal care during pregnancy have significantly less risk of child mortality.

11

Summary Findings and Policy Implications

The present research aimed to study the socio-economic demographic and health care determinants of infant and child mortality in rural India is based on the analysis of secondary data taken from the National Family Health Survey (NFHS) of India conducted during 1992-93 in 25 States. In order to have a better understanding of the variations in infant and child mortality rates among the various States of India, all the 25 States for which data are available for the present study are grouped in to three categories as Low, Medium and High Mortality Groups based on their level of under five mortality rate as per the NFHS, 1992-93. After having grouped the States in to three categories, the data related to rural areas were analysed separately for each group and compared.

As the variation in infant and child mortality rates are the reflection of the prevailing housing conditions of the area, fertility behaviour of women, utilization of maternal and health care services, immunization and breast feeding practices and nutritional status of children, a comparative analysis of the data related to the housing conditions; fertility levels, utilization of maternal health care services, immunization and breast feeding practices and the nutritional status of children under 5 years of age in the three mortality group of States was made.

11.1 Background characteristics of mortality groups

The results of the analysis of data on housing characteristics showed a substantial variations in the type of house, electricity, source of drinking water, persons per sleeping room, sanitation facility and place of keeping animals at night among the three mortality groups.

The proportion of kachcha houses (made from mud, thatches or other low quality materials) varied from 74 per cent for high mortality group to 42 per cent for low mortality group. The proportion of households having electricity facility varied from 64 per cent for low mortality group to 22 per cent for high mortality group. The mean number of persons per sleeping room varied from 3 for medium mortality group to 2.6 for low mortality group. The proportion of households having toilet facilities varied from 22 per cent for low mortality group to 10 per cent for high mortality group. With regard to place of keeping animals at night, the proportion of households keeping animals inside the house varied from 25 per cent for high mortality group to just 9 per cent for low mortality group.

The comparison of housing conditions among the three mortality groups revealed that the housing conditions were much better in the low and medium mortality group compared to high mortality group.

11.2 Fertility behaviour of women

As the infant and child mortality are closely associated with fertility, the fertility behaviour of women among the three mortality groups was studied in detail. The total fertility rates were in the expected lines with the observation of high mortality group experiencing high fertility(5.7) which was followed by medium(4.9) and low mortality groups(4.3). The crude birth rate, total fertility rate and general fertility rate were high for high mortality group followed by medium and low mortality groups. There was not much difference between the low and medium groups with regard to various fertility measures. The age specific fertility rates revealed that fertility was peak at 20-24 age group in all mortality groups. While the fertility decline was great at 30-34 age group in the medium and low mortality groups, it was great among women age 35-39 in the high mortality group, indicating the slow pace of fertility decline in the high mortality group. The differences observed in the total fertility rate among the three mortality groups narrowed down significantly at higher level of education, indicating education as an important determinant of fertility in all mortality groups. Fertility was high among Muslim women in all mortality groups.

The mean number of children ever born among women age 40-49 was 5.7 for high mortality group, 4.9 for medium and 4.3 for low mortality groups. The child loss as measured by the difference between the mean number of children ever born and surviving revealed that the child loss was high in the high mortality group followed by medium and low mortality groups. Nearly two-fifth (40 per cent) of births in the high mortality group, a little over one-fourth (28 per cent) in the medium mortality group and a little over one-fifth (21 per cent) in the low mortality group were higher order births (four and above). Contrary to expectations, the median duration of previous birth interval was high (32.6 months) in the high mortality group, followed by medium (31.4 months) and low (29.9) mortality groups. Women in the low mortality group started their child bearing a little later and stopped earlier than women in the medium and high mortality groups. The median duration of child bearing was 9.5 years for low mortality group, 11.4 years for medium mortality group and 14.2 years for high mortality group.

The results indicate significant variations in the child bearing practices of women among the three mortality groups. The medium mortality group is closely following the low mortality group interms of various fertility measures. However, women in the high mortality group experienced higher fertility and more child loss and exposed to longer duration of child bearing as compared to medium and low mortality groups.

11.3 Utilisation of maternal care services

Utilisation of maternal care services such as antenatal care visits, immunisation during pregnancy (Tetanus Toxoid), taking Iron and Folic Acid tablets, place of delivery and person attended delivery are likely to have significant influence on child survival. Hence, the variations in the levels of utilisation of various maternal care services among the three mortality groups were examined in detail. The results indicate marked differences in the utilisation of maternal care services among the three mortality groups. The utilisation of maternal care services was observed to be high in the low mortality group followed by medium and high mortality groups. The proportion of women who have received antenatal care visits at home was only 19 per cent in the high mortality group and 32 per cent both in the medium and low mortality groups. The proportion who have made outside visits for antenatal care was high in the low mortality group (70 per cent) which was followed by medium (51 per cent) and high (27 per cent) mortality groups. Both home visits and outside visits for antenatal care were very poor in the high mortality group indicating poor delivery of maternal care services and the poor knowledge of women on the importance of antenatal care visits in the high mortality group. Among those who have received antenatal care, the median number of antenatal care visits was slightly higher in the low mortality group as compared to medium and high mortality groups. There was not much difference in the median months of gestation at first antenatal care visit among the three mortality groups. It was about 5 months for all mortality groups.

Two fifth (40 per cent) of women in the high mortality group, nearly two-third (65 per cent) in the medium mortality group and a little over four-fifth (83 per cent) in the low mortality group have availed atleast one dose of TT vaccine during pregnancy. Substantial variation was also observed in the proportion of women who have availed Iron and Folic Acid tablets during pregnancy among the three mortality groups. Nearly three-fourth (74 per cent) of women in the low mortality group, nearly three-fifth (57 per cent) in the medium and a little over one-fourth (28 per cent) in the high mortality groups have availed Iron and Folic Acid tablets during pregnancy.

A majority of deliveries in all mortality groups took place at home. However, the proportion of institutional deliveries was comparatively high (37 per cent) in the low mortality group as compared to medium (19 per cent) and high (7 per cent) mortality groups. Higher proportion of literate women preferred to have institutional deliveries than illiterate women in all mortality groups. Home deliveries were more common among Scheduled Caste women than others in all mortality groups. Substantial variation in the proportion of deliveries attended by trained health personnel was observed among the three mortality groups. The proportion of deliveries attended by trained health personnel was only 15 per cent in the high mortality group where as it was 29 per cent in the medium and 49 per cent in the low mortality groups. While the proportion of deliveries attended by trained health personnel decreased with increase in the age of mother and birth order, it has increased with education and number of antenatal care visits in all mortality groups.

The findings revealed a substantial variation in the utilisation of maternal care services among the three mortality groups. The level of utilisation of maternal care services was more among mothers in the low mortality group than the mothers in medium and high mortality groups. In all, the results indicate that the high mortality group is in a most disadvantaged position in all aspects of maternal health care.

11.4 Immunisation and Breast Feeding

The coverage for BCG varied from 84 percent for children of low mortality group to 45 percent for children of high mortality group. The coverage for DPT (3 doses) varied from 79 percent for the children of low mortality group to 33 percent for the children of high mortality group. Similar variations were also observed in the coverage for polio and measles vaccines.

The variations in the proportion of fully immunized children varied from 60 percent in low mortality group to just 18 percent for children of high mortality group. Substantial differences were also observed in the proportion of children immunized against all vaccine preventable disease in the first year of life. In the low mortality group, 44 percent of children were fully immunized in the first year of life where as it was only 22 percent in the medium mortality group and just 10 percent in the high mortality group.

Sex differentials in the immunization coverage were observed in all mortality groups. Higher proportion of male children were vaccinated in all mortality groups. In all, female children, children of higher order births, children of illiterate mothers, children of Muslim mothers and children of SC/ST mothers seemed to have very less immunization coverage than others. The achievement of 52 percent of immunization coverage for the children of illiterate mothers in the low mortality group was higher than the immunization coverage among the children of mothers who had studied upto high school and above in high mortality group (49 percent). The results indicate the effectiveness of information, education and communication (IEC) activities of the programme personnel in the low mortality group. Improvement in the infrastructure facilities and the effective implementation of IEC activities will certainly help to improve the immunization coverage even in places where the formal education of mothers is at a very low level.

The analysis of data on the breast feeding practices of women revealed that breast feeding was near universal in all mortality groups. Not much variations were observed in the breast feeding practice and duration of breast feeding among the mothers in the three mortality groups. It is also observed that the duration of breast feeding by background characteristics of the mothers and children did not vary much in all mortality groups. Since the data related to rural areas and breast feeding is universal in rural India, not much variations were observed among the three mortality groups with regard to the breast feeding practice.

11.5 Nutritional Status of Children

The nutritional status of children as measured by the weight for height index revealed that the proportion of malnourished children was in the same level around 17-19 percent in all mortality groups. The proportion of severely malnourished was also in the same level of around 3 percent in all mortality groups. Thus the prevalence of malnutrition did not vary much among the three mortality groups. The percentage of both malnourished and severely malnourished children was observed to be more among male than female children in all mortality groups. Birth order and birth interval did not make much difference in the prevalence of malnutrition among children in all mortality groups. Education of mothers seemed to have substantial effect on the reduction of malnutrition among children in all mortality groups.

The results of the nutritional status of children under 4 years of age measured using weight for age index revealed that the proportion malnourished and severely malnourished children increased with the age of the child up to 12-23 months of age and showed a declining trend at higher ages of 24 months or more in all mortality groups. While a high prevalence of malnutrition was observed among male children in high mortality group, it was higher among female children in the medium and low mortality groups. Increase in birth order seemed to increase the prevalence of malnourished and severely malnourished in high mortality group.

However in medium and low mortality groups, though the proportion of malnourished increased with birth order upto 4-5, it has showed a declining trend for the birth order of 6 and above. While the proportion of severely malnourished increased with birth order in medium mortality group, it has showed a declining trend for the birth orders of 6 and above in low mortality group. The increase in birth interval seemed to reduce the prevalence of malnutrition among the children under four years of age in all mortality groups. Similarly, education of mother seemed to have substantial impact on the nutritional status of children in all mortality groups. While the prevalence of malnutrition is observed to be highest among the children of scheduled tribes in medium and low mortality groups, it was highest among the children of schedule caste in high mortality group. Overall the prevalence of malnutrition was comparatively lower among the children of low mortality group compared to children in high and medium mortality groups.

The prevalence of malnutrition among children in the three mortality groups as measured by height for age index was varying substantially with the observation of high prevalence among the children of high mortality group which was followed by medium and low mortality groups. The proportion of malnourished children increased with age and birth order in all mortality groups. While the prevalence of malnutrition was higher among male children in high mortality group, it was higher among female children in medium and low mortality groups. Increase in birth interval decrease the prevalence of malnutrition in all mortality groups. The increase in the education of mother resulted in the substantial reduction of malnutrition among children in all mortality groups.

11.6 Levels, Trends and differentials of infant and child mortality

The current levels, recent trends and differentials of infant and child mortality rates derived from the birth history data of ever married women revealed that deaths to children under the age of five had declined over the last fifteen years (1978-92) in all mortality groups. Though unequal between the mortality groups, the declines were substantial in all mortality groups. The infant mortality decline was 28 per cent in the high mortality group, 20 per cent in the medium mortality group and 18 per cent in the low mortality group.

The pace of infant mortality decline was more rapid in the high mortality group as compared to medium and low mortality groups. There was not much difference between the medium and low mortality groups in the pace of decline. Though the per cent decline of infant mortality rate was high in the high mortality group, the infant mortality rate continued to be high in the high mortality group as compared to medium and low mortality groups. The infant mortality rate during 1988-92 was 101 per 1000 live births in the high mortality group where as it was only 73 in the medium and 57 in the low mortality groups. The high mortality group have nearly double the infant mortality rate of low mortality group. The proportion of neonatal deaths to infant deaths was more than 60 per cent in all mortality groups.

The child mortality rate during 1988-92 was 48 per 1000 live births in the high mortality group whereas it was only 32 in the medium mortality group and 21 in the low mortality group. While the decline of infant mortality rate was high in the high mortality group, the decline of child mortality rate was high in the low mortality group. A decline of about 50 per cent was observed during 1978-92 for the low mortality group whereas it was 31 per cent and 30 per cent for the medium and high mortality groups respectively. It is also to be noted that there was not much difference between the medium and high mortality groups in the decline of child mortality rates over the period of 15 years preceding the survey (approximately 1978-92). The fast decline in the child mortality rate among the children of low mortality group indicates the improvement in the delivery of health care services and adoption of appropriate child care measures by the mothers in the low mortality group.

11.7 Socio-economic differentials of infant and child mortality

Both the infant and child mortality rates were observed to be higher among children of Hindu than other religions in all mortality groups. Children of mothers belonging to Scheduled Caste experienced high infant and child mortality rates in all mortality groups except in the medium mortality group where the child mortality rate was high among the children of mothers belonging to Scheduled Tribe. Increase in education of parents have depressing effect on infant and child mortality rates in all mortality groups. The variations observed among the three mortality groups narrowed down significantly when the education of parent was high school and above. The education of mother has more influence on infant and child mortality than the education of father. Infant mortality rate was low among the children of self employed mothers in all mortality groups. Child mortality rate was low among children of self employed mothers in the high mortality group and non-working (house wives) mothers in the medium and low mortality groups. Standard of living did not make much difference in the infant and child mortality rates in all mortality groups.

The infant and child mortality rates by socio-economic variables exhibit more or less a similar pattern in all mortality groups. However, the variation in the infant and child mortality rates by various socio-economic characteristics of the mothers among the three mortality groups was great. Both infant and child mortality rates were low for all socio-economic characteristics of mothers in the low mortality group as compared to the medium and high mortality groups. The findings indicate the need for programmes aiming at improving educational status and empowerment of women to reduce infant and child mortality rates in rural areas particularly in the high mortality group of states.

11.8 Demographic differentials of infant and child mortality

The univariate analysis of the infant and child mortality rates by selected demographic characteristics of the mothers and children among the three mortality groups revealed that both infant and child mortality rates were at low level in the low mortality group for all characteristics of mothers and children. Infant mortality rate was less among children of mothers age 20-29 years in all mortality groups. Child mortality increased with age of mother (upto age 40) both in high and medium mortality groups whereas in the low mortality group it was more or less at the same level for all age groups (upto age 40). Children of first and higher order births experienced high infant mortality in all mortality groups. Child mortality rates seemed to increase with order of birth in all mortality groups. Both infant and child mortality rates were high among children born less than 2 years following the birth of its preceding sibling in all mortality groups. The variation in the infant and child mortality rates observed among the three mortality groups narrowed down significantly with the increase in the duration of birth interval.

Fewer female than male die during infancy in all mortality groups, although the female mortality advantage reversed among children aged 1-4 years. The difference in male-female mortality observed at ages 1-4 years was nine times higher for high mortality group and six times higher for medium mortality group as compared to low mortality group. The variations observed in the excess female mortality at ages 1-4 years among the three mortality groups revealed that the sex bias was more prevalent in the high and medium mortality groups than in the low mortality group.

Variations in the infant mortality rates among the three mortality groups were substantial for children of both low birth weight and normal birth weight. Even among the children of normal birth weight, the chances of dying during infancy was more than four times higher in the high mortality group and more than two times higher in the medium mortality group as compared to low mortality group. In the case of child mortality, there was not much difference between the medium and high mortality groups. However, the chances of normal birth weight children dying during childhood was more than two times higher in the high mortality group as compared to the low mortality group.

The infant and child mortality rates by various demographic variables exhibit a similar pattern in all mortality groups. The observation of low levels of infant and child mortality rates for all characteristics of mothers and children in the low mortality group indicate the need for the change in the fertility behaviour of women, more specifically among women in the high mortality group, where there was more number of births among older women, and more number of higher order births. Improvements in the maternal and child health and family planning services are required to minimise the high risk pregnancies. Appropriate educational activities are required to educate women on the importance of avoiding too many, too close births in order to reduce the infant and child mortality. The excess female mortality observed in all mortality groups indicate the importance given to male children in all the groups.

11.9 Maternal health care and infant and child mortality

In all mortality groups, both infant and child mortality rates decreased with increase in antenatal care visits. Substantial variations were observed among the three mortality groups when there was no antenatal care visits. However, the differences narrowed down when the number of antenatal care visits was four and above. In all mortality groups, both infant and child mortality rates have declined considerably when the mother availed both antenatal and delivery care from trained health personnel. The variations observed in the infant and child mortality rates among the three mortality groups were great when the mother did not receive neither antenatal nor delivery care from trained health personnel. But the variations narrowed down significantly when the mother availed both antenatal care and delivery care from trained health personnel. While the infant mortality rate was high among children whose birth took place at home in the low mortality group, it was high among children whose birth took place at public sector facilities in the medium and high mortality groups. The results indicate the need for improvement in the quality of services provided by the public sector facilities in the high and medium mortality groups. This may also be due to the health care seeking behaviour of women. If the women did not avail any maternal care services and developed complications during delivery, the chances of survival for these group of children is very low even if their delivery took place at hospital. Hence, it requires further detailed investigation interms of quality of health care services and the health care seeking behaviour of women in the high and medium mortality groups.

Infant mortality rate was less among children whose delivery was attended by trained health personnel (Doctor/Nurse/Mid Wife) as compared to untrained personnel (relatives/others) in all mortality groups. Variations in infant and child mortality rates among the three mortality groups narrowed down when the delivery was attended by trained health personnel. Both infant and child mortality rates were observed to be high for births with delivery complications as compared to births without delivery complications in all mortality groups.

The results indicate the need for improvements in the availability, accessibility and quality of maternal health care services in rural areas with more emphasis in the high mortality group for an appreciable decline in infant and child mortality rates. Maternal education to women is also equally important to make women understand the importance of various maternal care measures and to utilise the needed services, which will result in the considerable reduction of infant and child mortality rates in rural India.

11.10 Infant and child mortality by exposure to mass media

Both infant and child mortality rates were low among children of mothers who had exposure to any mass media than to those who had not, in all mortality groups. Among those who had exposure to mass media, the infant mortality rate was comparatively low among children of mothers who had visited cinema once a month in the high and medium mortality groups where as it was low among children of mothers watching Television once a week in the low mortality group. The child mortality rate was comparatively low among children of mother watching Television once a week in all mortality groups. The results indicate the effectiveness of mass media in reducing infant and child mortality in Rural India.

11.11 Multivariate analysis of infant and child mortality

The effects of various socio-economic, demographic and health care variables on infant and child mortality were estimated using proportional hazard model in the multivariate analysis. It is observed that in the high mortality group, among the various socio-economic variables examined, caste, standard of living and education of mother have significant effect on infant mortality. It is found that children of Scheduled Tribe and other castes, children of mothers from households of high standard of living and children of literate mothers have significantly less risk of infant mortality. It is very surprising to note that the relative risk of infant mortality is significantly less among the children of Scheduled Tribe as compared to Scheduled Caste. Mother's age at birth, order of birth and immunization during pregnancy (TT) also have significant effect on infant mortality. Contrary to general expectations, hospital delivery seemed to have significantly high risk of infant mortality as compared to home delivery. This requires further investigation on the health care seeking behaviour of women during pregnancy and the availability and quality of services in the high mortality group of states. In all, the infant mortality in the high mortality group is significantly associated with different cultural practices prevailed among various caste groups, standard of living, educational status of mother, fertility behaviour of women (timing and number) and the use of tetanus toxoid during pregnancy.

In the medium mortality group, among the various socio-economic variables examined, only religion and caste seemed to have significant effect on infant mortality. Children of other religion (other than Hindu and Muslim) and other caste (i.e. other than SC/ST) seemed to have significantly less risk of infant mortality. Age of mother at birth, order of birth and sex composition of older surviving siblings were the demographic variables, having significant effect on infant mortality. The relative risk of infant mortality was significantly less among male children with all older surviving siblings female as compared to male children with mixed older surviving siblings. Among the maternal care variables, only Tetanus Toxoid injection seemed to have significant effect on infant mortality. In all, the infant mortality in the medium mortality group is significantly influenced by the cultural practices of various religions and caste groups, fertility behaviour of women (timing and number), sex composition of older surviving siblings and the use of Tetanus Toxoid during pregnancy.

In the low mortality group, caste, standard of living and mother's education emerged as significant socio-economic variables influencing infant mortality. Children of mothers belonging to ST, children of mothers from the households of medium and high standard of living and children of literate mothers have significantly less risk of infant mortality. Sex of the child, age of mother at birth, order of birth and sex composition of older surviving siblings were the demographic variables having significant effect on infant mortality. The significance of the high risk of infant mortality observed among the male children during infancy became non-significant due to the interaction between sex of the child and sex composition of older surviving siblings. It is observed that the infant mortality risk was significantly less among male children with all older surviving siblings female, as compared to male with mixed older surviving siblings . In the case of maternal care variables, hospital delivery and the use of Tetanus Toxoid during pregnancy seemed to have significant effect in the reduction of infant mortality risk.

In all, infant mortality in the low mortality group is significantly influenced by sex of the child, sex composition of older surviving siblings, order of birth, caste, standard of living, education of mother, place of delivery and immunisation (Tetanus Toxoid) of mother during pregnancy.

The effect of various socio-economic, demographic and health care variables on child mortality were also estimated using proportional hazard model in the multivariate analysis. The results indicate that in the high mortality group, education of mother was the only socio-economic variable having significant effect on child mortality. It is found that the children of literate mothers have significantly less risk of child mortality as compared to illiterates. Sex of the child, sex composition of older surviving siblings and order of birth were the demographic variables having significant effect on child mortality. The child mortality risk was significantly less among male children. It is also observed that the child mortality risk was higher among higher order births (three and above). None of the maternal care variables seemed to have any significant effect on child mortality in the high mortality group. In all, child mortality is significantly associated with education of mother, sex of the child, sex composition of older surviving siblings and order of births in the high mortality group.

In the medium mortality group, among the various socio-economic variables examined, religion, caste and mother's education have significant effect on child mortality. It is observed that the child mortality risk was significantly less among male children, children of mothers belonging to Hindu and other religions and children of literate mothers. Children of Scheduled Tribe have significantly higher risk of child mortality as compared to Scheduled Caste. None of the maternal care variables have any significant effect on child mortality. In all, child mortality is significantly associated with religion, caste, education of mother and sex of the child in the medium mortality group.

In the low mortality group, male children, children of mothers from the households of medium standard of living and children of mothers who have availed antenatal care during pregnancy have significantly less risk of child mortality.

Overall, the analysis of the data revealed that the low mortality group of states are placed in better position in terms of housing and environmental condition than the others. Women in high mortality group of states experienced high fertility, more child loss and exposed to longer duration of child bearing than women in medium and low mortality group of states. The levels of utilization of maternal and child care services were comparatively higher among the women in low mortality groups than women in high and medium mortality group of states. While the pace of decline of infant mortality is high in high mortality group of states, the pace of decline in child mortality is high in low mortality group of states during the 15 years period preceding the survey (1988-92). Though the decline of infant mortality in the high mortality group of states is greater than the decline in other two mortality group of states, the infant mortality continued to be high in the high mortality group of states. The multivariate analysis of data revealed the independent effect of various socio-economic and demographic factors on infant and child mortality in each of the three mortality group of states. The findings of the study provide useful information to suggest viable strategies to reduce infant and child mortality in rural India.

11.12 Policy implications

The findings of the study indicate vast variations in infant and child mortality rates among the three mortality groups. Though infant and child mortality rates have declined substantially in all mortality groups in the last fifteen years (1978-92), the levels observed for the period 1988-92 indicates that both the rates are significantly higher among the children of high mortality group as compared to medium and low mortality groups. Comparatively poor housing conditions, high levels of fertility and under utilisation of maternal health care services by women in the high mortality group are the possible reasons for the high levels of infant and child mortality rates in the high mortality group. Hence, special efforts should be taken to improve the housing conditions, reduce fertility (high risk pregnancies) and improve the availability, accessibility and quality of maternal health and family planning services in the high mortality group of states.

The child survival programme in India in the past was focused mainly on controlling immunizable and diarrhoeal diseases and more recently, on managing acute respiratory infections. The impact of these programmes have resulted in the reduction of post neonatal mortality rather than neonatal mortality especially in rural India. It is evidenced from the results of the present study that neonatal mortality continues to be high and constitute more than 60 per cent of infant deaths in all mortality groups. Hence the child survival programme in India should also focus on reducing neonatal mortality in rural India. Further reductions in infant mortality even in the low mortality group are expected only, if special intervention programmes, to improve maternal health are implemented.

The significant association of various demographic and maternal care variables with infant mortality observed in this study in all mortality groups suggest the need for high priority to implement reproductive health programmes more effectively and vigorously in rural India with special attention to the high mortality group of states.

The priority reproductive health needs include antenatal care, medical attention at birth and family planning services. Improving the availability and utilisation of these services are needed. A significant proportion of women in rural areas particularly in the high mortality group are reluctant to use medical maternal care services. They prefer to give birth at home with the assistance of untrained personnel rather than going for institutional deliveries. Hence, information on knowledge, attitude and access to maternal care services is needed.

The continued higher proportion of neonatal deaths could be addressed by ensuring that women in emergencies of pregnancy and child birth are better access to obstetric care, complications of pregnancy are detected early and treated promptly on the spot or by referral to higher level and increasing the proportion of women attended in child birth by trained health personnel. High risk pregnancies such as births among very young (<20 years) and very old (>30 years) women, too close (birth interval of < 24 months) and too many (more than 3 children), should be reduced in number by making the family planning services easily available, accessible and acceptable to women.

The significant relationship of either religion or caste with infant mortality indicate the prevailing traditional and cultural practices of mothers in the maternal and child care. Appropriate educational strategies are required to be integrated with the reproductive health programmes in order to remove wrong beliefs and ill-practices prevailing in rural areas among different cultural groups. As infant and child mortality are associated with education, living standard and employment status of women, special programmes aiming at improving the status of women through education and employment opportunities in rural areas are required to be implemented along with the reproductive health programmes.

The significantly excess female child mortality observed in all mortality groups indicate the prevalence of sex bias in rural areas. Empowerment of women and integration of women into development process will help to remove such sex bias in the long run.

The results strongly suggest that the health care delivery system in India must be area specific. The persistence of high infant and child mortality rates observed among the high mortality group of states deserves special attention. Time specific, special child survival programmes as suggested above need to be implemented in the high mortality group in order to achieve the desired level of infant and child mortality rates at an early date for India as a whole.

Appendix A

Study Design of National Family Health Survey

Objectives of the NFHS

The primary objective of the NFHS is to provide national-level and state-level data on fertility, nuptiality, family size preferences, knowledge and practice of family planning the potential demand for contraception, the level of unwanted fertility utilization of antenatal services, breastfeeding and food supplementation practices, child nutrition and health, immunizations and infant and child mortality. The NFHS is also designed to explore the demographic and socioeconomic determinants of fertility, family planning, and maternal and child health. This information is intended to assist policymakers, administrators and researchers in assessing and evaluating population and family welfare programmes and strategies. The NFHS used uniform questionnaires and uniform methods of sampling, data collection and analysis with the primary objective of providing a source of demographic and health data for interstate comparisons. The data collected in the NFHS are also comparable with those of the Demographic and Health Surveys (DHS) conducted in many other countries.

Questionnaires

Three types of questionnaires were used in the NFHS: The Household Questionnaire, the Women's Questionnaire, and the

Village Questionnaire. The contents and design of the questionnaires were based broadly on the DHS Model B Questionnaire, which is designed primarily for use in countries with low contraceptive prevalence. Keeping in view the Indian socio-cultural milieu and the objectives of the NFHS, additions and modifications were made to the model questionnaire. The questionnaires are largely pre-coded, with fixed response categories.

The household questionnaire was used to list all usual residents of each sample household, plus all visitors who slept in the household the night before the interview. Some basic information was collected on the characteristics of each person health of the household, as well as health status. The main purpose of this section of the household questionnaire was to identify women who were eligible to respond to the woman's questionnaire (ever-married women age 13 – 49years). In addition, the household questionnaire collected information on household conditions, such as the source of water, type of toilet facilities, materials used in the construction of the house, source of lighting, cooking fuel, ownership of agricultural land and livestock, ownership of various consumer durable goods, and characteristics of the head of the household such as religion, caste or tribal. The Household questionnaire also included household birth and death records wherein all the live births and deaths that took place within the last two years in the household were recorded.

The Woman's Questionnaire was used to collect information from eligible women-that is, all ever-married women, usual residents as well as visitors, age 13-49 years.

The village questionnaire was used to collect information on all villages covered in the NFHS. The village questionnaire included information on various amenities available in the villages such as electricity, water, transportation and educational and health facilities.

In addition to the above standard questions used in all the states of the NFHS, a set of state-specific questions was added in most of the states on issues of importance in those states. Accordingly, a set of questions on knowledge of AIDS was added to the NFHS in Arunachal Pradesh, Assasm, Delhi, Goa, Gujarat, Maharastra, Manipur, Meghalaya, Mizoram, Nagaland, TamilNadu, Tripura and West Bengal. The topics covered by state-specific questions in the order states are dowry in Bihar, age at marriage in Rajasthan, sex preference for children in Uttar Pradesh. International migration in Kerala, Green Cards in Madhya Pradesh, benefits received from antipoverty programmes in Karnataka and sex pre-selection and international migration in Punjab.

Sample Design

A uniform sample design was adopted in all the NFHS states (See Table 1 for a summary of the sample characteristics). The sample design adopted in each state is a systematic, stratified sample of household, with two stages in rural areas ad three stages in urban areas.

Sample Size and Allocation

The sample size for each state was specified in terms of a target number of completed interviews with eligible women. The target sample size was set considering the size of the state, the time and resources available for the survey and the need for separate estimates for urban and rural areas of the state. The initial target sample size was 3,000 completed interviews with eligible women for states having a population of 25 million or less in 1991; 4,000 completed interviews from large states with more than 25 million population; 8,000 for Uttar Pradesh, the largest state; and 1,000 each for the six small northeastern states (Arunachal Pradesh, Manipur, Meghalaya, Mizoram, Nagaland, and Tripura). In states with a substantial number of backwards districts[2] (Bihar, Madhya Pradesh, Rajasthan and Uttar Pradesh), the initial target samples were increased so as to allow separate estimates to be made for groups of backward districts.

The urban and rural samples within states were drawn separately and, to the extent possible, sample allocation was proportional to the size of the urban-rural populations (to facilitate the selection of a self-weighting sample for each state). In states where the urban population was not sufficiently large to provide a sample of at least 1,000 completed interviews with eligible women, the urban areas were appropriately over-sampled (except in the six small northeastern states).

The Rural Sample: The Frame, Stratification and Selection

A two-stage stratified sampling design was adopted for the rural areas; selection of villages followed by selection of households. Because the 1991 census data were not available at the time of sample selection in most states the 1981 census list of villages served as the sampling frame in all the states with the exception of Assam, Delhi and Punjab. In these three states the 1991 Census data were used as the sampling frame.

Villages were stratified prior to selection on the basis of a number of variables. The first level of stratification in all the states was geographic, with districts subdivided into regions according to their geophysical characteristics. Within each of these regions villages were further stratified using some of the following variables; village size, distance from the nearest town, proportion of nonagricultural workers, proportion of the population belonging to scheduled castes / scheduled tribes, and female literacy. However, not all variables were selected used in every state. Each state was examined individually and two or three variables were selected for stratification, with the aim of creating not more than 12 strata for small states and not more than 12 strata for large states. Female literacy was often used for implicit stratification (i.e., the villages were ordered prior to selection according to the proportion of females who were literate). Primary Sampling Units (PSUs) were selected systematically, with probability proportional to size (PPS). In some cases, adjacent villages with small population sizes were combined into a single PSU for the purpose of sampling selection. On average, 30 households were selected for interviewing in each selected PSU.

The Urban Sample: The Frame, Stratification and Selection

A three-stage design was adopted for the urban areas in each state: selection of cities / towns, followed by urban blocks and finally household. Cities and towns were selected using the 1991 population figures while urban blocks were selected using the 1991 list of census enumeration blocks in all the states with the exception of the first phase states. For the first phase states, the list of urban blocks provided by the National Sample Survey Organization (NSSO) served as sampling frame.

All cities and towns were subdivided into three strata: (1) self-selecting cities (i.e., cities with a population large enough to be selected with certainly), (2) towns that are district headquarters, and (3) other towns. Within each stratum, the cities / towns were arranged according to the same kind of geographic stratification used in the rural areas. In self-selecting cities, the sample was selected according to a two-stage sample design: Selection of the required number of urban blocks, followed by selection of households in each of the selected block. For district headquarters and other towns, a three-stage sample design was used: Selection of towns with PPS, followed by selection of two census blocks per selected town, followed by selection of household from each selected block. A household listing was carried out in the selected blocks, and an average of 20 households per block was selected systematically.

Sample Weights

At he national level, the overall sample weight for each household or women is the product of he design weight for each state (after adjustment for non-response) and the state weight. The calculation of the design weights at the state level is described in each state report.

The state weights are defined below:

Let P^i, be the projected population of the ith state[3]. Let P be the project projected population for all India. Then the state weight is calculated as followed:

$$W_i = \frac{\frac{P_1}{P}}{©(\frac{P_1}{P})}, i = 1,2,\ldots\ldots 25$$

Let N_{Hi} be the number of households with completed interviews in the ith state. Then N_{Hi} is the total number of households with completed interviews in the NFHS. The normalized state weight for the households is calculated as follows:

$$W_{Hi} = \frac{N'_{Hi}}{N_{Hi}} = \frac{W_i \text{ X } ÓN_{Hi}}{N_{Hi}}$$

Similarly, the normalized state weight for women is calculated as follows:

$$W_{wi} = \frac{N'_{wi}}{N_{wi}} = \frac{W_i \text{ X } \acute{O}W_{wi}}{N_{wi}}$$

Where N_{wi} is the number of women with completed interviews in the ith state.

Sample households and eligible women

The number of households and women interviewed in the NFHS are given in Table 2 ..

---

1. The Demographic and Health Surveys (DHS) program is an international project designed to collect comparable survey data across countries on fertility, family planning and maternal and child health.

---

2. The Ministry of Health and Family Welfare, Government of India, has defined backward districts as those having a crude birth rate of 39 per 1,000 population or higher, estimated on the basis of data from the 1981 population census.
3. The population was projected to November 1992, the midpoint of the field work dates for all the states except Punjab.

Table 1 Sample characteristics

STATE	*1991 POPULATI ON*	*TARGET SAMPLE OF WOMEN*	*ACHIEVED SAMPLE OF WOMEN*	*SELF-WEIGHTI NG*	*VARIABLES FOR RURAL STRATIFICATION*	*NUMBER OF AREA UNIT SELECTED*
Andhra Pradesh	66,508,008	4,000	4,276	Yes	Regions Distance from nearest town Village size Female literacy (implicit)	Urban:58 Rural: 100
Arunachal Pradesh	864,558	1,000	882	Yes	Regions Village size Female literacy (implicit)	Urban: 8 Rural : 56
Assam	22,414,322	3,000	3,006	No	Regions Village size Female literacy (implicit)	Urban: 50 Rural : 68

(Contd.)

(Contd. Table 1)

STATE	1991 POPULATION	TARGET SAMPLE OF WOMEN	ACHIEVED SAMPLE OF WOMEN	SELF-WEIGHTING	VARIABLES FOR RURAL STRATIFICATION	NUMBER OF AREA UNIT SELECTED
Bihar	86,374,465	5,550	5,949	No	Regions Proportion of SC/ST Village size Geographic location / female literacy (implicit)	Urban: 51 Rural: 134
Goa	1,169,793	3,000	3,141	Yes	Village size Geographic location Female literacy (implicit)	Urban: 63 Rural : 90
Gujarat	41,309,582	4,000	3,832	Yes	Regions Female literacy Proportion of SC/ST Village size (implicit)	Urban: 68 Rural : 76
Haryana	16,463,648	3,000	2,846	No	Regions Village size Female literacy (implicit)	Urban: 50 Rural : 68

(Contd.)

(Contd. Table 1)

STATE	*1991 POPULATION*	*TARGET SAMPLE OF WOMEN*	*ACHIEVED SAMPLE OF WOMEN*	*SELF-WEIGHTING*	*VARIABLES FOR RURAL STRATIFICATION*	*NUMBER OF AREA UNIT SELECTED*
Himachal Pradesh	5,170,877	3,000	2,962	No	Regions Distance from nearest town Village size Female literacy (implicit)	Urban: 46 Rural : 80
Jammu	3,504,290	3,000	2,766	No	Geographic location	Urban: 50 Rural : 68
Karnataka	44,977,201	4,000	4,413	Yes	Regions Village size Distance from nearest town Female literacy (implicit)	Urban: 68 Rural : 64
Kerala	29,098,518	4,000	4,332	Yes	Proportion of non-agricultural workers Geographic location Village size (implicit)	Urban: 58 Rural : 74

(Contd.)

(Contd. Table 1)

STATE	1991 POPULATION	TARGET SAMPLE OF WOMEN	ACHIEVED SAMPLE OF WOMEN	SELF-WEIGHTING	VARIABLES FOR RURAL STRATIFICATION	NUMBER OF AREA UNIT SELECTED
Madhya Pradesh1	66,181,170	6,400	6,254	No	Regions Village size Distance from nearest town Female literacy (implicit)	Urban: 76 Rural : 168
Maharashtra	78,937,187	4,000	4,106	Yes	Regions Village size Distance from nearest town Proportion of SC/ST Female literacy (implicit)	Urban: 78 Rural : 81
Manipur	1,837,149	1,000	953	Yes	Regions Village size Geographic location	Urban: 20 Rural : 50

(Contd.)

(Contd. Table 1)

STATE	1991 POPULA TION	TARGET SAMPLE OF WOMEN	ACHIEVED SAMPLE OF WOMEN	SELF-WEIGHTI NG	VARIABLES FOR RURAL STRATIFICATION	NUMBER OF AREA UNIT SELECTED
Megalaya	1,774,778	1,000	1,137	Yes	Regions Village size Geographic location	Urban: 12 Rural : 52
Mizoram	689,756	1,000	1,045	Yes	Regions Village size Geographic location	Urban: 30 Rural : 34
Nagaland	1,209,546	1,000	1,149	Yes	Regions Village size Geographic location	Urban: 12 Rural : 52
Orissa	31,659,73 6	4,000	4,257	No	Regions Proportion of SC/ST Village size Female literacy Geographic location (implicit)	Urban: 50 Rural : 94

(Contd.)

(Contd. Table 1)

STATE	1991 POPULATION	TARGET SAMPLE OF WOMEN	ACHIEVED SAMPLE OF WOMEN	SELF-WEIGHTING	VARIABLES FOR RURAL STRATIFICATION	NUMBER OF AREA UNIT SELECTED
Punjab	20,281,969	3,000	2,995	Yes	Regions Village size Proportion of SC/ST (implicit)	Urban: 44 Rural : 66
Rajasthan[1]	44,005,990	4,750	5,211	Yes	Regions Village size Distance from nearest town Proportion of SC/ST Geographic location (implicit)	Urban: 54 Rural: 114
TamilNadu	55,858,946	4,000	3,948	Yes	Regions Village size Female literacy (implicit)	Urban : 74 Rural : 100

(Contd.)

(Contd. Table 1)

STATE	*1991 POPULATION*	*TARGET SAMPLE OF WOMEN*	*ACHIEVED SAMPLE OF WOMEN*	*SELF-WEIGHTING*	*VARIABLES FOR RURAL STRATIFICATION*	*NUMBER OF AREA UNIT SELECTED*
Tripura	2,757,205	1,000	1,100	Yes	Regions Village size Geographic location	Urban: 12 Rural : 52
Uttar Pradesh	139,112,287	9,800	11,438	No	Regions Backward / Non-backward districts Village size Distance from nearest town Female literacy (implicit)	Urban: 30 Rural : 34
West Bengal1	68,077,965	4,000	4,322	No	Regions Female literacy (implicit)	Urban: 12 Rural : 52
Delhi	9,420,644	3,000	3,457	Yes	Geographic location	Urban: 50 Rural : 94

APPENDIX B

Appendix Table: Scores for the variables used in the computation of Standard of Living Index (SLI)

	Variables	*Scores*	
1.	Separate room for cooking	Yes	= 1
		No	= 2
2.	Type of house	Pucca	= 2
		Semi-pucca	= 1
		Katcha	= 0
3.	Source of lighting	Electricity	= 2
		Kerosene or gas or oil	= 1
		Other	= 0
4.	Fuel for cooking	Electricity or gas or bio-gas	= 2
		Coal or charcoal or kerosene	= 1
		Other	= 0
5.	Source of drinking water	Well or pipe or hand-pump, (Own)	= 2
		Well or pipe or hand-pump, (public)	= 1
		Other	= 0

(Contd.)

(Contd. Appendix-B)

Variables	Scores
6. Toilet facility	Own flush toilet = 3 Flush toilet (Public or shared) or own pit toilet = 2 Shared pit toilet or public pit toilet = 1 Other = 0
7. Ownership of livestock	Bullock = 2 Cow or = 2 Buffalo = 2 Goat = 1 Sheep = 1 Camel = 1

(Contd.)

(Contd. Appendix-B)

Variables	*Scores*	
8. Ownership of goods	Sewing Machine	= 2
	Clock / Watch	= 1
	Sofa set	= 2
	Fan	= 2
	Radio/Transistor	= 2
	Refrigerator	= 3
	Television	= 3
	VCR / VCP	= 3
	Bicycle	= 2
	Motor cycle / Scooter	= 3
	Car	= 4
Standard of Living Index (SLI)	Score Range	00 to 48
Categories of SLI	Range	
Low SLI	00 to 09	
Medium SLI	10 to 19	
High SLI	20 and above	

Bibliography

Abel Rajaratinam, 1988, "Impact of RUHSA'S health and development program on infant mortality": in Anrudh, K. Jain and Pravin Visaria eds Infant mortality in India: Differentials and determinants. Sage Publications, New Delhi 171-84.

Adlakha, A.L. and Suchindra, C.M., 1985, "Factors affecting infant and child mortality" Journal of Bio-Social Science, 174: 481-96.

Agarwal, D.K., Pandey, C.M., and Agarwal, K.N., 1995, "Vitamin A administration and preschool child mortality". Nutrition Research. 1995 May;155:669-680.

Agarwal D.K., Agarwal K. N., Satya K. and Agarwal S., 1998, "Weight gain during pregnancy : A key factor in perinatal and infant mortality. Indianpediatrics ISSN 0019-6061 Vol.35, no. 8, pp. 733-743 15 ref.

Ahmed Alkabir, 1984, "Effects of community factors on infant and child mortality in rural Bangladesh". WFS Scientific Reports, No. 56.

Amin S, 1990, The effect of women's status on sex differentials in infant and child mortality in South Asia. GENUS. 1990 Jul-Dec; 463-4:55-69.

Arnold, F., Choe, M.K. and Roy, T.K., 1996, "Son preference, the family-building process and child mortality in India". [Unpublished] 1996. Presented at the Annual Meeting of the Population Association of America, New Orleans, Louisiana, May 9-11, 1996. p. 49.

Arriaga, Eduardo, E., and Peter, O.Way., 1985, "Determinants of excess female mortality". Presented at the General Conference of the International Union for Scientific Study of Population, Florence.

Badari., S., Gopal, Y.S., and Devaramani, S.C., 1991, "Infant mortality, its components and correlates: findings from a longitudinal study in rural Karnataka, India". GENUS. 1991 Jan-Jun; 471-2:89-108.

Bailey, M., 1989, "Individual and environmental influence on infant and child mortality in rural Sierra Leona" : A multivariate analysis. Journal of Population Studies Taiwan 12 : 155-85.

Banerjee S., 2000, Sex disparity in infant and child mortality : India and major states. [Unpublished] 2000. Presented at the Millennium Conference on Population Development and Environmental Nexus, New Delhi, India, February 14-16, 2000. p. 18.

Battacharya B.N., Srivastava V.K. and Lamb I.M., 1980,. "Some sex differentials on infant mortality in rural areas". Journal of Family Welfare, 1980, December 272:34-42.

Bavedkar S.B., Bavedkar M.S., Kasla R.R., Ragunandana, K.J., Joshi S.Y. and Hatti G.S., 1994, "Infant feeding Practices in Bombay slums". Indian Journal of Practices. 1994. 31:1083-1087.

Behm and Hugo, 1979, "Socio-economic determinants of mortality in Latin America". Paper presented at the meeting on socio-economic determinants and consequences of mortality. World Health Organisation, Mexico.

Bhandari, B., Mandowara. S., Kumar. A. and Agarwal, 1989, "Under utilisation of MCH services - The major factor for very high IMR in rural Rajasthan". Indian Paediatrics 26 : 228-233.

Bhandari, B., Mandowara. S.L., Agarwal. H.R., and Jagder. D.K., 1988, "High infant mortality in rural areas of Rajasthan: An analysis based on prospective study". Indian Paediatrics 256 : 510-14.

Bhardwaj N., Hasan S.B., and Zaheer M., 1991, "Breast feeding and weaning practices: A rural study in Uttar Pradesh". Journal of Family Welfare, 1991. March, 311:23-29.

Caldwell, J.C., and Mc Donald, 1981, "Influence of maternal education on infant and child mortality : Levels and causes". International Population Conference, Manila Vol. 2, Liege : IUSSP.

Caldwell. J.C., 1979, "Education as a factor in mortality decline : An examination of Nigerian data". Population studies 33, No. 3 : 395-413.

Casterline. J.B., Cooksey. E.C., and Ismail. A.F., 1989, "Household income and child survival in Egypt". Demography 261 : 15-35.

Chen. C. Lincoln, Emdedul Huq., and Stan D'Souza, 1981, "Sex bias in the family allocation of food and health care in rural Bangladesh". Population and Development Review 71 : 55-70.

Chidambaram. V.C., McDonald. J.W. and Bracher. M.D., 1985, "Infant and child mortality in developing world : Information from the World Fertility Survey". International Family Planning Perspectives 111 : 17-25.

Chidambaram. V.C., McDonald. J.W. and Bracher. M.D., 1987, "Childhood mortality". In : The WFS : An assessment. Edited by John Cleland and Chris Scott in collaboration with David White Legge London. International Statistical Institute by Oxford University Press. 862-81.

Choe. M.K., 1987, " Sex differentials in infant and child mortality in Korea". Social Biology 34 1-2 : 12-25.

Choudhary. S.R. and Jayaswal. O.N, 1989, "Infant and early childhood mortality in urban slums under ICDS-Scheme - A prospective study. Indian Paediatrics 26 6:544-9.

Clark AW and Shreeniwas S., 1994, Class, maternal education and excess female child mortality in Gujarat State. Presented at Annual meeting of the Population Association of America May, 5-7,1994.

Cleland. J., 1991, "Socio-economic inequalities in childhood mortality: The 1970's compared with 1980's. In Demographic and Health Surveys World Conference Proceedings, Washington DC : 135 - 51.

Cleland. J. and Van Ginneken. J., 1989,"Maternal schooling and childhood mortality". Journal of Bio-Social Science 10 Suppl. : 13-34.

Das N.P., 1996,. "Differential impact of the programme vis-a-vis the socio-economic development in reducing infant mortality". [Unpublished] 1996. Presented at the National Seminar on "Role of the Non-Government Organisations in Accelerating the Pace of Decline in Infant Mortality and Fertility", organised by Population Foundation of India, New Delhi, India, July 29-30, 1996. 21 p.

Das, Talukder and Sella., 1992, Infant-feeding practices in rural Bangladesh. Indian journal of pediatricts, 59, 573-577.

Dasgupta. M., 1990, "Death clustering, mother's education and the determinants of child mortality in rural Punjab, India". Population Studies 443 : 489-505.

Deshpande R.V., 1998, "Determinants of child mortality: a district level analysis of major Indian states". JOURNAL OF FAMILY WELFARE. 1998 Jun; 442:43-53.

Dey D. and Bhavsar S, 2002,"Women's empowerment and its relevance to fertility and child mortality: an analysis based on NFHS-2, Gujarat data". [Unpublished] 2002. Presented at the 25th Annual Conference of the Indian Association for the Study of Population, International Institute for Population Sciences, Mumbai, India, February 11-13, 2002. 18 p.

Dhanalakshmi N., 1993, "Demographic correlates of infant mortality in rural areas" Population Education News. 1993 Oct-Dec; 204:21-3.

Dominique Tabutin., and Michel Williems, 1995, "Excess female child mortality in the developing world during the 1970's and 1980's". Population Bulletin of the United Nations No. 39 : 45-78.

Dyson. T., and Moore. M., 1983, "On kinship structure, female autonomy and demographic behaviour in India". Population and Development Review 9.1.

Ebrahim. G., 1982, "Delivery of perinatal care in developing countries". Journal of Tropical Paediatrics 28 : ii-iii.

Ecuador, "Demographic and Family Health Survey 1987" : Summary Report Quito, Ecuador, CEPAR 1989. 21P. Demographic and Health Surveys - DHS.

Fred Arnold., 1991, "Sex preference for children and its demographic and health implications" Demographic and Health Surveys, World Conference Procedings Washington DC. Vol. 1:249-61.

Gandotra. M.M. and Das. N., 1988, "infant mortality : An analysis of recent births in Gujarat". In, Anrudh. K. Jain and Pravin Visaria Eds infant mortality in India : Differentials and Determinants. Sage Publications, New Delhi - 297-321.

Ganjoo, C and Rowlands, R., 1988, "Breast feeding and weaning practices of urban housewives in Srinagar". The Indian Journal of Nutrition and dietetics, 25, pp. 354-356.

Gayatri ray and Reddy, D.C.C., 1988, "Some aspects of feeding and weaning practices in an urban slum community. Ind. J. of public health, Vol. XXXII, No. 41, 207-209.

George. T., Bicego. J. Ties Boerma, 1991, "Maternal education and child survival : A comparative analysis of DHS Data". Demographic and Health Surveys World Conference procedings, Washington DC. 177-204.

Germain. A., 1987, "Reproductive, health and dignity : Choice by third world women". Technical background paper prepared for the International Conference on better health for women and children through family planning, Nairobi, Oct. 5-9.

Ghai O.P., 1985, "Strategies to reduce infant mortality rate in India". INDIAN JOURNAL OF PEDIATRICS. 1985 Sep-Oct;52418:433-8.

Ghosh S, 1989. "Child mortality differentials: Census of India, 1981". INDIAN JOURNAL OF PEDIATRICS. 1989 Mar-Apr; 562:189-91.

Ghosh. S., 1991, "Discrimination all way" : Health for the Millions 172 : 19-23.

Griffiths P., Hinde A and Matthews, Z., 2001, "Infant and child mortality in three culturally contrasting states of India". Journal of Biosocial Science. 2001 Oct;334:603-22.

Grosse. R., and Auffrey. C., 1989, "Literacy and health status in developing countries". Ann Rev. Public Health 10. 281-298.

Gubhaju. B.B., 1986, "Effect of birth spacing on infant and child mortality in rural Nepal". Journal of Bio-Social Science 184 : 435-447.

Gujral, S., Chohan, A., and Gopaldas T., 1992, Age and sexwise child mortality and the influencing socio-economic factors in a rural and tribal population in western India. Indian Journal of Maternal and Child Health, 1992, October – December; 34: 113-7.

Gunasekaran S., Sankarapandian and Vasantha, L., 1995, Infant feeding practice is Tamil Nadu" Health and population perspectives and issues 23 1: 17-24, 2000.

Gunasekaran. S., 1988, "Correlates of infant mortality in Madurai District of Tamil Nadu" : In Jain, Anrudh. K and Pravin Visaria Eds. Infant mortality in India : Differentials and Determinants. Sage Publications, New Delhi : 247-57.

Hemant Tiwari, 1989, "Estimation of decline in the infant mortality rate in India due to fertility reduction" : The Journal of Family Welfare Vol. XXXV, No. 5, pp. 57.

Hobcraft. J.N., Mc Donald, J.W., and Rustein S.O., 1984, "Socio-economic factors in child mortality". A cross national comparison. Population Studies 38 : 193-223.

Idayatullah. A., 1986, "Child spacing, child survival and maternal health". In : Report of the European Parlimentarian's Forum on Child Survival, Women and Population : Integrated strategies. The Huage, Netherlands.

Jain. A.K., 1985, Derminants of regional variations in infant mortality in rural India". Population Studies Nov. 393 : 407-24.

James K.S., 2001, Gender differentials in child mortality in Andhra Pradesh: evidence from National Family Health Survey. Journal of Family Welfare. 2001 Oct;472:1-11.

Kabir Z and Long J., 2002, "Child mortality rates in rural India: an experience from the Ballabgarh project". Journal of Tropical Pediatrics. 2002 Jun; 483:178-80.

Kathrynkost. and Sajeda Amin., 1992, "Reproductive and Socio-economic determinants of Child Survival : Confounded, interactive and age-dependent effects. Social Biology, Vol. 39, No.12:139-50.

Khan M.E., 1993, "Cultural determinants of infant mortality in India". Journal of Family Welfare. 1993 Jun; 392:3-13.

Khan. M.E., 1988, "Infant mortality in Uttar Pradesh : A micro level study". In Anrudh K. Jain and Pravin Visaria Eds. Infant mortality in India. Differentials and Determinants. Sage Publications, New Delhi. 227-46.

Kishor S., 1993, "May God give sons to all": gender and child mortality in India. American Sociological Review. 1993 Apr; 582:247-65.

Kishor S., 1998, Gender differentials in child mortality: A review of the evidence. In : Women's Health in India: Rise and Vulnerability. Edited by Monica Das Gupta, Lin Coln C.Chen, T.N. Krishnan. New Delhi,India.Oxford India.19-54.

Kishor S and Parasuraman S., 1998, Mother's employment and infant and child mortality in India. International Institute for Population Sciences, 1998 Apr. 40 p. National Family Health Survey Subject Reports No. 8

Koenig. M.A., campbell. O., Phillips. J.F., and D'Souza. S., 1988, "Birth intervals and childhood mortality in rural Bangladesh". Population Council's International Program on Mortality. Paper No.23.

Koeing. M.A., and Stan D'Souza. S., 1986, "Sex differentials in childhood mortality in rural Bangladesh". Social Science and Medicine 221 : 15-22.

Kwast. B.E., 1988, "Unsafe motherhood : A monumental challenge". A study of maternal mortality in Addis Ababa, Leiderdrop.

Ladusingh, L. and Singh, C.H., 2006, "Place, community education, gender and child mortality in north-east India" Population, Space and Place. 2006;12:65-76.

Lahiri, S., and Dutta P., 2002, Sex-preference and child mortality in some selected Indian states : an analysis based on NFHS data during 1992-93 and 1998-99.

Lahiri S and Ram U., 2004, "Infant and child mortality: programs and achievements." [Unpublished] 2004. Presented at the Seminar on Follow-up of the National Population Policy 2000: Focus on EAG States, Mumbai, India, October 25-27, 2004. [29] p.

Leslie. J., and Gupta. G.R., 1989, "Utilisation of formal services for maternal nutrition and health care in the third world". International Centre for Research on Women. Washington DC.

Luis Tam, 1991, "Intermediate and under lying factors associated with infant mortality in Peru 1984-86. Proceedings of the Demographic and Health Surveys World Conference. Washington DC.

Mahadevan. K., 1986, "Mortality, biology and society : Analytical framework and conceptual model". In Mahadevan. K Eds. Fertility and mortality Theory, Methodology and Emperical issues. Sage Publications, New Delhi. 239-301.

Mahadevan. K., Murthy. M.S.R., Reddy. P.R., Reddy. P.J., Sivaraju.S. and Gowri. V., 1985, "Infant and childhood mortality in India" Mittal Publications, New Delhi.

Maine. D, and Mc Namara. R., 1985, "Birth spacing and child survival". Columbia University, Centre for Population and Family Health, New York.

Meegama. S.A., 1980, "Socio-economic determinants of infant and child mortality in Sri Lanka : An analysis of post-war experience". World Fertility Survey Scientific Reports No.8.

Miller B., 1985, "The unwanted girls. A study of infant mortality rates, Manushi". 1985 Jul-Aug;54:18-20.

Miller. B.D., 1989, "Changing patterns of Juvenile sex rations in rural India, 1961 to 1971". Economic and Political Weekly 2422 : 1, 229-36.

Ministry of Health and Family Welfare (MoHFW)., 1992, Module for Health Worker, New Delhi : National Child Survival and Safe Motherhood Program, MoHFW.

Minja Kim Choe, Hao Hougsheng., and Wang Feng, 1995, "Effects of gender, birth order and other correlates on childhood mortality in China". Social Biology, Vol. 42, No.1-2:50-64.

Mosley and Lincoln Chen, 1984, "An analytical frame work for the study of child survival in developing countries. In child survival: Stratagies for research". W. Henry, Mosley and Lincoln Chen Eds. Population and Development Review. Vol.10 Supplement: 25-45.

Mrinal Kanti Chatterjee, 1990, "Feeding pattern practiced by the mothers attending an under five clinic", Indian journal of public health, Vol. XXXI, No. 4, pp. 113.117.

Muktaparashar and Mayachoudhary, 1986, "Weaning and feeding practices of urban, rural and tribal children". The Ind. J. of Home Science, Vol.16, No: 273, pp.166-169.

Nath, D.C., Land, K.C., and Singh, K.K., 1994, "Birth spacing, breastfeeding, and early child mortality in a traditional Indian society: a hazards model analysis". SOCIAL BIOLOGY. 1994 Fall-Winter; 413-4:168-80.

Neena Joshi, Saraswathi G. and Bhawani Belavaely, 1999, "Maternal Nutrition, breast feeding and growth of young children among urban population a prospective case study". The Ind. J. Nutr. Dietete, pp. 39-182.

NFHS., 1998-99, "Breast feeding practices", International Institute for population sciences, Mumbai, India, 2000.

Nina, S. Dodd and Sunanda Datta, 1993, "Effect of the socio-economic level on the infant weaning practices in Maharastrians". The Ind. J. of dietetics, pp. 25, 259.

Palloni. A. and Tienda. M., 1986, "The effects of breast feeding and pace of child bearing on mortality at early ages". Demography 23:31-52.

Pandey, A., Choe, M.K., Luther, N.Y., Sahu, D. and Chand J., 1998, "Infant and child mortality in India". Mumbai, India, International Institute for Population Sciences, 1998 Dec. 99 p. National Family Health Survey Subject Reports No. 11.

Panikar P.G., 1985, "Health care system in Kerala and its impact on infant mortality". In: Good health at low cost, edited by Scott B. Halstead, Julia A. Walsh, and Kenneth S. Warren. New York, New York, The Rockefeller Foundation, 1985 Oct.:47-55. A paper presented at a conference held at the Bellagio Conference Center, Bellagio, Italy, April 29 - May 3, 1985, sponsored by The Rockefeller Foundation.

Patel R.M., 2000, [Unpublished] Determinants of infant mortality in Gujarat. Popline document number 194415.

Paul. B., 1991, "Health service resources as determinants of infant death in rural Bangladesh : An empirical study". Social Science and Medicine. 321 : 43-49.

Pebley. A.R and Millman. S., 1986, "Birth spacing and child survival". International Family Planning Perspectives 12, No.3 71-79.

Petto. G.H., 1987, "Cultural issues in maternal and child health and nutrition". Social Sciences and Medicine. 25: 553-59.

Population Research Centre, Baroda, 1983, "Some determinants of infant mortality in Gujarat". Baroda Reporter. 1983 Aug;16:1-8.

Prakasam, C.P., Sinha, U.P., and Sridhar V.S., 1991, "Determinants of child mortality in selected states of India". Bombay, India, International Institute for Population Sciences, 1991. 27 p.

Rajaram. P., 1990, "Child survival Maternal factors". Indian Journal of Maternal and Child Health 12 : 39-45.

Rajaratinam. T., 1989, "Socio-cultural and ecological determinants of infant mortality in rural areas of Tamil Nadu". Ph.D dissertation submitted to Sri Venkateswara University, Tirupati.

Rajna P.N., Mishra A.K., and Krishnamoorthy S., 1998, "Impact of maternal education and health services on child mortality in Uttar Pradesh, India". Asia-Pacific Population Journal. 1998 Jun;132:27-38.

Ram. F., Girimaji. J.H. and Umamani. K.S., 1985, "Infant and childhood mortality in Karnataka : Levels trends and differentials assessed through indirect techniques". Health and Population : Pespective and issues 83 : 168-80.

Rao P.S., 1991, "Sex differentials in infant mortality". [Unpublished] 1991. Presented at the International Union for the Scientific Study of Population [IUSSP] Committee on Anthropological Demography and ORSTOM Seminar on Socio-Cultural Determinants of Morbidity and Mortality in Developing Countries: the Role of Longitudinal Studies, Saly Portudal, Senegal, October 7-11, 1991. 18 p.

Rao S.R., Pandey, A., and Shajy K.I., 1997, Child mortality in Goa: a cross-sectional analysis. SOCIAL BIOLOGY. 1997 Spring-Summer; 441-2:101-10.

Ravindran. S., 1986, "Health implications of sex discrimination in childhood : A review paper and an notated bibliography" : Unpublished paper, WHO/UNICEF/FHE 86.2.

Reddy, P.H., and Sholapurkar, M.V., 1983, "Type of birth attendant and infant mortality in rural Karnataka". Demography India. 1983 Jul-Dec;122:214-24.

Registrar General of India, 1987a, "Fertility and child mortality estimates of Tamil Nadu". Office of the Registrar General. Demography Division. Census of India 1981., Occasional Paper No.4 of 1987.

Registrar General of India, 1987b, "Fertility and child mortality estimates of Madya Pradesh". Office of the Registrar General, Demography Division, Census of India 1981. Occasional Paper No.7 of 1987.

Registrar General of India, 1987c, "Fertility and child mortality estimates of Uttar Pradesh". Office of the Registrar General, Demography Division, Census of India 1981. Occasional Paper No.8 of 1987.

Registrar General of India, 1987d, "Fertility and child mortality estimates of Hariyana". Office of the Registrar General Demography Division, Census of India 1981. Occational Paper No.10 of 1987.

Registrar General of India, 1987e, "Fertility and child mortality estimates of Karnataka". Office of the Registrar General of India, Demography Division, Census of India 1981. Occasional Paper No. 11 of 1987.

Roy. T.K. and Jeyachandran, V., 1996, "Is living condition important for determining fertility and childloss experience?". An Empirical Investigation based on NFHS. Paper presented at XIX. Annual Conference of IASP, held at M.S. University of Baroda, February 26-28, 1996.

Rutherford. R.D., Choe. M.K., Thapa. S., and Gubhaju. B.B., 1989, "To what extent does breast feeding explain birth interval effect on early childhood mortality?" Demography 263 : 439-450.

Rutstein, 1984, "Infant and child mortality : Levels, trends and demographic differentials". Revised edition. WFS Comparative Studies No. 43.

Rutstein Shea Oscar, 1984, "Infant and child mortality : Levels, trends and demographic differentials" WFS Comparative Studies No. 24.

Sandhya S., 1991, "Socio-economic and cultural correlates of infant mortality: a demographic appraisal". New Delhi, India, Concept Publishing Company, 1991. p. 128.

Sangeethapanday, Tripathi, S.K. Tandon and J.Mishra, C.P., 2001, "Weaning in the perspectives of breast feeding in rural area". The Ind. J. of Nutrition dietiects, 39, 223.

Sarojadahiya and Sehgal, 2001,"Infant feeding practices of working and non-working urban mothers", Ind. J. of Nutrition ditetics. Vol.39, No.8 pp. 367-69.

Schultz. T., 1984, "Studying the impact of household, economic and community variables on child mortality". In child survival strategies for research Eds WH. Mosely and L.C. Chen. Population and Development Review No. 10 Supplement 225-36.

Schultz. T. and Paul, 1985, "Household economic and community variables as determinants of mortality". In International Population Conference, Florence, 1985, Vol.2. Liege : International Union for the Scientific Study of Population.

Sharma, R. and Kumar, 1991, "Breast feeding pattern in urban infants in Patna", Indian journal of pediatric, 3, pp. 31, 35, 51.

Singh K and Srivastava P., 1992, The effect of colostrum on infant mortality: urban rural differentials". Health and Population: Perspectives and Issues. 1992 Jul-Dec;153-4:94-100.

Singh K.P., 1989, "Green revolution and child survival in the State of Punjab. In : International Population Conference, New Delhi, Sep. 20-27, 1989" International Union for the Scientific and Study of Population, Belgium 379-88.

Singh. K., Viegas. O.A., and Ratnam. S.S., 1987, "Health Rationale for family planning in : High risk mother and new borns: Detection management and prevention". Ed. by Abdel. R., Omram, Jeem Martin and Bechir Hamza. Thun Switzerland, ott, Verlag.

Srinivasan,S., 2000, "Determinants of infant and child mortality in Tamil Nadu and Uttar Pradesh". Mumbai, India, International Institute for Population Sciences, 2000 April 18. 23 p.

Srivastava, J.N., and Saksena, D.N., 1981, "Infant mortality differentials in an Indian setting: follow-up of hospital deliveries". Journal of Biosocial Science. 1981 Oct;134:467-78.

Srivastava. J.N., 1990, "Impact of birth spacing on child survival in rural Uttar Pradesh". Demography India : 191 : 141-146.

Suhasini Ramisetty, 1988, "Impact of action programme on health, hygiene feeding practices of mother in slum areas". The Ind. J. of Home science, Vol.18:2.

Tulasidhar, V.B., 1993, Maternal education, female labour force participation and child mortality: evidence from the Indian census. Health Transition Review. 1993 Oct;32:177-90.

UNICEF, 2005, State of the World's Children 2005.

United Nations Secretariat, 1988a, "Sex differentials in survivorship in the developing world : Levels, regional patterns and demographic determinants". Population Bulletin of the United Nations 25: 51-64.

United Nations Secretariat, 1988b, "Sex differentials in life expectancy and mortality in developed countries : An analysis by age groups and causes of death from recent and historical data". Population Bulletin of the United Nations 25 : 65-107.

Utomo. B. and Iskandar. M.B., 1989, "Socio-economic differentials in infant and child mortality in Indonesia in the 1970's : Trends, causes and implications". In differential mortality : Methodological issues and Bio-social factors. Eds Lado Ruzicka, Guillaume Wunsch and Penny Kane. Oxford Press : 145-55.

Vijay L.Grover, Pragti Chhabra and Aggarval O.P., 1997, "Knowledge, Attitude and Practices of breast feeding in a rural area of East Delhi". Health and Population-perspectives and issues 2027: pp. 45-56.

Whitworth A and Stephenson R., 2002, Birth spacing, sibling rivalry and Child Mortality in India.

Winikoff. B., 1987, "The effect of birth spacing on child and maternal health International Journal of Gynecology and Obstetrics, 25 Suppl. : 219-38.

Zubair Kabir, Jean Long, Venkadara P., Reddaiah, John Kevany, Suresh K., and Kapoor, 2003, "Non-specific effect of measles vaccination on overall child mortality in an area of rural India with high vaccination coverage": a population based case control study, Bulletin of the world health organization, 2003, 81: 244-250.

Wilke L., Grover, [illegible] and [illegible] C.P., 1997. [illegible] Knowledge, Attitude and Practices of [illegible] [illegible] from East Delhi [illegible] and [illegible] [illegible] 19: 56.

Zohair K.M., [illegible] [illegible] [illegible] 2002. Non-specific effect of measles vaccine [illegible] with high [illegible] A [illegible] case control study. [illegible] 2001.

Index